D0426410

DONATED
MATERIAL

# FATAL
# JOURNEY

# FATAL JOURNEY

THE FINAL EXPEDITION OF
HENRY HUDSON—
A TALE OF MUTINY AND MURDER
IN THE ARCTIC

*Peter C. Mancall*

BASIC
BOOKS

A Member of the Perseus Books Group
New York

Books published by Basic Books are available at special discounts for bulk purchases in the United States by corporations, institutions, and other organizations. For more information, please contact the Special Markets Department at the Perseus Books Group, 2300 Chestnut Street, Suite 200, Philadelphia, PA 19103, or call (800) 810-4145, ext. 5000, or e-mail special.markets@perseusbooks.com.

Designed by Pauline Brown
Type set in 11.5 point Caslon.

Library of Congress Cataloging-in-Publication Data

Mancall, Peter C.
  Fatal journey : the final expedition of Henry Hudson—a tale of mutiny and murder in the Arctic / Peter C. Mancall.
    p. cm.
  Includes bibliographical references and index.
  ISBN 978-0-465-00511-6 (alk. paper)
  1. Hudson, Henry, d. 1611. 2. America—Discovery and exploration—British. 3. Explorers—America. 4. Mutiny. I. Title.

E129.H8M358 2009
910.92—dc22

2009003072

10 9 8 7 6 5 4 3

*For Lisa*

*Evil appeareth out of the north,*
*and great destruction.*
—JEREMIAH 6:1

# Contents

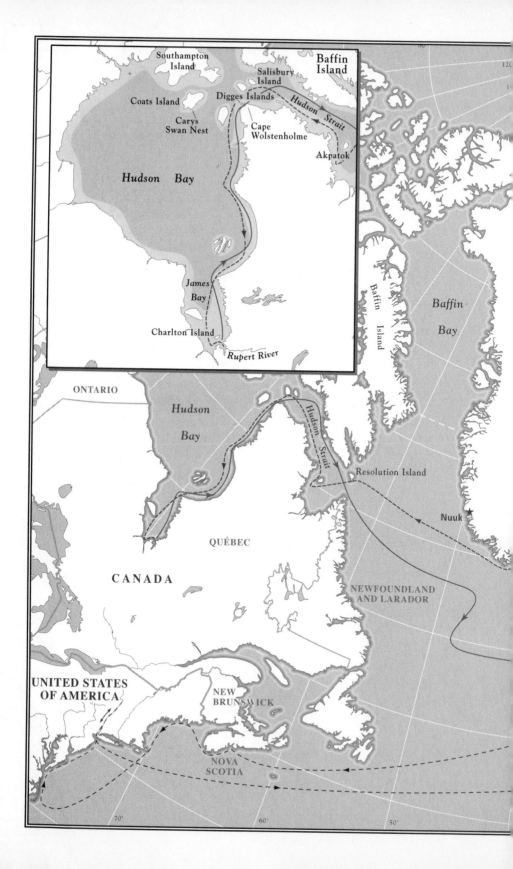

Southampton
Island

Baffin
Island

Salisbury
Island

Coats Island

Digges Islands

Hudson Strait

Carys
Swan Nest

Cape
Wolstenholme

Hudson    Bay

Akpatok

James
Bay

Charlton Island

Rupert River

ONTARIO

Hudson

Bay

Baffin

Island

Baffin

Bay

Hudson Strait

Resolution Island

Nuuk

QUÉBEC

CANADA

NEWFOUNDLAND
AND LARADOR

UNITED STATES
OF AMERICA

NEW
BRUNSWICK

NOVA
SCOTIA

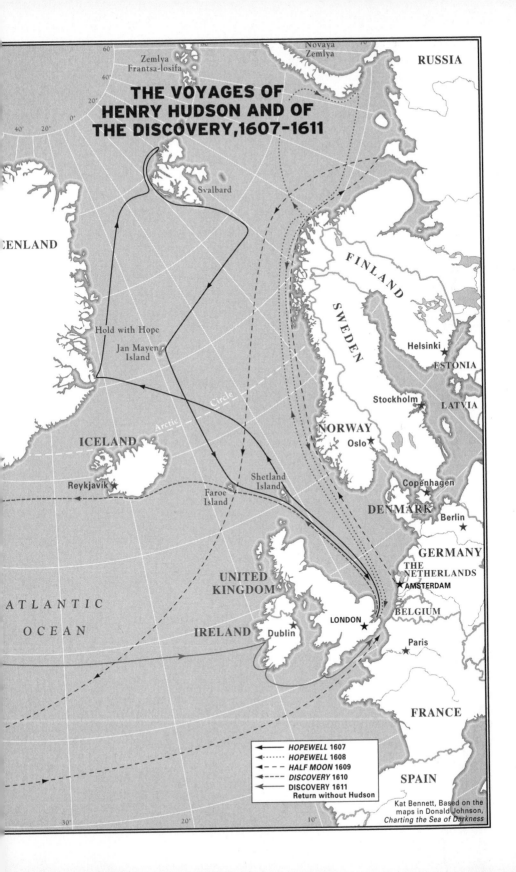

# THE VOYAGES OF
# HENRY HUDSON AND OF
# THE DISCOVERY, 1607–1611

RUSSIA

Novaya
Zemlya

Zemlya
Frantsa-Iosifa

Svalbard

FINLAND

SWEDEN

Helsinki

ICENLAND

ESTONIA

Hold with Hope

Stockholm

LATVIA

Jan Mayen
Island

NORWAY

Oslo

Circle

ICELAND

Copenhagen

Reykjavík

Shetland
Island

Faroe
Island

DENMARK

Berlin

GERMANY

ATLANTIC

THE
NETHERLANDS

UNITED
KINGDOM

AMSTERDAM

BELGIUM

OCEAN

IRELAND

Dublin

LONDON

Paris

| | HOPEWELL 1607 |
|---|---|
| | HOPEWELL 1608 |
| | HALF MOON 1609 |
| | DISCOVERY 1610 |
| | DISCOVERY 1611 |
| | Return without Hudson |

FRANCE

SPAIN

Kat Bennett, Based on the
maps in Donald Johnson,
*Charting the Sea of Darkness*

# I.

# *Mutiny*

JAMES BAY, JUNE 1611

*L ike the needle of a compass,* Henry Hudson was always attracted to the North. In 1607, he led a mission that he
hoped would take him from England over the top of the world
and past the pole toward East Asia. It would be the first of four
voyages that would make him one of the most intrepid and important explorers of his age—even as he failed in his quest to
find a northern route to the coveted riches of the East, and even
though his final voyage ended in mutiny, mystery, and quite
possibly murder.

Like all European explorers of the sixteenth and seventeenth centuries, Hudson knew that fame and immense riches
would accrue to the one who found a new and quick route to
the vast markets of spices and silks in East Asia and the Southwest Pacific. For almost a century, the English had sought a
shortcut to the "South Sea," the term Europeans used for the
Pacific Ocean. Explorers recognized that discovering the route
would bring glory to their realm and abet the larger Protestant
mission of rescuing Christendom from the thrall of Rome. Of
course, Hudson's backers had other goals too, notably making
an enormous fortune by controlling the trade between East Asia
and England. The English East India Company, organized only

a few years earlier, had already begun sailing vessels home from the Spice Islands laden with pepper, cinnamon, cloves, and nutmeg. But they had to follow the long course from India around Africa before arriving in London—a journey through thousands of miles of open seas that put them at risk of assault by Barbary pirates who had the unfortunate habit of taking English sailors captive and selling them as slaves. Hudson realized that a northern passage—despite the risks every sailor confronted in the Arctic—could cut the time substantially, and thereby increase profits by reducing the costs of any venture. A man of few words but of evident ambition and significant experience with the sea, he could have become as famous as Sir Francis Drake and possibly won great wealth.

That 1607 expedition to sail past the pole failed, and Hudson turned home. But he was not a man who easily gave up. The next year he launched another expedition from England in search of the Northeast Passage, a water route long theorized to exist leading through seas north of Russia to East Asia. Hudson could not find a path through the pack ice that blocked the route, and once again he returned to England. It would take almost 300 years before Europeans managed to plow through and circumvent the ice blocking the passage from the Atlantic to the Pacific north of Russia.

Despite his failures, Hudson's reputation remained intact. He had attracted the attention of potential investors who saw him as a leader who took informed, calculated risks, the kind of man who could safely lead an expensive, speculative foray into unknown waters without loss of life or a waste of his backers' funds. In 1609, the Dutch East India Company—the leading competitor of the English mercantile house—hired Hudson to lead another journey in search of the Northeast Passage. Hudson guided the 80-ton *Halve Maen* (*Half Moon*) toward that potential route, but along the way he gave up on it and instead sailed across the Atlantic. He had hoped to find an entryway to the much-fabled Northwest Passage somewhere north of Virginia, where the English had only recently established a colony based at Jamestown. Hudson eventually sailed into modern New York harbor and then up the river that now bears his name, a journey that earned him a permanent place in American history. On his return he landed in England, where he reported that he hoped to return to America soon.

At the time of his fourth voyage in 1610, no English mariner of the age knew the North Atlantic as well as Henry Hudson. His boldness in leading ships northward season after season had revealed him as a man willing to take risks in the effort to explore new territory and bring home both hard-won knowledge and the promise of profit. Remarkably, none of Hudson's men perished on his expeditions of 1607 and 1608. He had proved he knew what it took for his men to survive. He knew how to overcome what, 300 years later, the American novelist Jack London would identify as "the Fear of the North," the terrifying "child of the Great Cold and the Great Silence." He acknowledged and anticipated the terrors that shrouded the Arctic once the sun, perpetually visible during the prime sailing months, made its inevitable dip below the horizon and virtually disappeared for months. The darkness that followed could seem inescapable to those unfamiliar with northern rhythms. Ship candles and oil lamps provided small solace in an enduring gloom that, for those trapped in ice and snared by darkness, could feel like an interminable prison sentence, one that could incite despondency, fury, and madness.

By the time Hudson sailed, English mariners did have some understanding of what they would find in the Arctic. Norse sailors had traversed the northern reaches of the Atlantic in the centuries around the year 1000, and in the process had established outposts in Iceland, Greenland, and Newfoundland. But they had abandoned their efforts west of Iceland well before 1500. In the years following the journeys of Christopher Columbus, the English had sponsored expeditions captained by the Venetians John and Sebastian Cabot, but those journeys did not lead to any sustained efforts to explore North America for another two generations. Martin Frobisher sailed the North Atlantic in the mid-1570s, and on his third journey he brought home 200 tons of ore that had glistened in the midsummer sunshine, only to discover with dismay that it was worthless— tons of rock, no gold. Sir Humphrey Gilbert, half-brother of Sir Walter Ralegh, sailed to Newfoundland in 1583, but two of his three ships, including the one he was on, sunk on their return. The English mariner John Davis led three journeys in the mid-1580s in search of the Northwest Passage; he explored the west coast of Greenland, sailed north into the strait that now bears his name, and also navigated the eastern shores of Baffin Island and modern Labrador.

Hudson had learned a great deal from these other explorers before he set off to find the Northwest Passage on the 55-ton bark named *Discovery*. Prior to his 1609 journey, he had met Captain John Smith, a veteran of voyages to the new English colony on the banks of Chesapeake Bay, who was eager to share his theories about the possible water route through North America. Hudson quite likely knew Richard Hakluyt, England's preeminent authority on overseas navigation. Hakluyt had published numerous accounts of journeys to the Northwest Passage and inspired potential explorers and a wider audience with the texts he edited and reprinted in his collections. Hudson had also befriended some of Europe's most sophisticated mapmakers. From such authorities he gathered the most complete and up-to-date information pointing to the existence and location of the Northwest Passage.

The Atlantic had become a second home to Hudson, who had spent almost as much time there during these years as he had on land. That experience burnished his reputation and allowed him to gain funding from some of London's best-known investors. Among them was Thomas Smythe, one of three principal backers of the voyage of the *Discovery* in 1610. Smythe was already one of the dominant forces in English

Richard Hakluyt never traveled farther than Paris, but his books inspired generations of English readers to think about the world beyond their borders. One of those readers sketched this scene in a copy of Hakluyt's first book, *Divers Voyages touching upon America and the Ilands adjacent* (London, 1582). *Yale Center for British Art, Paul Mellon Collection*

overseas trade. He became the first governor of the East India Company on December 31, 1600, and except for a period from 1605 to 1607, he would serve in that capacity until 1621. In 1609, Smythe had become treasurer of the Virginia Company, the joint-stock effort responsible for the English settlement at Jamestown. He was also a member of the Company of Merchant Adventurers and one of the governors of the Levant Company.

More crucially, Smythe was a governor of the Muscovy Company, an enterprise with long connections to Hudson's family and to efforts to find the Northeast Passage. He served in Parliament and would later become governor of the Somers Island Company, which would try to organize an English colony on Bermuda. Smythe embraced the opportunities opened by long-distance trade and took a personal interest in sailing and the sea. Sailors or their wives could often be found at his house. He kept in contact with the captains he backed, and he shared information with Hakluyt, among others, thereby helping to keep the idea of long-distance trade in the minds of policy makers and the public. That Hudson won funding from Smythe signaled that his venture had the approval of one of the most illustrious and commercially minded men of his age. Even more important, that financial support allowed him to stock the *Discovery* with the provisions he thought he would need for his passage through the Arctic.

But no matter how well provisioned Henry Hudson was with knowledge, experience, financial backing, food, water, and weapons, he knew that such advantages took a ship commander only so far. In the end it was Hudson—not Europe's mapmakers or Hakluyt or Smythe—who had to lead an expedition into waters that were unknown to Europeans. No plan was foolproof. Hudson knew well how human error, the vagaries of the weather, a troublesome crew, or encounters with little-understood peoples could undermine any voyage. As a veteran of three earlier journeys, Hudson understood the risks he would soon face.

❧

During the summer of 1610, Hudson guided the *Discovery* across the Atlantic to the Canadian coast, entering the body of water now known as Hudson Strait and into modern Hudson Bay. Few Europeans had seen these waters before. It is possible that a Portuguese expedition had entered the strait much earlier, and that Frobisher did as well, though there is little evidence that either ventured into it very far. Frobisher named an alleged passage from the Atlantic to the Pacific "Frobisher's Straightes," but that moniker was the product more of his imagination than his observations. Davis had sailed across the opening to Hudson Strait, but he chose to continue south toward the coast of Labrador before heading back toward England. Hudson was the

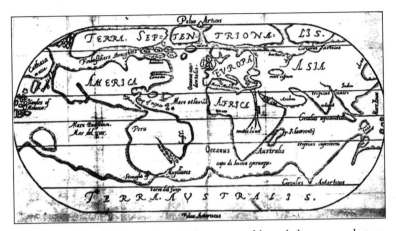

When Hudson set sail in April 1610 he possessed knowledge garnered at sea and acquired from books and maps available in England. Among the works he might have seen was this map from the journeys of Sir Martin Frobisher, who had named an alleged route through North America after himself. From George Best, *A true discourse of the late voyages of discoverie, for the finding of a passage to Cathaya, by the Northweast* (London, 1578). *Huntington Library*

first English mariner to sail deep into the strait, which divides modern Baffin Island from the Ungava Peninsula.

When the *Discovery* arrived in Hudson Bay, Hudson must have beheld its vast expanse with excitement, anticipation, and a real, if premature, sense of accomplishment. On July 5, in a moment of perpetual light, he wrote in his log that the ship had passed near unforested plains covered with snow, a place so appealing that he had named it "Desire Provoketh," or "Desire Provokes" (modern Akpatok Island). A month later, the *Discovery* edged its way through a deep, narrow strait and entered into what one of Hudson's contemporaries called "a spacious Sea." This body of water was so extensive that Samuel Purchas, who later chronicled Hudson's journeys, believed that the mariner "had won the passage." One can barely imagine the emotion he must have felt at the moment. He had finally found what he had spent years looking for: the seaway that would take him through the North American continent to the Pacific—the long sought-for opening to the East Indies and its fabled riches.

Yet finding this possible route westward would have been meaningless if Hudson now faltered or failed. It was already August and he needed time to guide the *Discovery* through the frigid Canadian bays and into warmer waters before the Arctic winter closed the seas and locked his men into a world of ice, skin-freezing winds, darkness, and possible death.

Once he sailed into the bay, Hudson made some calculations about the ship's location and attempted to determine whether the *Discovery* could complete its mission to make it through the Northwest Passage before winter. He knew that the Arctic summer was brief, and that at extreme northern latitudes he might run into ice within days. In 1610, Europeans had no perfect way to judge their longitude because the tools to calculate it—notably an accurate sea clock known as a chronometer—had not been invented. So although Hudson believed that the Northwest Passage existed and that sailing through it would lead him to the South Sea, he was unsure if the crew had enough time to complete the journey before winter fell upon them. In the comparative warmth of midsummer, he realized he had come to his expedition's decisive moment.

Hudson was faced with two alternatives. The simpler, safer decision would be to turn the ship around and return to England before ice choked off all routes. The riskier and bolder option was for the men to winter in the region and proceed on their journey to Asia the following spring (or summer) when the ice thinned. Hudson had not yet spent a winter in Arctic conditions, and he feared that he and his men might meet their death in these icy waters. Still, he believed that the mission could succeed. But before making his final decision, he consulted his crew to make sure they supported his plan. He encouraged the men to debate whether they should turn back to England before the advance of the winter ice sheet, or wait winter out and continue their search for the passage. Though some dissented, Hudson gained the backing of the crew to push on-ward. It would be a choice that many of them came to regret.

By November, Hudson had guided the *Discovery* as far south as he could. They reached what is now called James Bay, the large body of water that stretches southward from Hudson Bay. Hudson's men probably positioned the *Discovery* close to the deeper (but rockier) eastern side of the bay. The site would have been better than the more shallow, silt-filled waters to the west, which would have prevented the ship from getting close to the shoreline. (The men would have known about the depth from looking at the color of the water, which in western James Bay can be milky white because it is so shallow.) The trick to survival in the Arctic, they understood, was to get a ship as close as possible to land so that they could find at least some supplies before the cold came down, and perhaps even during the winter when they could venture out. They would need wood to keep their fires burning all winter. They would have to hunt deer, caribou, bear, rabbits, or even rodents, both for the protein their bodies craved and for the fur and skins that could ward off the cold. But getting close to land was tricky even in the eastern part of the bay, since submerged rocks threatened to rip apart the *Discovery*'s hull. Sailing into James Bay made sense if Hudson was looking for warmer climes (though in this re-gion it did little good), but the uncertain flooring here made it a risky place—though no one on the ship could have known it at the time.

Hudson had reason to think that survival in this locale was manageable. According to one account, the *Discovery* had reached 52° north, approximately the same latitude as London, which, by the prevailing European logic of the time, meant that cli-mate conditions should not have been much worse than they were at home. This same reasoning had prompted the era's En-glish colonists to imagine planting olive trees and grapevines near Chesapeake Bay, which happened to share the latitude of southern Europe. Like other explorers and geographers of his

European sailors needed to find ways to ground their ships safely to avoid the enormous pressure that ice could exert against a hull during the winter. The Dutch explorer Willem Barentsz, who had survived his first two voyages in search of the Northeast Passage, died on his third attempt when his ship was so damaged by the winter ice that his crew needed to scrap it, using its wood to build small open boats in which they paddled for home. From *Warhafftige Relation: der dreyen newen unerhörten* (Noribergae, 1598). *Huntington Library*

time, Hudson was unable to take into account the fact that the circulation of winds in the Atlantic pushed warm air toward Europe and made it a more tolerable (and inhabitable) place than locales on similar latitudes in North America. Perhaps Hudson had guided the *Discovery* southward because he hoped to find a more temperate area for winter, even if, as he must have realized upon coasting the shores of James Bay, it was unlikely that he would find an opening to the Northwest Passage from there.

But as Hudson soon learned, the weather in James Bay was unlike that of England. Though Hudson was far south of the Arctic Circle, James Bay is part of Canada's Arctic Archipelago marine ecosystem, and its environment resembles territory farther north. As in areas above the circle, winter descends rapidly here. Ice forms quickly and moves aggressively. Winds in James Bay blow from the north all year long, pushing the Arctic air that dominates the climate. Ice sheets typically last into July. The water temperature rarely rises above 45°F. Once the *Discovery* became surrounded by the pack ice in November, the crew faced a winter worse than they or Hudson could ever have imagined.

❧

Europeans who embarked on voyages to northern waters could prepare themselves for the challenges they knew they would face. Those who thought they might have to spend the winter in a frozen land came prepared with supplies to build shelter. But Hudson had anticipated making it through the Northwest Passage before winter set in, and there is no record that the *Discovery* carried all that it needed for its crew to construct a dwelling suitable for the Canadian Arctic. Moreover, these were men who knew how to work the rigging on a three-masted ship, how to drop an anchor so that it could be retrieved, and how to use a seine to haul in fish to supplement the stored food below decks. They could probably capture a shark. But none of them, as far as the surviving records indicate, had any experience building a house, and certainly none of them knew how to erect one on the rocky, windswept shores of a bay 3,000 miles from home.

Building a shelter was only the first act in the effort to survive. During the winter the winds would have battered the walls and no doubt opened holes in the sides. Maintenance could not have been easy. According to a surviving report of another European ship marooned in ice, constructing a winter abode posed novel risks for those who hoped to survive until the next thaw. Iron nails froze to the inside of cheeks when carpenters absently put them in their mouths while they were working; detaching them opened bloody sores unlikely to heal quickly. Ice sheathed the interior walls of the best-built shelters. Clothes and shoes froze solid. Every movement could be painful. Men accustomed to the relative security of an English winter might have felt they would never escape or survive its torments.

No account survives of the conditions endured by Hudson and his men that winter. The extant documents either end before the onset of winter or offer no sustained observations of daily life during those frozen months. But other travelers to the region did write about the horrors that extreme cold produced. During winter there, as one later observer lamented, it was awful enough to huddle in a shelter put together from the materials available on an English sailing ship. Even with the door shut tight and a fire burning, it was nearly impossible to chase away the frigid cold. But that was more tolerable than venturing outside to gather firewood or hunt for game. Fierce winds battered English bodies that were accustomed to the far more moderate London winter rather than to the snow, howling gales, and temperatures that regularly sank well below 0°F. They probably wore leather coats and mittens lined with lamb skins and tried to keep their feet warm with socks made out of coarse woolens. These were men who could cope with gales on the sea but had no experience trudging through deep snow.

Winter winds forced men back inside as quickly as possible, trapping them in their own frosty company, in quarters rank with the smells, mutterings, prayers, quarrels, complaints, and grudges of twenty or so men uncertain of their own survival. Anyone who wandered too far away from their makeshift shelters could get caught in a squall and buried by drifts, which could reach 30 feet around Hudson Bay—a fate that befell later travelers in the region. Most unfortunate were the men who had to climb on board the ice-bound ship to retrieve supplies. Severe frostbite followed exposure to bitter winds that froze human skin and eyes. The bitter cold of James Bay eventually became so well known in England that Robert Boyle, one of the leading scientists of the Royal Society in the seventeenth century, used reports from English travelers there to define what "cold" actually was. Boyle understood that the English did not experience deep cold at home, but that in northern regions the cold could be "Stupendious," and it made sense to him to write a treatise explaining its properties, just as scientists had been doing in their attempts to understand other natural phenomena.

No one knows for certain what transpired among the crew of the *Discovery* during those dark, frozen months. But one can only imagine that the daily struggle for survival put immense stress on the relationships between the crew members and with the captain who had brought them here. During the winter the ship's gunner died, and several others became either ill or injured—unable, it seems, to be able to do any of the tasks necessary to help the small community stay alive. Others remained healthy, no doubt keeping the shelter intact and scrounging for firewood or food when the weather permitted. The infirm and the healthy had one thing in common: All of them waited, week after week, for the ice to crack.

When the days started to lengthen, tensions began to break out. By late spring some of the able-bodied men were grumbling about Hudson's decision to dole out any of the *Discovery*'s diminishing stores to their ailing comrades. The complainers saw no use in providing nourishment to men who were not doing their share of the work, and who quite possibly were unlikely to survive another voyage. A winter of privation and tension had convinced some of the men that the only sensible option would be to return to England, and for that they would need as much food as possible. Understanding that Hudson was not about to abandon his desire to find the passage or his

By the time the *Discovery* embarked on its search for the Northwest Passage in 1610, books were in circulation that reported the opportunities and dangers that awaited them in northern waters. The crew of Willem Barentsz's expeditions in the 1590s told of their success in hunting walrus as well as of the dangers posed to unwary men who encountered polar bears, including one man who had lost his life. The account of Gerrit de Veer, a ship's carpenter on Barentsz's first two expeditions, provided illustrations of what the men had seen. From *Warhafftige Relation: der dreyen newen unerhörten* (Noribergae, 1598). *Huntington Library*

decision to feed all of the men on the ship, the discontented took matters into their own hands and plotted mutiny.

Hudson understood that the Arctic posed risks to Europeans who ventured there, but he never expected that the greatest threat to his own life would come from his own men. Before the *Discovery* became trapped in ice, he believed that he had the support of the crew and was making plans to continue his expedition the following summer. That proved to be a fatal miscalculation.

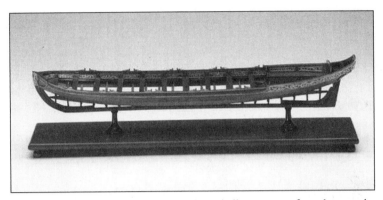

European sailors used shallops to explore shallow water, often along rocky coastlines. The kind of shallop on the *Discovery* could probably hold up to ten men. *National Maritime Museum, Greenwich*

By around June 10 the ice had thawed and the *Discovery* was free. Two weeks later, just as Hudson would have been making his final calculations to sail his ship toward the East Indies, the angry men rebelled. They lowered Hudson, his seventeen-year-old son, and seven other men onto a small boat known as a shallop, which was tethered to the ship. Then the rebels cut the rope and sailed away. As Hudson watched the vessel fade from view, he faced the most severe trial he had ever known.

❧

In the autumn of 1611 seven men and one boy from Hudson's crew returned to England on the *Discovery*. They told about the mutiny and claimed that the perpetrators had all died in the weeks since the rebellion. Their story, not surprisingly, aroused suspicions that lingered for years. Doubts about the veracity of their account remained until, six years after their return, four of the survivors found themselves in the High Court of Admiralty. They had been charged with the murder of Henry Hudson, who was never seen again.

Four hundred years later, mysteries remain about the events of that fateful summer of 1611. As one recent environmental writer put it, "in the Arctic nothing is ever really lost." Daylight is abundant in James Bay around the time of the summer solstice. In that bright landscape it is difficult to keep a secret. What caused the men on the ship to turn against their captain, an action which should have earned them the noose? Shipboard mutinies have come to capture the modern imagination, thanks to the 1789 rebellion against William Bligh on the *Bounty*, but they were in fact very rare in Hudson's age. It was not until 1689 that English lawmakers enacted their first statute specifically designed to punish mutineers. When writers or dramatists (including Shakespeare) used the term "mutiny" during Hudson's lifetime, they tended to refer to insurrections on land, not at sea. Only one attempted mutiny had occurred on an English ship within recent memory of the English. That effort, against Sir Francis Drake during his circumnavigation of the earth from 1578 to 1580, failed, and the leader of the putative insurrection went to the gallows.

What happened to the men on the shallop? What caused the insurrection? These questions gripped the High Court of Admiralty as it sought a final resolution to the mystery of the events in James Bay in June 1611. It would be several years after the return of the *Discovery* before English authorities pieced together the narrative from the small number of survivors who had witnessed the mutiny and apparent murder of Henry Hudson.

The full extent of Hudson's saga reveals one of the darker chapters of the European age of discovery. Now mostly forgotten, this tale illuminates the early English colonial period as much as the history of Jamestown, Plymouth, and Massachusetts Bay. Those settlements succeeded, though along the shores of the Chesapeake it was a hard-won victory for the English, who witnessed many of their fellow colonists succumb to disease during Jamestown's first years. Still, the high human cost of early Virginia paid off—at least for some—with the development of the tobacco trade in the 1610s. Plymouth and Massachusetts earned their place in American lore as targets for religious migrants who, our national narrative tells us, helped establish the principle of freedom of religion. Taken together, the nascent settlements along the Chesapeake and in New England mark the origins of a nation that has long embraced both its thirst for profit and its desire for religious freedom.

But these colonies survived thanks to luck. The English (and the Dutch) succeeded in planting along the Atlantic coast because they found environments similar to those they'd had at home. They knew enough about wind patterns in the Atlantic basin for their ships to get back and forth regularly, thereby providing economic, political, religious, and psychological links to their respective homelands. More important, these colonists were, in the words of one noted historian, "beneficiaries of catastrophe." They unwittingly transported lethal microbes that took a horrific toll on the continent's indigenous peoples and thereby made it easier for the newcomers to succeed.

Henry Hudson and the men who went with him on the voyage of the *Discovery* were not so lucky. English colonists elsewhere prospered when the population of indigenous peoples shrank. Hudson, by contrast, needed the help of Inuit and Crees who had little interest in his fate. The environment he entered allowed little margin for error. In an age of discovery when so much seemed possible, Hudson's experience reveals the limits of what Europeans could achieve. The only way to survive in those cold lands was to maintain contact with others; once those bonds became severed, an individual or a small group faced the imminent risk of death, as countless explorers have realized. Hudson learned that lesson too late to make it home again. But the mystery of his disappearance provides a new way to think about the nature of English colonization and the fates of those whose visions of glory perished in the Arctic.

## II.

# The Age of Spices

London, c. 1607

*efore he left on his first journey*, Henry Hudson lived in a city awash with mercantile enthusiasm and maritime pride. By the early seventeenth century, London had become one of the most important commercial entrepôts in Europe. Ideally situated for taking advantage of emerging transatlantic business opportunities, the city boasted a new commercial exchange created to facilitate the active participation of merchants in long-distance trade. One contemporary author commented that London had become "the most famous and the most principal place here in England,"* and his book gave specific details about the distance between the capital and "certain principal places here in *Europe*, and also in *Africa*, and in *Asia*, and also in *America*." When ships that brought English goods to the shores of North America, Africa, India, and the Spice Islands returned laden with valuable fish and exotic goods, news of their

---

* Here and below, some quotations have been silently modernized. All italics within quotations are preserved from the original sources.

arrival raced through the streets and captured the attention of the city. One visitor to London marveled that up to 2,000 English ships might be at sea at any given time. Another observer noticed that the grounds of Whitehall featured animals imported from India, a living sign of the acquisitive impulses of the age.

In 1610 when Hudson was fitting out the *Discovery* for his fourth expedition, a Londoner with enough money could find anything and everything he or she might want to buy without ever leaving town. Keepers of cabinets of curiosity—including Walter Cope, whom Hudson knew—filled their collections with unusual natural wonders and the handiwork of distant peoples. Cope, for example, had the horns of a rhinoceros and a bull seal and the alleged tail of a unicorn, as well as a Madonna made from feathers, a goosefoot cap contructed in China, and a chain from India made from monkey teeth. That local customers could purchase such items was a testament to the success of the realm's mariners and merchants, who had embraced long-distance travel and trade. "The English Ships touch also at Nycobar, and at other places," one chronicler noted in a long description of the extent of trade at the time, "and by their painful and industrious travail, have discovered great Kingdoms, and strange Nations, besides many other Ports, and Provinces, rich and full of Traffic, to the great honour of this Kingdom and Nation."

Chief among these provinces were the Spice Islands, those fragrant lands of the East Indies, including Banda, Java, and the Moluccas, that supplied Europeans with natural products that enhanced their diets and, reputable authors claimed, cured a wide range of bodily ailments. The costs of conducting such expeditions could be heavy, but the rewards went beyond the material. Commerce made London the envy of the rest of England. The king and his subjects could indulge their acquisitive fantasies because of the enterprise of the sailors who were willing to try their luck. The English also profited from the ventures previously made by other Europeans, especially the Portuguese, who had pioneered the seaways to the East Indies and made long-distance voyages more tempting.

The sailors who signed aboard a ship to India or the Spice Islands understood that a long, arduous, and often perilous journey lay ahead of them. But they and the merchants who sponsored their voyages also knew that cinnamon, cloves, peppers, and other exotic flora had captured the imagination of the English, and that much money was to be made in satisfying the newly sophisticated national palate. These luxuries had captivated Europeans since the Middle Ages. The desire to obtain spices had driven the Portuguese eastward over a century before Hudson embarked on his search for a swifter passage to the Spice Islands, and the same quest had propelled Christopher Columbus to sail west looking for East Asia. By the latter decades of the sixteenth century, the Portuguese had emerged victorious in this race, but their success only intensified the Western European demand for spices and other products from faraway lands. In the 1610s, American tobacco would join these imports. At the time of Hudson's four voyages, flavorful eastern plants stood alongside sugar (which was then produced in southern Europe, the eastern Mediterranean, and the Canary Islands) as the most valuable flora to arrive on England's docks. Hudson devised his ambitious plans to sate England's expansive tastebuds.

❧

For the people of Renaissance Europe, spices pleasured the palate, doctored the body, and salved the soul. English botanists embraced the revolution in their field long before Hudson came on the scene, and they popularized their theories via the printing press. William Turner, who identified himself as the physician to the Duke of Somerset, produced the first part of his *New Herball* in 1551, drawing primarily on knowledge of European plants by such venerable authorities as Pliny the

Elder, Dioscorides, and Galen. Turner died in 1568, the year of his final work, which informed readers about nutmeg and mace from the Banda Islands and guiacum from Java and Sri Lanka.

The expansion of demand for information about plants prompted a small boom in publishing by the end of the century. In 1597, William Langham published *The Garden of Health*, a book testifying to the faith in medicinal uses of plants that prevailed in Hudson's era. Most of this knowledge had developed over centuries—at least since antiquity, when healers looked to herbs for *materia medica* to cure the enormous range of ailments that beset human bodies. Like Turner's, Langham's catalog noted that the vast majority of plants believed to have curative powers could be found in Europe, but that enterprising botanists and others seeking new ingredients for their storehouses of treatments remained open to new possibilities.

Those possibilities materialized with the arrival of cinnamon, nutmeg, mace, cloves, and peppers from the Southwest Pacific. Before 1500, those plants trickled into Western Europe via an overland trade system that stretched across southern Asia to Venice, and from there to towns and cities across the continent. Near the dawn of the sixteenth century, Portuguese explorers had found ways to reduce the time of transit by hauling these plants through the Indian Ocean, around Africa, and then to Lisbon. Northern Europeans paid dearly to obtain the spices because of the extraordinary curative powers they were believed to offer. Some spices had by then already become well known and widely used by Europeans. A Catalan cookbook of recipes for the king of Naples written in 1500 included 125 recipes featuring cinnamon.

Langham's book assured its readers that cinnamon soothed upset stomachs, strengthened the brain and liver, helped prevent dropsy, and eradicated pain in the lungs, guts, and breast. A concoction rubbed in the mouth could both freshen breath and whiten teeth. Cloves were especially useful in battling illness or ailments caused by cold. Taken properly, a mixture containing cloves could ease digestion and improve eyesight, improve the taste of meat and medicine, and comfort the stomach of someone who had just vomited. Cloves also combined well: A mixture of cloves and peppers could cure agues and other unspecified ailments, Langham declared, and cloves with mace could help to solve the problems of a "weak" brain. Mace had a wide variety of uses of its own as well. Its oil could be rubbed on the stomach to chase away nausea and improve digestion. Chewing mace could "strengthen the brain." Mace boiled in combination with fennel and wine produced a liquid that would combat heartburn, colic, and "all griefs of the spiritual members." A powder made from mace, sugar, long pepper, and pomegranate could be used to counter a lethal disease known as black jaundice, possibly the ailment now known as Weil's disease, which was common in northeastern England and caused by contact with infected rat urine.

Nutmeg was even more variously helpful. According to Langham, it alleviated tensions caused by gas and had benefits for a woman's belly, liver, and urinary tract (for those who "piss by drops"). It could be employed to treat other "secret griefs" of both sexes. When consumed in a cordial, nutmeg eased headaches, ameliorated the disease known as the "bloody flux" (probably dysentery, identified by the bloody diarrhea of its victims), treated dropsy, and reduced vomiting. Pounded into a powder with mint, it addressed the afflictions of a cold head or a poor memory. Chronically ill patients could sip it in a broth, and it was a favorite for those who suffered from ringworms or freckled faces. Insomniacs could take a mix of nutmeg, almonds, and hempseed to help them sleep. Perhaps most remarkably, a patient suffering from internal bleeding could eat chopped nutmeg, which would cause him to expel blood and render him "as clean as ever he was." This treatment could be repeated until the patient was healthy again.

But of all these imports, none was more important than pepper. In addition to its culinary properties, learned authors raved about its extraordinary medicinal capacities. It could be ground for use in salves (known as "treacles") useful for curing both venomous bites and poison. Mixed in a drink, it could break a fever. With honey it soothed lungs, lessened coughing, and could even reduce tumors and other swellings. Chewed with raisins, pepper could "purge" a brain. Long peppers were useful in eye ointments. Someone suffering from ringworms could kill them by holding a mix of peppers and hot wine in the mouth before spitting it out. A salve made with peppers was a useful antidote against gout. Onions and peppers mixed together could help ease sciatica. In all, Langham enumerated sixty-three possible uses for peppers, either on their own or combined with other substances, for ailments as diverse as bloody flux, excessive gas, headaches, catarrh (called "rheume"), scrofula, tonsillitis (known as "squincy" or "quinsy"), canker sores, colic, ringworms, and leprous facial sores.

English readers with access to John Gerard's lavish *Herball or Generall Historie of Plants,* published in London in 1597, learned more about the provenance of these plants in India or the Spice Islands—information that enhanced the allure of the exotic locales. Cloves, Gerard reported, could be harvested in Zeilan (Ceylon), on Java, and in the Moluccas between mid-September and late February. The matured buds fell to the ground when someone beat the trunk of the tree. Gerard reported that the medicinal benefits of cloves were many. Cloves eased digestion, cleared the urinary tract, and strengthened the liver, heart, and stomach. Portuguese women who had moved to the East Indies had learned how to extract a sweet-smelling liquid from still-green cloves, which they used to make an effective cordial with alleged benefits for the heart. The locals would extract the juice of the clove, too, work it about in their hands and then apply it to open wounds (as the English did with balsam).

Gerard declared that the best nutmeg came from the island of Banda, though the plant also grew on the Moluccas (now known as the Moluku Islands) and Zeilan. The harvest came in September when the tree's branches were full of ripe fruit. Pepper could be found in the East Indies, too. Though Europeans had known since antiquity that some pepper could be found in Africa, the so-called bastard pepper grew only in the Moluccas, where its vines tended to wrap themselves around the Areca tree, which Gerard believed imparted a bitter taste to the plant. The peoples of the East Indies would roll pepper into a ball and leave it in their mouths, the way the English did sugar candy or licorice. The locals in the Spice Islands believed that the plant refreshed them and improved their memory. Gerard also praised cardamom, which he called the "grain of Paradise," also found in the broad region from Calicut to Cananor, Malavar, and Goa. The herb ripened in September. When chewed, it released watery and "pituitous humours," and if combined with the wine known as sack, the plant battled ague, eliminated seizures (perhaps caused by epilepsy), and comforted feeble stomachs. Unlike Langham, Gerard also included illustrations of each of the plants he described—a useful feature for those of his readers going to the markets in search of the newest arrivals from the East Indies.

❧

Hudson's voyages occurred during a time of English optimism. The island nation was finally gaining the maritime might that could lead it to greater prosperity and power. Only in the previous generation had the English mastered the art of building their own substantial ships, rather than purchasing them from elsewhere. Now they built larger and larger vessels. The East India Company, the most promising of all of the economic enterprises in London at the time, had just taken delivery of a 1,200-ton ship, "the greatest and fairest Ship that ever was made in this kingdom by Merchants," according to one contemporary chronicler. They went on to commission a 250-ton pinnace to accompany the great ship on its voyage to the East.

King James himself endorsed such ventures. He recognized that it was crucial for the English to be able to conduct trade in the Spice Islands. By improving the chances for this English company to succeed, the monarch also hoped "to prevent both the Turk, and the Persians of their richest Trade." If he succeeded, he would have simultaneously hindered England's foes and advanced the cause of Protestant Christianity. James was so enthusiastic about the new ship's prospects that he traveled to Deptford for its launch. He and his son toured each of its rooms and then shared a banquet put on by the captain at a grand table on the half-deck, the long wooden boards set with fine china overflowing with delicacies.

The display of food laid out for the king reflected James's long-standing interest in the wider world and what the English could extract from it. Like his predecessor, Queen Elizabeth, James understood that the expansion of commercial opportunities during the sixteenth century had permanently altered European societies. The English monarchs were also well aware that Iberians had benefited the most from long-distance trade. The Spanish had first brought the riches of the Western Hemisphere to Europe, while the Portuguese had mastered the journey to India and the Spice Islands. James himself knew firsthand the kinds of wonders that inspired such trade. Only a few years earlier he had offered guests at a state dinner a melon and oranges, telling one (in the words of a witness) "that they were the fruit of Spain transplanted into England."

The English embraced long-distance trade later than the Iberians, but by the early seventeenth century the king's subjects eagerly sought goods wherever they could be found. James supported the East India Company, which had been chartered by Queen Elizabeth in 1600, with every means at his disposal. In December 1609 he granted the company a monopoly on the sale of pepper in England. He gave Sir Thomas Smythe, the governor of the company and one of Henry Hudson's backers, a golden chain with a jewel containing the monarch's portrait. He named the company's great 1,200-ton ship the *Trades Encrease* and the pinnace the *Peppercorne*. In response to his generosity and enthusiasm—to say nothing of the legal privilege the company obtained, which granted it an enviable position in the domestic market—the leaders kissed the king's hand.

The ships sailed off in March 1610, just as Henry Hudson was preparing for his fourth effort to reach the East Indies, though in a ship that was about one-twentieth of the size of the *Trades Encrease*. Intent on returning with an enormous cargo of spices, the two ships crossed the Red Sea, and then decided to sail for Bantam, the city on Java where the East India Company had set up a trading factory in 1603. Of course, no one who watched these ships sail down the Thames from Deptford toward the English Channel on that March day in 1610 could have known that the *Trades Encrease*, like so many other enterprising vessels, was doomed. It sank near Bantam. Most of those on board drowned. But the business of trade continued; by 1615, the *Peppercorne* was already on its next voyage from London to the East Indies. By then the managers of the East India Company had learned how to turn a regular profit by establishing a carrying trade between East Asian ports, thereby allowing it to raise funds to purchase spices for the English market even when there was little regional demand for English manufactured goods.

During James's reign, at least ninety-five ships sailed out of the realm bound for the East Indies, and London cemented its status as the leading port in England. The king's support for the East India Company represented only one aspect of his enthusiasm for expanding his realm's economy. James was also keen to develop a domestic silk industry, as the Spanish and Portuguese had already imported silk from East Asia and had mastered the art of producing it at home. According to the chronicler Edmund Howes, the king was eager to find an occupation for "his poorest Subjects" while bringing profit to the realm. To advance his goal, he imported hundreds of thousands of young mulberry trees from France, which he then had planted across England. Soon some of his industrious servants were tending to silkworms and launching an industry. James's desire to improve the realm's finances went even further in May 1609 when he issued a proclamation barring the subjects of any other realm from fishing off the coasts of Ireland, Scotland, or England without a special license.

But royal or entrepreneurial excitement about new possibilities did not always guarantee success. Not all trade ventures prospered—including those spawned by the silkworm business, which never lived up to their promoters' dreams in the seventeenth century. By 1610, the king and his advisers had quite likely come to have doubts about the new settlement at Jamestown in North America. Organized by the Virginia Company and planted on the banks of the James River in 1607, that outpost of the realm was hardly a source of pride. Few women wanted to go there, and most of the men found their dreams of economic gain dashed by the realities of the toxic swamp where the English had decided to settle themselves. Though it would take time before London would learn that about half of these early emigrants to North America had died within two years of their arrival, the early news coming back to England was already so dreadful that the Virginia Company put out a pamphlet aimed at refuting the "scandalous reports" that had brought "disgrace [to] so worthy an enterprise." It was perhaps the only promotional pamphlet in English history to boast of a place that only one colonist there had engaged in cannibalism. In its early years, Jamestown was simply a disaster for the English: Colonists there fought with the Powhatans, who controlled the region, and virtually all the settlers who died succumbed because they did not know where to find clean water to drink.

Yet even a tragedy like the sinking of the *Trades Encrease* or the reports of mortalities at Jamestown could not diminish the enthusiasm of the king and the public for long-distance trade, especially toward East Asia, and for the expeditions of Hudson and of other explorers who established new routes to destinations in the Spice Islands and beyond. The East India Company's efforts to mount large expeditions to the islands of the

Southwest Pacific became public spectacles. Pamphlets describing each of the early missions appeared from printers' shops in London, a sign of the reading public's sustained interest in the business.

❦

By the time Hudson began his expeditions, he had access to extensive information about the North Atlantic, thanks to what he had learned from a century of explorers. Under Queen Elizabeth, who had died in 1603, the English embraced the idea of long-distance trade and even colonization of distant lands. Many explorers and merchants had ventured to the Americas, Russia, the Levant, and Africa. Sebastian Cabot claimed he had found the Northwest Passage at the end of the fifteenth century, and for the next hundred years geographers and the makers of maps and globes included alleged routes from the Atlantic to the South Sea. The English also sent explorers to survey the far margins of the Atlantic itself. The 1536 expedition led by Richard Hore to Newfoundland became widely known in England; at the end of the century, Hakluyt traveled 200 miles to interview the only surviving member of the crew. Transatlantic ventures did not always end well, as Hakluyt knew when he mourned the death of friends and associates lost at sea on a trip to Newfoundland in 1583.

After the East India Company's chartering in 1600 by Queen Elizabeth, merchants associated with the venture began to gather as much information as they could about the places that existed abroad and how to get there most efficiently. Hakluyt hauled a stack of large books to one memorable meeting of the company's directors to support his claims about the commodities to be extracted from specific locales. The directors needed to be convinced, especially since funding explorers could be expensive, as they discovered firsthand soon enough: The company estimated the costs of one 1602 journey at £3,000 (approximately $800,000 in modern currency). No group of merchants would have made such an investment without the belief that their funds would bring a substantial return. Their backing allowed George Weymouth to brave peril and sail farther north and west than any English sailors had gone earlier. He piloted his crew beyond Greenland and left a log about what later explorers might find. Like those who had sailed before him, Weymouth never found the Northwest Passage. When Henry Hudson sailed, it remained the greatest prize any explorer could find. Hudson knew well the everlasting fame that would come to the one who found the fabled water route.

English sailors had been traversing those waters for generations, often in search of cod or other marine life that could be salted and brought home to market. Over time, many of those who had traveled there, along with practical scientists and geographers working in London and on the continent, had described likely routes for a passage to the East Indies. Danger still existed, of course, especially for those who were leading their vessels into waters that Europeans had not yet explored. Faulty equipment made it difficult for captains always to know where they were, a problem compounded when less experienced sailors used cross-staffs to plot their location. The cross-staff, commonly used on European ships at the end of the sixteenth century, allowed a crew to determine latitude by judging the height of either the Sun or Polaris (the North Star) and then calculating their position from that assessment. An English ship like Hudson's crossing the Atlantic at this time would also have carried a good compass and possibly an astrolabe, a tool that could be used to measure the altitude of celestial bodies and thus could provide clues to the location of a vessel at sea. The equipment might not work correctly in every instance— some writers complained about the inaccuracies of navigational devices—but they would have been sufficient to guide Hudson's crew and allow them to estimate the ship's latitude.

Hudson also benefited from the work of a number of English scholars whose studies had convinced them that a water

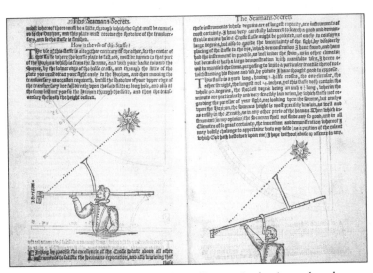

European sailors managed to travel vast distances in the sixteenth and seventeenth centuries with only rudimentary navigational tools. Among these implements, the most widely used was a cross-staff. Directions for using the tool could be found in John Davys's small pamphlet entitled *The Seamans Secrets*, published in London in 1599. *Huntington Library*

route to East Asia existed and could be found. Ever since news of Columbus's first voyage had spread across Europe at the end of the fifteenth century, the English had looked on warily as Spain and Portugal, with the explicit support of the Vatican, sought to divide up the Western Hemisphere. But it was Columbus's original desire to find a quick water route to East Asia that was of the most interest to the English. As early as 1527, the geographer Robert Thorne had argued that the English could get to the Spice Islands of the Southwest Pacific by traveling via the Arctic. Like other European geographers, Thorne believed that ice would not block the way of any sailors who managed to get into this far northern sea. As he confidently put it, there was no "Sea innavigable." In 1582 Hakluyt reprinted Thorne's theory along with a recent map by the geographer Michael Lok, which depicted a vast ocean that connected the

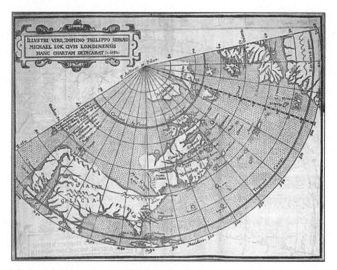

Michael Lok's map of 1582 contained visual proof of the existence of a water route from Western Europe to the Pacific Ocean. From Richard Hakluyt, *Divers Voyages touching the discoverie of America, and the Ilands Adjacent* (London, 1582). *Huntington Library*

Atlantic to the Pacific. Since Hakluyt knew Hudson, it is likely that the man gathering information about routes toward the Spice Islands would have consulted this book, among others. If an explorer like Hudson could get through, the English would not only have a new and shorter passage to the rich region, but circumvent the Portuguese and Spanish, who dominated the shipping routes via either the South Atlantic or around Africa and India.

Thorne was not the only English authority who speculated about the existence of a water route to provide quicker access to the rich East Asian silk and spice markets. Martin Frobisher commanded three expeditions to search for the Northwest Passage in the 1570s; his adventures led to at least four published accounts. Sir Humphrey Gilbert, who would drown in 1583 while attempting to return from a voyage to Newfoundland, wrote an influential pamphlet in 1576 arguing for the existence of the Northwest Passage and enumerating the great gains to come to Elizabeth's realm if her subjects sailed through it. John Davis captained three journeys in the mid-1580s and a decade later wrote a tract arguing for the existence of the Northwest Passage. These works convinced the English that they possessed the requisite skills and knowledge to find the route.

The notion of an ice-free polar region resulted from theoretical speculation and inexperience. The idea caught on among some Europeans because it made a certain sense: Endless sunshine in the Arctic summer would warm the waters and prevent the formation of ice. But the theory persisted because virtually no one in Western Europe had deep experience with the far north. William Bourne, a leading authority on navigation in Elizabethan England, wrote in 1574 that though it might seem foolish to think that sailing across the pole might be possible, he was convinced that "the long continuance of the Sun" made it likely that far northern waters would take time to freeze after they had been warmed during the summer. If Bourne, the author of a guide to seafaring that went through three editions in the late sixteenth century, thought the route possible, then potential explorers like Hudson had all the justification they needed for attracting the capital necessary to fund an expedition. Cartographers, too, propelled the idea along, perhaps none more prominently than Hudson's associate Petrus Plancius, whose 1594 map of the world depicted both a navigable Northwest Passage and an open polar sea, as did Gerard Mercator's view of the northern part of the globe. Though some, such as the prolific author Thomas Blundeville, an expert on navigation (as well as horses), disputed the possibility of a warm polar sea, the idea continued to attract adherents until the nineteenth century, when extensive European explorations proved once and for all that no such ice-free body of water existed.

The desire to find the Northwest Passage brought together complementary strands of English thought, including economic imperatives, geographical speculation, and propagation of Protestantism. The drive for easier trade with the East Indies provided

Gerard Mercator died in 1594, but this map of the northern part of the world, which appeared in his posthumously published atlas with the title "Polus Arcticus," revealed the purported existence of an ice-free polar sea. From Mercator, *Atlas sive Cosmographicae Meditationes de Fabrica Mundi et Fabrica Figura (Duisburgi Clivorum*, [1595]). *Huntington Library*

the most immediate motive. Private companies involved in long-distance trade had been vital to the economic development of London and had earlier supported the founding of the Royal Exchange. Geographical theories suggesting an ice-free Arctic made northern journeys more attractive than the known routes farther south. All that was needed were individuals willing to try, in the face of earlier disappointments, to mount expeditions that all knew could end in economic ruin or disaster.

But for Hudson and the merchants who supported him at the dawn of the seventeenth century, the sense of possibility, tirelessly propelled by Hakluyt (who had just witnessed the appearance in print of the last major volume of his immense travel collection), became ever more tempting. The English had been slow to embrace serious exploration of much of the Atlantic basin, and slower still to mount expeditions to establish colonies. Perhaps explorers might find not only the elusive passage but territories for possible colonies and new sources of natural resources that could be harvested and sold for great profit back home—notably, locales for hunting seals (for their furs), whales (for their oil and to make ambergris), and walrus (prized for their tusks, which Europeans believed possessed medicinal properties).

Despite the risks, George Weymouth traveled toward what he hoped was the Northwest Passage in 1602. If he had been able to provide proof that he made it to the South Sea, the East India Company would have paid him £500, an enormous sum. Upon his return in the autumn, John Chamberlain, an inveterate letter writer who often paid attention to the departure and arrival of ships from London, noted that "Our discoverers that went to seek out the Northwest passage are returned *re infecta*"—with the business unfinished—"but yet may shew that they will proceed afresh the next year." The first published account of Weymouth's journey, written by the ship's chronicler, James Rosier, appeared in London in 1605. The mission to what Weymouth called the "North part of Virginia" went to modern-day Maine and included a voyage up the St. George River. Rosier reported few problems and included a note on the many natural resources to be found there, from a thick grove of trees to abundant animals, birds, and fish. Visitors, he claimed, would find "excellent sweet and strong" tobacco, the plant then just beginning to spread through England, as well as the medicinal plant angelica, plants to make dyes, and abundant berries. Weymouth even brought back five of the Abenakis, including one he labeled their "commander" and three he called "gentlemen," a term that to Rosier's readers connoted solid social standing. The last of these "Americans," to use the term that Europeans commonly employed in the sixteenth century for the indigenous peoples of the Western

Hemisphere, was a "servant" named Sassacomoit, whose presence signaled a stratification of this indigenous society that would have made sense to the English.

Weymouth was not the only English mariner willing to seek fame and fortune looking for the Northwest Passage. In 1606, four years after Weymouth set sail, an explorer named John Knight, who had served on a 1605 expedition to Greenland, commanded the 40-ton *Hopewell*—perhaps the pinnace that Hudson would captain in 1607—in a search for the Northwest Passage. His luck was not as good as Weymouth's. The surviving journal from his expedition details the persistent problems caused by ice. Even worse, Knight and a small party that accompanied him on a shallop to explore the Labrador coastline never returned after an encounter with a group of Montagnais (or possibly Naskapis or Beothuks). The survivors of the mission faced the High Court of Admiralty on their return, but there was no evidence to charge them with any crimes. Accounts from these expeditions circulated in London and probably passed from hand to hand among the community of shipmasters and those who funded them. The Flemish cartographer Petrus Plancius purportedly gave Weymouth's log to Hudson in 1609 when the English captain accepted a commission from the Dutch East India Company to find the Northeast Passage. By then Hudson would have read Rosier's account. These works would have taught him about the threats that his English expedition faced.

Thorne had proposed the theory of an ice-free Arctic, which Hakluyt promoted, but it was the actual travelers who saw firsthand what an explorer would encounter when trying to find a water route to the East Indies. The Arctic might in theory be an open ocean, but those who went there recognized that there was no easy route to the Pacific through it, or at least none that had yet been found. Weymouth's journey, which revealed that ice could bedevil even an expedition that sailed well south of the Arctic, would not in itself have disproved existing arguments about an ice-free polar sea.

Sea captains with access to inexpensive and practical books knew that the farther north they sailed the more likely it became that they would run into ice and other climate-related threats. This late sixteenth-century English guide provided a schematic map of the world with a warning of the cold that explorers would find near the poles. From John Davis, *The Seamans Secrets* (London, 1599). *Huntington Library*

Hudson's information was not limited to reports generated by English sailors. By the time he became a ship captain, he was integrated into an international community of European geographers and explorers who often shared accounts of their travels and routes as well as geographical research. The workings of this network can be seen in the ways that details about particular places moved from one written account to another. In 1560, an unknown scholar obtained a small treatise by a native of Greenland named Iver Boty, which had been written in Norse, and translated it into German (or High Dutch). The Amsterdam-based Willem Barentsz translated the tract into Dutch (called Low Dutch) that same year. The German version continued to circulate and fell into the hands of Jodocus Hondius, another Flemish cartographer. A merchant named William Stere translated the Dutch version into English for Hudson in 1608. But Hudson also had access to Barentsz's earlier translation, which he borrowed from Plancius. Eventually, the English version of the manuscript, along with other tracts that provided details of Hudson's own journeys, came into the possession of Hakluyt. Information about the North Atlantic moved from one hand to another, spreading ideas among geographers and ship captains across national boundaries and language barriers.

❧

By the time Hudson set sail in April 1610, the spices grown on tropical islands in the Southwest Pacific had become not just a commodity but an obsession for people across England. Physicians sought them to harvest their medicinal value; cooks wanted the zest that enlivened otherwise dull dishes; social elites wanted to extract their scents to help deflect the common smells of their world. The desire for exotic and rare flora was permeating all strata of society.

The urge to acquire spices was not new—as early as 1541 the cosmographer Roger Barlow had urged Henry VIII to find a northern route to the Pacific Ocean. The plans fell apart when the king refused to meet the demands of a ship pilot from Seville who had offered his services for the mission. But by the early seventeenth century trade in spices had become an economic and social imperative. Compounding the craving for the spices was the English need to find new markets for its woolens. Their hopes for a rapid passage to the East Indies was a matter of national competitiveness as well; if English ships managed to make it to the Spice Islands and back via the theorized polar route, the spices on board could come to market without the markups imposed by Portuguese or other middlemen. The effort to control the trade had implications, too, for English Protestants, who did not want to see Iberian Catholics profit at their expense.

The lust for spices provided an unavoidable push for explorations of new routes. In 1595, a decade after he returned from his voyages, John Davis told the Privy Council that English ships traveling through the channel he explored (modern Davis

Strait) would find markets for goods produced at home. More important, they would return with "all Indian commodities in the ripeness of perfection." The quick passage of spices homeward would make the queen's realm "the storehouse of Europe, the nurse of the world, and the glory of all nations." Spreading exotic spices throughout Europe would be England's way to advance a divine agenda by distributing the benefits of God's bounty to all. Merchants and artisans would grow richer, as would the state itself. Davis was so confident that he wrote a pamphlet summarizing his knowledge of global geography, declaring that there were no natural barriers blocking English ships from speedy journeys to China, the Spice Islands, the Philippines, or India. Travel through a northerly route would allow the realm's mariners much quicker access to the East Indies than the slow route around Africa.

In the years that followed, the East India Company mounted one large expedition after another through the South Atlantic, around the Cape of Good Hope, and through the Indian Ocean toward various destinations. Unlike expeditions to find the reputed Northwest Passage, these voyages tended to include substantial ships with large crews. On the company's third journey, which lasted from 1607 to 1610, some of those on board even staged performances of Shakespeare's *Richard II* and *Hamlet*. Such spectacles would never be seen on the more meager decks of the ships that Hudson commanded.

III.

# The Northern Sailor

LONDON, AMSTERDAM,
AND THE ATLANTIC, 1607–1609

*Henry Hudson grasped* the significance of finding a quick water route to the spice markets of the East Indies. He was in an ideal position to advance the nation's quest because, almost unique among Europeans of his age, he was a man who felt comfortable sailing through the frigid waters of the North Atlantic. His studies and early travels had convinced him that mastering the Arctic would ensure the future of England's spice trade. His expeditions all began with high hopes for wealth and renown, and although he did not achieve his greatest goal—finding a passage to the East Indies—he provided in-depth reports of Arctic locales that had been little understood by Europeans earlier. His name would eventually attach to the most important sites he explored—the Hudson River, Hudson Strait, and Hudson Bay. But as important as his first three voyages were, equally vital to the captain himself were his growing command of the sea, the cold, his ship, and his crew—even as he sought to accommodate the needs of his sailors, who did not always share his ambitions.

When Hudson took command of his first ship in 1607, Europeans believed that there were, in essence, four possible ways to reach the East Indies. The first, which countless merchants had by then traversed, was an overland route, a tiresome and often dangerous journey that was also expensive because it required a cargo of spices to change hands multiple times. The second option was to sail southward along the western coast of Europe, across the Mediterranean, down the western coast of Africa, past the Cape of Good Hope, through the Indian Ocean, and finally to the Southwest Pacific. Though the sea route was twice as long—20,000 miles from Banda to Western Europe compared to 10,000 miles for the overland trail—over time it became both quicker and less expensive to use. Such travel was by then well-charted and profitable, though still time-consuming, expensive, and risky. The third possibility was to sail west across the Atlantic, southward along the coast of South America, and then through the Straits of Magellan. But this was a dangerous route, especially in the fierce waters separating South America from Antarctica. The fourth alternative was a northern route through the Arctic. Various maps circulating at the time of Hudson's early voyages suggested this to be the quickest path—if only Europeans could get into the ice-free polar sea, which meant they had to figure out how to survive the ice and cold that ringed the Arctic and might, some still feared, cover it entirely.

By Hudson's time Europeans had been sailing to the East Indies for more than a century. In 1498—only five years after Christopher Columbus returned to Spain and told his tale of finding lands that Europeans did not know existed—the Portuguese captain Vasco da Gama had pioneered the sailing route around Africa to the Indian Ocean. A generation later, Ferdinand Magellan had led his expedition westward, southward around South America, and across the Pacific to the Philippines. The commander died in a skirmish on Mactan Island, in the Cebu province of the Philippines, but the survivors of the assault on his small fleet continued to sail westward until they reached Europe. In the decades that followed, the Portuguese mastered the routes from Europe to the Southwest Pacific and established Europe's first genuine maritime empire.

But the English did not benefit directly from these oceanic triumphs. In 1600 Queen Elizabeth chartered the East India Company, which almost immediately launched annual expeditions to India and the Spice Islands. Over time, the operation enabled the English to participate more directly in trade in the East Indies, and eventually Hakluyt produced a book to meet the linguistic needs of those who would sail there. Yet even under the best circumstances the English never had the strategic advantages of Iberians, especially the Portuguese, who had mastered the route and established outposts in Africa and South Asia to supply their ships.

Under these circumstances, some of the English came to realize that their strategic advantage lay in sponsoring missions that would chart a more northerly route. When they looked at their maps, they saw three possibilities. The shortest distance to the East Indies was across the North Pole. The next shortest route led through the waters north of Russia and into the Northwest Pacific. The third route lay through the interior of North America.

From 1607 to 1609, Henry Hudson looked for all three of them.

❧

Little is known about Hudson's life before his first attempt to navigate northward to Asia in 1607. The date and place of his birth remain uncertain, as does his family background. He was probably born in the 1560s, and it is possible that in 1584, when he was a teenager or young man, he lived in the small coastal hamlet of Longhoughton (or nearby Bowmer), midway between Newcastle-upon-Tyne and Berwick-upon-Tweed on the Northumberland coast of the North Sea, in an area then known as the East Marches. If this is the case, he could have become accomplished in navigating along rocky coastlines and coping with bitter winters—two sets of skills that would have been of great use to someone who dreamed of leading a ship through the North Atlantic. He also could have undergone at least minimal military training, another experience that would have made him more attractive to potential investors.

Hudson made his first confirmed appearance in the historical record in 1607 as the master of a ship called the *Hopewell* bound for China and Japan via the North Pole—possibly the same ship that Knight had led to the Labrador coast in 1606. Presumably Hudson had been involved with earlier ventures in exploration, because it is virtually impossible that an inexperienced sailor could have otherwise obtained the financing to captain such an expedition. Perhaps he had been involved in earlier English voyages in search of the Northwest Passage, though no evidence confirms such theories. But the silence in the records is not impenetrable. It is likely that he was a member of a family that had supported overseas exploration and mercantile investments that stretched from Brazil to Newfoundland to Muscovy (Russia) in the middle decades of the sixteenth century. Possibly born in London (if not in Northumberland), Hudson had three sons with his wife Katherine: John, his father's constant companion on his adventures; Richard, who eventually traveled with the East India Company to Japan and India (where he died in 1644); and Oliver, about whom little is known.

History may not record much about Hudson's private life, but he left detailed narratives of his journeys of 1607 (written with the assistance of a crewman named John Playse) and 1608. Robert Juet, his mate, wrote an account of their 1609 voyage to the mid-Atlantic coast of North America. Those narratives fell into the hands of Richard Hakluyt, who in his efforts to promote overseas exploration and commerce, passed them to Samuel Purchas, the Anglican priest who acquired many of Hakluyt's manuscripts, and Purchas published them in 1625. Hudson was not a particularly elegant writer, and Juet possessed minimal talents, though he could evoke a scene vividly and he kept a day-by-day accounting of much of the 1609 expedition. Whatever their limitations as literature, their reports and a small number of other surviving documents still transport the reader to the often brutal seascape of the North Atlantic in the opening years of the seventeenth century.

⁊

On April 19, 1607, Henry Hudson led a party of eleven men to St. Ethelburga's Church on Bishops Gate Street in London, where they joined the congregation for Communion, probably seeking divine protection from the unknown menaces they might encounter. The modest church had once served the spiritual needs of the nuns of St. Helen. One chronicler writing in 1603 described the church as having seven rooms for alms in the house associated with the leather sellers' company, one of many guilds in London at the time.

Hudson's son John, who was then only fourteen years old, attended church with the party. Within days, he would become the crew's youngest member. His father was grooming him for a life of sailing long distances and braving nature at some of its fiercest points. Four days after the church service, Hudson guided the *Hopewell* down the Thames. The captain's plan was simple: He would lead the ship due north, across the pole, in the hope of soon arriving in East Asia. The scheme was audacious but appealing—or at least it was to the ten men who attended the service and joined Hudson for the mission, and presumably to those who provided financing for the expedition.

Hudson docked first at Gravesend, where he probably finished stocking up on supplies for the long journey. They cleared the port on May 1. For the next three weeks, the ship sailed northward, but apparently nothing of interest crossed Hudson's mind, since the next entry in his journal was dated

45

the twenty-sixth, when the crew reached 60°12′N at a point 6 leagues (18 miles) east of the "Isles of Shotland" (presumably modern-day Shetland). Ever the explorer, Hudson took a sounding and reported that the ship was in 64 fathoms; the sea floor there was "black, oozy [muddy], sandy, with some yellow shells." Such comments, which appeared frequently in accounts of the captain's journeys, reveal that Hudson, like other mariners, understood that the success of any voyage depended on knowing what lay beneath them, especially since the color of the water provided direct clues to potential unseen risks. Four days later, the *Hopewell* reached 61°11′N, but then the winds turned against them and they made no progress for the next four days. Hudson could not have known it yet, but this pattern of progress and delay would bedevil him on all his journeys. Such thrall to the whims of weather was familiar to many Europeans who sailed the North Atlantic.

Soon the winds picked up and the *Hopewell* began to make progress again. By June 8, they reached 65°27′N, the latitude of Iceland, and three days later they crossed the Arctic Circle and reached 67°30′N. Hudson reported that the crew spotted a pod of six or seven whales, which caused the ship no problems. That night the crew faced gale-force winds that continued the next day. By the time night fell on the twelfth, a dense fog had besieged the ship.

That night Hudson reported that land lay ahead of the ship, as well as ice. The fog had not lifted, so the crew steered toward the north in hopes of avoiding catastrophic collision with ice or shoreline. They managed to avoid crashing into the nearby rocks, but the bitter winds froze their sails and shrouds (the rope rigging that held the sails to the mast). The skies cleared by eight in the morning, giving them a view of the island they had narrowly avoided. They beheld what Hudson called "a very high Land, most part covered with Clay, with much Ice lying about it." A whale swam near the shore and birds flocked to it. Following the pattern of other European explorers, Hudson and his mates named the places they encountered that did not yet exist on their map. They called the headland "Young's Cape," presumably after James Young, one of the men on board. Nearby rose a steep mountain—"round like a Castle" as it was described by Hudson and his chronicler Playse (who helped the captain with the first part of the narrative)—which the English named the Mount of God's Mercy. Then it began to rain, which continued into the night and turned to snow the next day as the ship ran closer to the island.

Soon, unsurprisingly, the winds picked up again. It was so blustery on the fourteenth that the crew feared the *Hopewell* would be driven into the rocks, so they hauled in their sail. The men did not even try to raise sail the next morning because the winds were too strong. Instead, they allowed the boat to drift while they waited for favorable breezes. The rains came heavy that night, but the men had no choice but to wait out the storm and hope for better conditions. It was, they knew, the only way to reduce the risk of a wreck in these forbidding seas, amid such brutal coastlines.

The ship managed to resume course by the seventeenth, with winds sufficient to drive them along for several days. But the rain and fog kept returning, and it was often difficult for them to know where they were. In this age when navigators relied on a cross-staff or an astrolabe, each of which required clear skies to work, days of miserable weather could thwart even the most skilled sailors. At one point, crewmen caught a glimpse of land, but before they could determine if it was Greenland or another island, the fog forced them to change directions once again. Soon they spotted three more whales. The crew must have rejoiced that the waters had calmed. They continued to sail northeast through the fog.

On May 20, Hudson estimated that the *Hopewell* should be close to Newland (modern Svalbard), a cluster of islands barely known by Europeans at the time (and to this day among the most remote places on earth). The sun broke through the clouds for the first time in eighteen days. "We saw many Birds with black backs, and white bellies in form much like a Duck," Hudson wrote. "We saw also many pieces of Ice driving at the Sea." But soon, not surprisingly, the fog settled in again, persisting until the morning of the twenty-second. Hudson estimated that the ship was at 72°38´N when they sighted "a main high Land, nothing at all covered with snow." On the northern side of this landmass rose tall mountains, which, Hudson noted, were not snow-capped, a crucial marker of the climate. This land seemed to lie at 73°N, but he could gain no further purchase of it because ice jutted out near the shore, fog blocked their vision, and variable winds made sailing difficult and precarious.

Hudson thought this route might lead into the rumored open sea, which would have sped his journey if he was right. But he could not be certain because he lacked an accurate map of the region. As he wrote in his report, the crew had found land that was not even marked on the navigational charts, called "cards," that they had brought with them. Hudson's men could not touch down on this remote land, but he thought it might still be a place worth knowing and certainly worth future exploration. The ship continued on toward the northeast, though the crew spotted ice frequently. The men had ventured into territory that, as far as they knew, had never been named by Europeans, and so they labeled this northern land Hold with Hope and noted that it lay at 73°N. Early seventeenth-century cartographers identified this location as a remote corner of northeastern Greenland, perhaps near modern-day Kap Parry (not far south of the present-day place known as Hudson Land).

Hudson believed that this newly charted land needed to be described in some depth. His report of it fits into the long-standing tradition among European explorers of providing firsthand accounts of their travels and of the places they discovered—a literary practice that predated even Columbus's first narrative, which was printed in 1493. These observers recognized that readers craved direct observations and valued

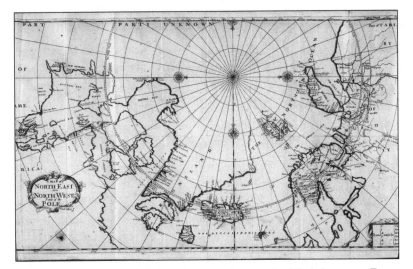

Hudson's first journey sailed through waters that remained little known to Europeans for generations. Hold with Hope is the place-name farthest north on the east coast of Greenland in this late seventeenth-century map. From *An account of several late voyages & discoveries to the south and north* (London, 1694). *Huntington Library*

them over summaries of travel literature by Europeans who had not ventured abroad. The desire for eyewitness testimony fueled a continent-wide publishing trend to label new accounts as "true" reports in order to differentiate them from the fables spun by earlier writers (such as the one by the fourteenth-century English fabulist Sir John Mandeville, who filled the account of his purported travels with reports of monsters he claimed to have seen). By the latter decades of the sixteenth century, printers realized there was an enormous market for narratives that were alleged to be truthful, and so they frequently added claims about a report's veracity to the title of a work. Chroniclers of Frobisher's journeys to the North Atlantic in the 1570s employed the technique, as did the English mathematician Thomas Harriot, who titled his 1588 book *A Briefe and True Report of the Newfound Land of Virginia*. Such accounts were most popular when observers chronicled the natural resources to be found and provided details about indigenous peoples.

For Hudson, the desire to describe places had a special urgency. He wanted to let others know whether it was possible to survive in northern territories rife with ice-strewn bays and beset by fierce storms. He pointed out that when the ship had sailed past the Mount of God's Mercy and Young's Cape that each was mostly covered with snow and the temperature bitter. But that was not the case at Hold with Hope. Instead, the location felt temperate. Nor was there much wind; the ship remained essentially in place for two days. Soon enough, the winds returned, as did the rain, which Hudson likened to an English thunderstorm.

On June 25, Hudson reported that the *Hopewell* had reached 75°N and fog had arisen that night. He then remarked that the English used the word "night" to mark a certain time of day, but that such a term had little meaning here, because the sun never dipped below the horizon. When the mist cleared the next day, he reported that three grampuses played near the ship, and later he observed small flocks of birds he described as having white bellies, black beaks, and spear-shaped tails—in all likelihood thick-billed murres, which return to the area each summer to breed. Hudson surmised that land was nearby, believing that birds, unless they were migrating, tended to remain close to shore—but his crew could not see it. The next day the ship reached 76°38′N and the men spotted yet more birds, including some of apparently the same kind as sighted the previous day, but with red heads. They had seen these birds when they passed the Mount of God's Mercy in Greenland, but not in such numbers.

The next day they reached 78°N and sailed into a thick fog. They could not see where they were, but Hudson thought they had approached a temperate land—which would give him further confirmation that the polar sea was warm enough to be navigable. Hudson thought they should be near Vogel Hooke. But over the next two weeks they managed to move only mar-

European travelers frequently reported on the creatures they encountered in the North Atlantic,
such as the whale, narwhal, gram-
pus, and walrus depicted in this
later scene of a whale hunt. The
birds in the foreground, probably
ptarmigan and thick-billed murres, were frequent visitors to the
region during the summer. From
Jean Bernard, *Recueil de Voyages*
(Paris, 1716). *Huntington Library*

ginally northward. The men had to keep a constant watch
against the jagged ice that threatened the *Hopewell;* occasional
stiff winds froze their sails. On the morning of July 9, Hudson
noted a large quantity of driftwood floating near the ship. The
men took advantage of it to plug a leak and mend the *Hopewell*'s rigging. They remained amid these "Islands of Ice" for
another day, with seals and walruses paddling nearby.

At this point, the nature of Hudson's report itself changed.
The early section had reflected Playse's voice, though it is impossible to separate Hudson's observations from his assistant's.
But the latter part came from Hudson himself, and the phrasing changed, at least in some places, to include the first-person
voice. "I steered away North ten leagues," Hudson wrote on
July 11, a sign that he was in command of both the journey
and its account. By then he would have been increasingly concerned about the pace of his voyage, with its outcome increasingly in doubt.

The *Hopewell* continued to edge northward, reaching
79°17′N, but Hudson reported "we had the company of our
troublesome neighbours Ice with fog." He wrote that they saw

51

many seals and also bear tracks on the frosty island when some men rowed ashore. Some of the crew had managed to find the remains of a bear, which they soon devoured. It was a mistake. Soon many of them became ill from eating the apparently rotten meat. Within two days, the ship reached 80°N—and headed straight for an iceberg. Fortunately, a small gale allowed them to steer clear of the obstacle. At midnight the boatswain William Collins spotted Newland, the land they had passed seven weeks earlier, now illuminated by the half-light of midsummer.

Every hour brought new opportunities to observe a region never before described by an English traveler. Aware of the importance of keeping a record of his journey, Hudson filled his report on a daily basis. Certain themes appeared time and again. He always noted remarkable events on board, like the time on July 13 when the ship reached 80°23′N and happened upon yet more whales. One of the men thought it was an ideal opportunity to fish. But a whale grabbed the line instead, apparently breaking it. The crew took a sounding and found the vessel in waters more than 100 fathoms deep, which led them to believe they were in a sound, not a bay. As they looked inland they saw valleys and swamps filled with snow, even though, Hudson wrote, "we found it hot." They were in the midst of the Arctic summer, yet they could never get far from the ice or the fear of being driven onto a rocky, icy coastline.

As the *Hopewell* lay at anchor at Newland, four of the men went on shore. After hiking in the summer heat, they returned to report that they had seen deer (perhaps caribou), whale bones, the tracks of bears and other creatures, "Rote-geese," and driftwood. They had also quenched their thirsts in a freshwater stream. They brought back a pair of walrus tusks still embedded in a jaw as well as what Hudson termed "a Stone of the Countrey." The ship remained in the area, and the next day Hudson estimated that the land stretched north to 81°. He was fairly certain of his location, as he had confirmed the ship's whereabouts with his cross-staff. His crew saw more seals than at any other point on their journey. As it turned out, this moment marked one of Hudson's first notable achievements on this voyage. No European would reach this latitude again for another two centuries.

But that accomplishment meant little to a man who had sailed north hoping to find the quickest way to the spice markets. Hudson's notes would show the English the possibilities for venturing into the Arctic during the summer. His observations would have real value to others in the realm who might want to fish or hunt seals or walrus. Yet this was little consolation to him. He had fitted out the *Hopewell* for a journey across the pole, not a scientific expedition. But he did learn something important for his own purposes. An open polar sea might exist, but the route they tried did not lead to it: They had moved north as far as the season safely allowed. Hudson felt he had no choice but to turn around and head for home. They steered a course back toward Cherie's Island (also known as Bear Island). On August 15, they docked at the Faro Islands. A month later they sailed up the Thames and landed at Tilberie Hope.

Four and a half months had elapsed since Hudson had taken Communion at St. Ethelburga's Church and asked God to protect his crew and provide success to his mission. He had led the small crew of the *Hopewell* farther north than any English sailor had ventured before. Hudson did not reach the pole—he turned back well before his trajectory could prove itself to be a route leading to the East Indies. But he had lost no men, he had charted territory rich in seals, whales, and birds, and he had described remote and potentially resource-rich lands in greater depth than any European before him. The numbers of whales and seals would have excited those who heard his report; their presence opened up the possibility of new, profitable businesses. Promoters of English expansion would have welcomed Hudson's careful recording of latitudes, depths, and distances, which all contributed to the growing stock of English knowledge about the North Atlantic. That was an achievement that would later benefit the realm's other sailors and explorers, especially when the report appeared in print in 1625. On a more personal level, the expedition had one other benefit: Hudson had proved that he was up to whatever challenges he might face in the North Atlantic.

❧

There is no record of what Hudson did after his return to London in September 1607. The appearance in the Thames of the *Hopewell* did not elicit any surviving commentary, unlike the return of ships from the East Indies, which arrived overflowing with the promise of their aromatic treasures. Nor did his journey attract even the level of attention that ships returning from the struggling new English settlement at Jamestown did. Perhaps Hudson met with Hakluyt or some other advocate of colonization or gatherer of geographical knowledge. It is likely that he left in London at least one written account of his journey toward the North Pole. Any experienced sailor would have wanted posterity to have a record of heroic actions, even if, as was always possible with long ocean journeys, the explorer himself never returned home, even if his ship did. Perhaps Hudson met with London's cartographers to tell them what he had seen so they could include the information on their charts, but there survives no map or card from his hand.

The 1607 journey increased Hudson's ambition for exploration. The next year he organized another expedition bound for northern waters and again fitted out the *Hopewell*. Having presumably concluded that he could not succeed by following his previous year's route across the pole, he now chose a different strategy to reach the East Indies. This time he decided he could reach the Spice Islands by sailing through the Northeast Passage, which geographers had argued existed along the northern edge of the Eurasian landmass. Others, including English sailors employed by the Muscovy Company, had previously tried to find it. They all had failed. So had the Dutch explorer

Willem Barentsz, whose experiences—including the ones leading to his unfortunate demise in 1597—contributed to Hudson's store of knowledge about the route.

Barentsz also had sought the coveted route east, in his case to provide better access for the Dutch, who shared the trans-European passion for spices. No Dutch explorer was more determined to succeed than Barentsz, who made three separate journeys looking for the Northeast Passage. During 1594 and 1595 he got as far as Novaya Zemlya (known then as Nova Zemsla) before ice blocked his way. Still, he came back with details about the great bounties to be found in the Arctic, especially its large herds of walrus. He also told about the danger from polar bears, which killed two of his men in 1595. He fared worse on his third journey, when his ship became surrounded by ice near Novaya Zemlya in July 1596. As winter settled in, Barentsz and his men decided to break up what remained of their vessel to build a house in an effort to stave off the cold. Most managed to survive the winter, but after ten months without a thaw sufficient enough to allow them the warmth they needed for the labor of rebuilding their boat, they decided instead to try to sail home in two open shallops. A week into the trip, Barentsz died, as did many of the others. Twelve men managed to make it home to tell the tale of what had happened.

Among the veterans of Barentsz's expeditions was a carpenter named Gerrit de Veer. He had traveled with Barentsz in 1594 and 1595 but had not gone on what proved to be the explorer's last attempt. After news had reached Amsterdam about the disaster, de Veer wrote a chronicle of the three trips, including Barentsz's fatal journey, which soon found a wide audience. A German edition appeared in Noribergae in a 1598 collection by the Dutch engraver Levinus Hulsius (who also illustrated an edition of Sir Walter Ralegh's account of his meandering journey up the Orinoco during his exploration of Guiana). That same year, printers in Amsterdam published editions in French, Latin, and German. From then on, the circulation of de Veer's chronicle grew across Europe. Two separate editions in Italian appeared in Venice in 1599, the same year the first copies came rolling off the press in Paris. In 1602, two separate editions appeared in Nuremberg, and four years later an Italian version could be found in a new edition of Giovanni Battista Ramusio's *Navigationi e Viaggi*—a book whose first edition (published in the middle decades of the sixteenth century) had been one of the geographical monuments of the European age of discovery. The first English translation appeared in 1609—the year that Hudson set off on his task for the Dutch East India Company—but in all likelihood Hudson had learned about the expeditions before then.

The appeal of de Veer's accounts of Barentsz's three Arctic voyages was based on the incredible nature of the accounts themselves, augmented by the vivid illustrations in many editions. The images evoke the bounty to be harvested in the Arctic, suggesting as well the seeming ease with which hunters could take walrus, which lolled on the shore in great herds and moved slowly enough in the water that men in rowboats could attack them. But de Veer also showed the risks of these ventures. An encounter with a polar bear could be fatal to an unarmed man. Worse still, as Barentsz's death proved, were the dangers faced by those unlucky enough to be trapped by the ice. The pressure of the ice could destroy the hull of a ship and force men onto a frozen wasteland where bears prowled.

Stories of the failures of other explorers did not deter Hudson, who set off from St. Katherine's Pool on the Thames on April 22, 1608, with a crew of fourteen, again including his son John. Hudson and his men faced few obvious challenges during the first few weeks of the journey. Of course, they encountered fog, and occasionally struggled to find decent winds, but it was not until the fourth week of May, approximately on the twenty-first, that the crew began to feel the effects of the chill northern air. On May 25, Hudson reported that Philip Stacie, the ship's carpenter, had become ill. Three or four others also seemed to

be suffering from what the captain believed was a malady arising from the onset of the frigid conditions. By the end of the
month, the weather had taken a turn for the worse, with snow
on May 30 and again on June 1, when the crew ran into a "hard
gale." By June 3, they had rounded the North Cape (modern
Nord Kap, the northernmost part of Norway). Fortunately,
Stacie was sufficiently recovered by June 4 to make a mast "for
our ship-boat," but the same day, the ship's cook and one other
crew member fell ill. By that point, the ship had made it past
74°N with relative ease.

From early June to early July, Hudson pursued two tasks.
First, and most important, he tried to find a way to guide the
*Hopewell* through the Arctic region, which even in the middle
of the summer was sufficiently cold for snow to fall and ice to
form along the side of his ship, though some days were warm
and pleasant. The *Hopewell* had to navigate its first ice field on
June 9, which the crew managed to do, but the sailing never became easy. Hudson's job was to explore the region and identify
profitable commodities that might be harvested there. His men
disembarked long enough to investigate some of the lands they
were passing, and realized that other humans had been there
before them, including some who had left a cross standing, the
sign of Christian visitors. Along the shoreline, his crew found
long grasses as well as whale fins, deer antlers, and the tracks of
fox and bear. They also came back with birds and eggs and reported they had seen great flocks of other birds, evidence of the
Arctic's summer fecundity. The report indicated that future expeditions into the area would be more likely to succeed, because later crews could supplement their stored food with fresh
sources of meat. Seals basking in the sun attracted attention
too. But Hudson was particularly excited about the sightings of
large numbers of walrus. He understood that harvesting their
tusks would be a boon for physicians, who ground them down
for their medicinal properties, and for artisans, who made
knives and combs from the ivory. That market could possibly

generate sufficient profits to cover the cost of a future venture into the region. Hudson by then knew much about what might be found in northern waters and along nearby shorelines. But there were still surprises, among them the sighting of a mermaid.

On June 15 one man had spotted her out in the water, not far from the boat. He called to the others "to see her, one more came up, and by that time she was come close to the ships side, looking earnestly on the men." Hudson reported that soon a wave came and flipped her over, offering the men a view of her torso. He described her as resembling a woman from her navel to her head, and about the same size as the men on the ship. She had long black hair, which contrasted with the whiteness of her skin. When she descended into the water again, the men studied her tail, which had the shape of a porpoise's but the speckling common to a mackerel. Hudson added that the witnesses to this magical creature were Thomas Hilles and Robert Rayner.

Why would Hudson provide the names of the witnesses? Presumably he thought that spreading tales about mermaids would not do much for his credibility. Still, many Europeans did believe in the existence of such creatures. During the sixteenth century, cosmographers had speculated about the existence of mermaids in their treatises about the natural history of the sea, often providing some illustration of what such a creature might look like. A sign of a mermaid in London helped customers locate at least one printer's shop. Whether he intended to or not, Hudson had in fact employed the same strategy that Sir Walter Ralegh had used a decade earlier when he explored the Orinoco Basin. Ralegh declared that there were some in the area who had witnessed monsters roaming the forests, but he never claimed to have seen them with his own eyes. Hudson could report on the possibility of mermaids, and offer a description of them, without implicating himself in the dissemination of rumors of mythical beasts. In an age in which many explorers were keen to offer readers "true" accounts of what they had seen, perhaps he feared that his report would be dismissed if he recorded that he had seen mermaids with his own eyes.

By early July, Hudson understood that he had reached a pivotal moment. He realized that the rivers he had seen flowing into the Barents Sea could not be followed far enough to make them serious candidates for an eastern passage, and that currents and tides would work against any ship that tried to ascend them. More troubling was the continued threat posed by the ice, including large floes propelled by a river toward the *Hopewell* on July 2. The ice, Hudson wrote, was "driving upon us, very fearful to behold." But the ship was firmly moored in open water with a double anchor, and the men managed to use spars to fend off any shards that came too close. For twelve hours they fought a defensive action against the ice until the currents subsided. Within a few days, Hudson concluded that the Northeast Passage could not be found. Some of his men, who had taken a shallop to explore one river, reported that there was no way through. "[W]e presently set sail with the wind at North North-west," a dejected Hudson wrote in his journal, "with sorrow that our labour was in vain." Hudson was especially disappointed by his inability to go through the sound and into "a more Easterly Sea." They had not found the accessible Northeast Passage that the cartographers had posited on their maps.

Still, Hudson knew he had encountered a land with much to recommend it. "Generally, all the Land of *Nova Zembla* that yet we have seen, is to a man's eye a pleasant Land," the captain recalled. Much of the mainland was free of snow and covered with grass, and he had observed many deer browsing there. Some snow lay on the hills, but even there he saw bare spots. Yet experience had taught him much about this part of the world and its ubiquitous dangers. He had now encountered much of the geography of the Arctic Circle, and his observations led him to a single conclusion: Ice would prevent any access to the South Sea. He remained puzzled about the inaccuracies on the maps generated on Barentsz's journeys and wondered if the Dutch had misread the variation of their compass.

During their return across open sea, Hudson continued to make observations about the weather and the ship's latitude, thereby adding yet more details to the growing body of information he had gathered about these infrequently traveled seas. On July 17, his men spotted land and estimated that they were near Ward-house. Ten days later, Hudson reported that the crew began to light candles once again at the end of the day, which they had not had to do since mid-May, when the *Hopewell* had sailed into a region of perpetual summer daylight.

On August 7, Hudson reached London, put an unknown number of his company ashore, and continued on the *Hopewell* until he reached Gravesend on August 26. He gave each of his men a certificate indicating that no one on board had forced him to abandon the mission. It was a curious statement, and one that he quickly explained in his account of the journey, which he apparently gave to Hakluyt. When he was at Novaya Zemlya on July 6, he reported, he had realized that he was not going to find the Northeast Passage, and at that moment he contemplated reversing the ship's course and heading toward the Northwest Passage instead. But he feared that the winds might turn against them, a common occurrence that he understood too well by that point. He knew it would take immense effort to get past a place called *Lumleys Inlet*, "and the furious over-fall" identified by the English captain John Davis years earlier—now the opening of Hudson Strait. It was too late for such a radical change in course, as Hudson knew. But he recognized that the trip so far had taken just over half of the time he had allotted for it, and he had only made it through the briefest part of his proposed circuit because of the "contrary winds" that had slowed the progress of the *Hopewell*. He had then taken it upon himself to do all he could to save the lives of the men on his ship from the immediate menace of icebergs and the impending onslaught of autumn cold. He needed to preserve the "Victuall, Wages, and Tackle," and the only way to do so was to beat a hasty retreat. It would have been "foolish," he wrote, to waste more time trying to go farther before real problems arose.

Hudson's second journey, like his first, had ended with failure. He had not made it through the Northeast Passage, though he still maintained that it existed, even if he saw no way for the *Hopewell* to traverse the contrary winds and currents through the straits at Novaya Zemlya. It was possible that a craft equipped for a different kind of journey might have made it farther up the river where Hudson had abandoned his quest, but that remained a theoretical possibility.

Though he had failed to meet his ultimate objective, his report on the journey gave those who read it confidence in his abilities. He had found no shortcut to the East Indies, but he had astutely recorded in detail the flora and fauna he observed, aware of the potential market for the region's resources—especially walrus tusks. His comments about the apparent fertility of the land also confirmed the theory that the long summer days near the pole warmed the climate considerably, making it feel hot and facilitating possible excursions from the Atlantic to the Pacific.

Just as important, Hudson had now completed his second northern journey and he had not lost a single man. Indeed, by his own account, he valued their safety more than the possibility of finding success if it meant taking unjustified risks. Such a venture was not worth putting lives in jeopardy. When he offered his men those certificates in London, he was also, in his own way, protecting them: No one could accuse them of turning against him or persuading him to abandon his journey. They were, to a man, loyal to the captain, and he to them—even to the point of making sure to preserve sufficient food for their homeward voyage. Hudson's allegiance to his men and his strong concern for their welfare suggests much about how he balanced his sense of honor with the intensity of his ambitions—and it casts into even greater contrast his men's rebellion in James Bay after he kept them largely safe through the hard Arctic winter of 1611.

❧

On April 6, 1609, Hudson embarked on his next expedition. But this time he departed from Amsterdam, in the employ of the Dutch East India Company and with a mixed Dutch and

English crew. He did not leave a complete record of his own of the journey, though extracts from his writing have survived. Instead, the major extant account, which is far more detailed than the reports of his previous two expeditions, came from the hand of Robert Juet, Hudson's mate, who had also been on his crew for the 1608 expedition and would later play a pivotal role on his final journey. Also writing a brief history of the expedition was Emanuel van Meteren, the Dutch consul in London from 1583 until 1612, whose account was presumably based on what he was able to reconstruct from the sailors after their return. None of those who boarded the 80-ton *Halve Maen* (*Half Moon*) could have known that they had joined what would become Hudson's most famous journey—a voyage that made history by charting part of the mid-Atlantic coast of North America, helping to propel eventual Dutch colonization of the region.

Like London, Amsterdam had become a center of commercial enthusiasm and consumer opportunity. Over the seventeenth century, it would play a pivotal role in the Dutch "Golden Age," which would witness a phenomenal passion for tulips at home and a remarkable expansion of long-distance commerce. At the time Hudson was sailing, Dutch and English authorities had much in common, including a desire to promote the spread of Protestant Christianity. The Dutch also loathed the Spanish, with whom they were at war during much of the first half of the century, and that enmity mirrored Elizabethan sensibilities that had shaped English policies toward North America in the sixteenth century. The commercial powers in Amsterdam and London shared the belief that Henry Hudson was the man to advance their nation's overseas agenda. The faith in Hudson's abilities went farther still. Before he set sail, the French also considered hiring him on the advice of an Amsterdam-based merchant named Isaac Le Maire, who knew both Hudson and the geographer Plancius. That overture never resulted in a contract, however, which left Hudson in the employ of the Dutch East India Company.

Most of the English and Dutch men aboard the *Halve Maen* were probably sailors-for-hire who loitered the docks awaiting their next voyages. One of them was likely a carpenter capable of repairing the ship and constructing shallops for quick trips ashore. Another invariably knew how to use a cross-staff and compass to track the ship's latitude. The Dutch East India Company probably made sure there was a surgeon on board to set broken bones and catch early signs of frostbite or scurvy, which could render a crewman useless. Some of the men might have been good at fishing with nets to supplement the ship's stores with fresh protein. The ablest among them apparently knew how to bring in a whale—no mean feat, given that some leviathans could stretch as long as the ship itself—though there is no evidence of any whaling on this journey. They were a typical crew, able but anonymous; none was sufficiently famous to have had his portrait painted, not even Hudson himself.

The merchants who underwrote Hudson's expedition wanted the English captain to find a quick water route to East Asia. They had dictated that he begin where Barentsz had failed and where he had turned back the previous year. Following orders, Hudson began the journey by sailing east, renewing his efforts to find the Northeast Passage. But again the route proved impassable. As van Meteren put it, Hudson "found the sea as full of ice as he had found it in the preceding year, so that they lost all hope of effecting anything during the season." The Dutch consul added that some of Hudson's men had previously spent time in the East Indies and found the frigid conditions of the Arctic unbearable. Unhappy with their predicament, the men began to argue. Hudson offered them a choice: They could either sail westward toward the fortieth parallel to territory where the English captain John Smith (who had gone to Jamestown in 1607) had advised him that a route through the continent might be found. Or they could instead sail through the Davis Straits, which ran up the west coast of Greenland (and, Europeans believed, toward the open sea) but were much farther north. They opted for the mid-Atlantic route, which all would have guessed would pose fewer problems with the weather.

Van Meteren's account is so brief that it barely does justice to the journey. Fortunately, Juet wrote a long report, but, alas, he was not always very descriptive or evocative. He offered no details about the first part of the expedition, simply writing "because it is a journey usually known, I omit to put down what passed." Only when the ship had sailed farther north did he bother to note that they had had "*much trouble with fogs, sometimes, and more dangerous of Ice.*" Finally, after they had passed the North Cape of the northern Norwegian province of Finmark, he began to record his observations. Like other sailing reports, including Hudson's, Juet's account typically made note of storms and winds, provided calculations of the latitude at specific points, and offered corrections to charts or cards that seemed erroneous. When the *Halve Maen* passed the Faro Islands in late May, for example, Juet noted that they "found them to lie out of their place in the Sea Chart fourteen leagues too far Westerly." The men foraged on shore there, filling their casks with fresh water for the long journey across the open ocean.

By early June, the ship was sailing south by southwest; Hudson estimated that the vessel was at 60°58′N. On the night of June 1 they lit candles in the part of the ship known as the "bittacle," where they kept the compass. The next day, the men thought they spotted Buss Island, which had first come to the attention of Europeans when Sir Martin Frobisher had reported its existence in 1578. On June 3, Juet reported that the men believed themselves to be near Buss Island, "but could not see it." That was hardly surprising, since the island did not actually exist. Frobisher had been in error.

By early July, the crew had arrived along the outer shores of Newfoundland. Juet soon reported that the men found themselves amid "a great Fleet of French-men, which lay Fishing on the Bank" at 43°41′N. He reported that they did not speak to these other Europeans, who had come to the region to harvest cod from the continental shelf. As the *Halve Maen* proceeded southward, the crew followed the example of the Frenchmen and tried their luck with fishing, to great success. Juet reported that on July 8, the men fished for five hours and caught 118 "great Cods" and then took twelve more after a break. They also saw huge schools of herring, but did not report catching any of them. The men fished again the next day, but brought in a smaller haul because they did not have enough salt to preserve more fish. At 44°27′N they again encountered a French fishing ship. They engaged in conversation with its crew—though Juet did not report what they discussed. Soon they fished for yet more cod. Hudson no doubt knew that it was the most profitable natural resource the English had yet harvested in North America. In the days to come they would haul in lobster and halibut as well.

More important, the *Halve Maen* soon began to encounter Algonquians, probably Micmacs, the indigenous people of Nova Scotia; the ship could have been in that area if Juet's latitude recordings were accurate. By 1609 Europeans sailing across the Atlantic would have had some idea of what these Americans would be like. Travel accounts like Thomas Harriot's, which became the most famous depiction of any indigenous North American population in this era, told about their economic and spiritual practices and also their willingness to trade with visitors—a cultural trait that many European sailors welcomed after weeks at sea even if it meant inviting strangers on board. One morning, six of the locals paddled out to the ship. "We gave them trifles, and they eat and drank with us," Juet reported, adding that the Indians told Hudson and his crew that they were near copper, silver, and gold mines. The Europeans also learned that the Americans had been trading with the French. Juet believed they were telling the truth because one of the Indians had acquired at least a small French vocabulary. The crew saw the business for themselves soon enough, when they noticed that the Indians brought beaver and other pelts to the French, who traded knives, axes, kettles, beads, and red gowns. The men on the *Halve Maen* began to trade with the locals too. But they were less diplomatic than the French and came to the conclusion that the Americans were going to rob them. Taking matters into their own hands, Hudson's men launched a pre-emptive raid on one local settlement.

The *Halve Maen* cruised on a mostly southward course toward the opening to the Northwest Passage that Smith thought existed around the fortieth parallel. On August 2, at approximately 41°56′N, the crew once again spotted land—presumably the outer shore of Cape Cod. The next day, they sailed farther south, and when they got close to the coast, they sent a small party ashore to survey the area. Soon they thought they heard other Europeans, but discovered Americans instead, likely Pokahokets or Narragansetts. The locals seemed pleased to meet the Europeans, who welcomed one of them onto the deck of the *Halve Maen*. The crew gave him some meat, and Hudson offered him glass buttons. When the man returned to the shoreline, he signaled back to the boat that this was a place where the Americans fished. The English would have realized that this was the territory that their countryman Bartholomew Gosnold had found in 1602 and named Cape Cod in recognition of the storied schools of the fish swimming off its shoals. Juet's report noted that the Americans here possessed tobacco— the plant in the Western Hemisphere that Europeans had come to crave more than any other for its supposed medicinal value and the pleasant sensations it aroused. They smoked it from red copper pipes fashioned with earthen bowls. "The Land is very sweet," Juet wrote.

On they went, heading farther south. By August 18, the ship crossed over what Juet called the "Barre of *Virginia*"— along today's Eastern Shore of the Chesapeake—which he understood to be "the entrance into the *King's* River in *Virginia*, where our *English*-men are." Several nights later, on the twenty-first, they encountered another storm sufficient to cause damage to their vessel. On August 24 they reached 35°41′N, offshore from the outer banks of modern North Carolina and close to the site of the earlier, disastrous English settlement at Roanoke. Soon the *Halve Maen* reversed direction and headed north, reaching latitude 40°30′N, approximately the coastal border of present-day New York and New Jersey, on September 3. The men had great luck catching mullet and salmon, and on the fourth they hooked a ray so large that it took four men to haul it to shore.

That same day, the men of the *Halve Maen* came into contact for the first time with the Munsees, a group of Delawares (also known as Lenapes) who lived near that harbor. The English had arrived on the shores of the ancestral Delaware territory, which the locals called Lenapehoking, or "the Land of the People." Juet reported that the Munsees were happy to see the English and offered the newcomers green tobacco in exchange for beads and knives. The English found them "very civil" and noted their large supply of maize. The woods nearby had tall oak trees, a sign of the richness of the area's soils. The next day, September 5, members of the crew went back onto the land, where they met American men, women, and children, for another gift of tobacco; some of the Indians also went on board the *Halve Maen,* many of them wearing feather mantles and furs and skins, and several gave Juet dried currants, which he reported "were sweet and good." The women who came on board offered hemp. But despite the peaceful exchanges, the English and Dutch men on the ship once again felt that the locals could not be trusted.

The following day Hudson sent a party of five to the shore again to scout the territory. Their explorations went well for a while. They found plentiful flowers and grasses as well as "goodly Trees, as ever they had seen, and very sweet smells came from them." As they returned from rowing into what Juet called an "open sea," they were approached by twenty-six local men paddling toward them in two canoes. As night fell it began to rain, and the Munsees attacked, injuring three sailors. One of them, a man named John Coleman, who had probably sailed with Hudson in 1607, took an arrow in his throat and soon died. They buried Coleman nearby, naming a point of the land after him, and maintained a vigilant watch the entire night.

To Juet's way of thinking, the assault they suffered was unprovoked. But the Europeans did not yet have sufficient understanding or knowledge of the Americans to identify precisely who among the indigenous peoples were their enemies. They continued to meet with the locals, some of whom even came on board the ship. The crew watched them warily, always trying to figure out which of them (if any) had killed their shipmate. Tensions grew over the next few days, and the English and Dutch decided the time had come to leave. They began to sail up a large river, presumably because they believed that it led to the Northwest Passage. As they sailed up what would later become known as the Hudson River, the captain and his men met more of the Indians, some of whom offered not just tobacco but wheat, the kind of hospitality typically offered by the Algonquian peoples who controlled this part of the American mainland. But the Europeans, even as they accepted their gifts, had grown more wary and distrustful. "They appear to be a friendly people," Hudson later remarked, "but have a great propensity to steal, and are exceedingly adroit in carrying away whatever they take a fancy to."

The assault that took Coleman's life in September confirmed the crew's misgivings about Americans. Thereafter, even peaceful meetings with locals heightened their anxiety. On September 9 the Europeans, fearful that two canoes filled with men aimed to attack them, tried unsuccessfully to capture several of the locals. Three days later the men of the *Halve Maen* faced the largest group of Algonquians they had yet encountered when twenty-eight canoes carrying men, women, and children paddled out to the ship. Juet believed that they had come "to betray us." But the *Halve Maen* anchored and the two parties did trade with each other, presumably on the shore. The sailors acquired beans and oysters from the Indians, and Juet was impressed with the Americans' yellow copper pipes. Over the next few days, after the *Halve Maen* had gone another 4 miles upriver and anchored, other Indians arrived, trading oysters, pumpkins, maize, and tobacco to the English in exchange for what Juet called "trifles." The English also replenished their casks with fresh water. Most of the natives the English encountered offered hospitality and sought trade, though ill will remained. On September 15 Juet noted that the sailors had again tried to take two locals captive, but they also escaped and swam to shore, cursing the visitors. As the ship sailed farther upstream the men met other groups of Americans, who also offered what they had, including grapes. Some brought out beaver and otter pelts, prompting the English to trade beads, knives, and hatchets.

As the English continued up the river, they realized they had ventured into the midst of a series of indigenous communities. Juet did not provide the names of these groups, but in all likelihood the *Halve Maen* had sailed into the territory of the Catskills and Mahicans. Hudson and his men were extremely suspicious of the locals they were encountering, especially after the violence and tensions of the last weeks, but they also wanted to continue to travel and trade among them safely. But they did not know who they could trust and who would turn on them. To find out if these Indians "had any treachery in them," Hudson and Juet hatched a plan: They would invite some Indians on board, get them drunk on aquavit and wine, and see how they behaved. Though the Indians became intoxicated, they continued to behave in ways that impressed the English. Juet noted that the wife of one man sat as "modestly" as an Englishwoman "in a strange place."

Hudson's guests had not been drunk before. Native Americans in this region had never even tasted alcohol before Europeans brought it there in the seventeenth century, and the

European-driven liquor trade did not develop in earnest until after the mid–seventeenth century. They seemed confused by the effects of the aquavit and wine. Still, after they went home they returned to the ship bearing strings of shells known as wampum, a sign of their appreciation of the English arrival. Soon after, other locals visited the *Halve Maen* and offered more wampum, tobacco, and food to the visitors. One made a speech describing the nearby countryside. The Indians, according to Juet's account, treated Hudson with "reverence."

By late September, the *Halve Maen* had ventured as far as it could up the great river. Hudson had dispatched a small group to paddle upriver to take a sounding, and they returned with the news that only 25 miles farther upstream the river was only 7 feet deep. At that moment, Hudson and the others knew that this could not be the Northwest Passage, at least not a channel deep enough for an oceangoing ship. On the twenty-third, the men turned the ship around near modern-day Albany and began to retrace their route downstream.

Hudson had failed again, but he realized that the lands he had seen offered much to his investors. As the *Halve Maen* descended the river the men paid careful attention to the landscape, especially the flora. They saw fertile fields and forests thick with oak, walnut, chestnut, ewe, and "trees of sweet wood in great abundance, and great store of Slate for houses, and other good stones." They traded and ate with the same peoples they had encountered on their upriver journey. They marveled at their success fishing in the river, where they caught mullet and bream, and appreciated the willingness of the Indians to trade furs for "Knives and trifles." Their river journey also convinced some of the men that the valley would be a good place to settle. "This is a very pleasant place to build a town on," Juet wrote—the first time anyone on one of Hudson's expeditions mentioned the subject of colonization. The nearby mountains might contain minerals, Juet mused, and he believed that some of the local stones were strong enough to cut through steel or iron.

On October 1, the crew hosted visitors whom Juet identified only as the "people of the Mountain" who seemed not to have encountered the *Halve Maen* or its men earlier. The Europeans purchased some small skins from them. As the group remained on board, Juet wrote, one local man paddled his canoe close, leaped onto the rudder of the *Halve Maen,* and climbed into the window of the cabin, where he stole Juet's pillow, two bandoliers, and two shirts. One of the sailors shot him in the breast and killed him. The other visitors then immediately jumped off the ship into the river. The English gave chase, leaping into a shallop, and one of the Indians grabbed hold of their rowboat and tried to overturn it. The ship's cook chopped off the man's hand with a sword, and the man soon drowned. The others swam away. The Europeans had seen enough. They mounted the *Halve Maen* and hurried downstream.

But sailing downstream did not solve the Europeans' problems with the locals. Word of the hostilities quite likely passed down through the valley, in all likelihood in advance of the ship itself, and roused other communities. A group that had had prior contact with Europeans, including one man who had been on board the ship before it ascended the river, paddled to the *Halve Maen* in two canoes and shot at the ship with their bows and arrows. The crew fired back with guns, killing two or three of the attackers. More than a hundred others on the shoreline then launched a barrage of arrows toward the Europeans. Again the sailors returned fire. Juet claimed that he used a light cannon, called a falcon, to kill three of the Indians, while others onboard shot three or four more with muskets. When the skirmish abated, the *Halve Maen* sailed away, finally reaching a place the locals called *Manna-hata.* They met with no other locals and sailed on without further violence. On October 4 the ship reached the river's mouth, set their sails, and headed into the Atlantic.

Hudson began the return journey pondering a dilemma. Should he head to Amsterdam to admit his failure, or hatch a new plan, turn the ship, and try again? After six months at sea and two different attempts to locate a route to the East Indies, he had found neither the Northeast nor the Northwest Passage. His English and Dutch crewmen also debated the ship's next destination. The Dutch argued for setting a northward course to Newfoundland, passing the winter there, and launching another search for the Northwest Passage the next spring. Hudson gave in to English opinions and judged such a course unwise. "He was afraid of the mutinous crew," the Dutch consul and historian van Meteren later reported, "who had sometime savagely threatened him." The captain worried about mutiny, but also about running out of food over the winter, thus starving his crew either to death or to such debility that they could neither carry on nor return to Europe.

Hudson had an alternate plan. The ship could winter in Ireland and then proceed to Dartmouth in early spring to prepare for the next year's search for the passage. If he could launch an expedition into the North Atlantic by mid-March, sail northwest, and hunt whales until mid-May, he might then make another stab at finding the entrance to the Northwest Passage. Assuming this strategy worked, he would have the entire summer to search for another opening to the Northwest Passage before the advance of the winter ice made northern routes impassable.

But he never pursued the scheme. For reasons no one bothered to explain, the *Halve Maen* sailed eastward and reached Dartmouth, a deep-water port in southwestern England, on November 7. Hudson soon returned to London, where he told others about his journey, his crew's inability to handle the cold at the start of the trip toward the Northeast Passage, his trip to the coast of Newfoundland and the stop in New France, his journey past Cape Cod and the Chesapeake, and finally, his expedition inland up "a goodly river" (which did not yet bear his name). He also revealed that he remained well connected in London, with ties to the antiquarian Sir Walter Cope, a friend of Hakluyt's who kept one of the city's most famous cabinets of curiosity, and Sir Thomas Chaloner, a chemist who became a courtier and close associate of King James I. Hudson told at least one acquaintance that he planned to return soon to the American coast.

❧

Hudson docked his ship in a capital city celebrating its new status and prosperity. Earlier in the year, Londoners had commemorated the completion of a new gallery of fine shops that were, as one of the annalists of the day put it, "richly furnished with Wares." On April 10, the opening day, the royal family and many aristocrats gathered there to hear speeches, receive gifts, and observe "ingenious devices." King James watched the celebration and welcomed the establishment of what he called "Britains Burse," a place for mercantile exchange. The next month, James issued an order barring ships from other European nations from fishing along the coasts of England without a new license. The decree sparked joy across the land, as the people of London, in particular, believed they would grow richer than at any time "within man's memory," according to the chronicler Edmund Howes. Experiments in the production of alum (which could be used in dyes, leathermaking, medicines, paper production, and even for fire protection) had proved so successful that the king banned the importation of any into England. He rewarded those who had been involved in developing the industry and then engrossed it for himself, loading the material into storehouses. The king also offered to repay a substantial loan to the city's merchants, but they refused to take it. The "wondrous increase of traffic and Navigation," they told the monarch, had made repaying the debt irrelevant.

But economic success did not bring universal prosperity. The number and condition of London's poor elicited concern from, among others, the directors of the Virginia Company. In 1609 they made a formal request to the lord mayor to support shipping some of the "swarm of unnecessary inmates"—who were "a continual cause of dearth and famine, and the very original cause of all the plagues that happen in this kingdom"—to the nascent Chesapeake colony. The domestic problem was not new. Unemployed and underemployed men, in particular, had aroused concern since the middle decades of the sixteenth century, and the problem had only grown worse with the expansion of London's population. The establishment of Jamestown offered a specific destination for these unwanted individuals who, as some feared, would otherwise resort to a life of crime and end their days at the gallows.

By the time Hudson arrived in London, the days were getting shorter and winter had begun to set in. London's air lay heavy with smoke from countless wood fires burning to keep people warm. Across the countryside English farmers had finished their harvests and turned their attention to stocking up fodder for their livestock.

Down by the docks, sailors traded stories about what they had seen, some of them surely telling tales of encountering whales, hunting polar bears, catching fish beyond their wildest dreams, and fighting feather- and leather-clad Americans whom they also got drunk. Hudson was a familiar figure along the wharves, and his adventures and discoveries became part of the lore of the harbor. When he was recruiting men for his journeys, he would have wanted them to know what kind of experiences his crew had had on previous expeditions. He knew that on a small ship it would be crucial to have sailors with sufficient skills to handle the often arduous chores that lay ahead, as well as the daunting hardships they might have to endure. He wanted sailors bold enough to want to embark with him into unknown realms. He also wanted to prevent the kinds of disputes over destinations that had threatened the *Halve Maen*.

As King James's subjects bore down for another winter, the merchants involved in long-distance trade clustered to make plans for spring, when sailors were more likely to make journeys across the Atlantic. Scholars of navigation and exploration might have very well been conveying news of Hudson's exploits and information to guilds or businesses—organizations like the East India Company, which had hired Hakluyt to provide guidance for its ventures earlier in the century. At times, the world of the sailors and the scholars intersected; Hakluyt purportedly went down to the docks at Wapping to speak to those who had returned from journeys like the ones Hudson had led. In an age when literacy was not universal, especially among laborers who had no access to formal education, knowledge of the sea circulated orally from one traveler to another or from seaman to chronicler. For the city's burgeoning mercantile community, the possibilities for commercial growth seemed to have no limits.

By the spring of 1610, Hudson was ready to embark on a new expedition—but the English government prevented him from leaving the country and even halted his efforts to communicate with the Dutch merchants who had funded his most recent expedition. "Many persons thought it strange that captains should thus be prevented from laying their accounts and reports before their employers," van Meteren noted, "having been sent out for the benefit of navigation in general." But the English apparently had little interest at that moment in offering up details of Hudson's journey to the Dutch, quite probably—as the consul himself concluded—because they were hatching plans to explore this part of "Virginia" that Hudson had seen, notably the river that had commanded so much of his attention.

In 1616, the *Halve Maen,* now under a different commander, disappeared off the coast of Sumatra in western Indonesia, a reminder of the range of English ambitions and the costs of the desire among Europeans in general to extend trade and political ties around the world. The English did mount other expeditions toward Virginia. But Henry Hudson would not again commit himself to exploring that region. There was no point. He had cruised along the mid-Atlantic coast without finding the passage that John Smith had told him was there. To be sure, he was impressed by what he had seen. "It is as pleasant a land as one need tread upon," he wrote, "very abundant in all kinds of timber suitable for shipbuilding, and for making large casks or vats." But even though he thought that copper and iron could be found there, he never made any plans to return. He was an explorer, not a potential colonizer.

Hudson had learned much on his first three expeditions—about the weather, maintaining good relations with a crew, the natural resources of the Arctic, the benefits and dangers of encounters with indigenous peoples beyond Europe's shores, and the skills needed to preserve a ship in difficult climates. He had also learned to seek unexplored routes toward the Northwest Passage. These experiences built his confidence and fueled his passion for travel to the north.

IV.

# The *N*orth Atlantic

*O*n *April 17, 1610,* Henry Hudson led the *Discovery* out of the docks at St. Katherine's toward his destiny. His goal was straightforward. A group of twenty-four merchants, politicians, and gentlemen—who would later form the North-West Passage Company—had commissioned him to find the elusive Northwest Passage, the water route through the North American landmass that would allow European ships to travel from the Atlantic to the Pacific and then to the East Indies.

Others had tried before, of course. The English mariner Martin Frobisher had led three expeditions into the frigid waters of the northern Atlantic in the mid-1570s. During their journeys the sailors encountered Inuit on rocky islands southwest of Greenland, and some of the men thought that they might be monsters, which Europeans believed lived at the edges of their world. During the voyage, when an examination of an old woman's feet convinced them that the Inuit were in fact humans, Frobisher brought three of them back to England, where they became instant curiosities. Their capture and display proved temporary. All of them soon died—a man from injuries sustained when he was captured, and a woman and her infant child of some unidentified ailment, which could have been one of several Old World diseases that felled Americans in the sixteenth century. Queen Elizabeth wanted to see them but never had the chance.

Though Frobisher had not found the Northwest Passage, books printed to celebrate his journeys included maps depicting a passage labeled "Frobisher's Straightes," a body of water that began in an island-choked channel southwest of Greenland and proceeded almost due west to the Pacific. Nor was Frobisher the only European mariner in search of the route. In 1609 a Spanish cosmographer and navigator named Lorenzo Ferrer Maldonado had offered the Spanish court a report of his purported journey through the passage nineteen years earlier. He claimed that this route was connected to the Strait of Anian, a large inlet that the Spanish already believed was the outlet from the passage to the South Sea. The circulation of the manuscript in the months before Hudson's departure suggests that Ferrer Maldonado's alleged journey had interest for many well beyond England's shores.

There is no indication that Hudson knew of the Ferrer Maldonado manuscript, but certainly he had studied the texts generated by Frobisher and other English explorers, notably John Davis and George Weymouth. Experienced sailors like Hudson pored over contemporary maps, all of which agreed on the existence of the Northwest Passage. When Hudson guided the *Discovery* with its crew of twenty-two men and two boys out of London that April, he was perhaps the most skilled explorer in England, the heir of a maritime tradition that some English promoters of expansion believed gave them an advantage over other Europeans, notably the Spanish and Portuguese. He was the most qualified man in Europe to find the Northwest Passage.

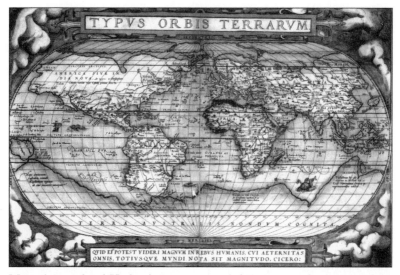

Maps that predated Hudson's journeys revealed the supposed existence of the Northwest Passage, though no one who made them had any evidence beyond the geographical theories that had circulated for decades. This map appeared in Abraham Ortelius's *Theatrum Orbis Terrarum* (Amsterdam, 1570), one of the most important European atlases of the late sixteenth century. *Huntington Library*

Hudson knew from his three previous journeys that excitement about new prospects did not guarantee their success. A great ship like the 1,200-ton *Trades Encrease* could sink, and there was no way to know whether Jamestown, with its dying settlers, would endure or become another Roanoke. Overseas ventures, he understood, sometimes met with disastrous ends.

Yet even tragedies did not diminish the enthusiasm of the king, the realm's merchants, and the public for long-distance trade, especially to the East Indies. Cinnamon, cloves, peppers, and other exotic flora still gripped the imagination of the English. The East India Company's efforts to mount large expeditions to find more convenient ways to get to the source of these exotics became public spectacles. At the same time, the English sought legal assurances that they could participate in the trade on an even footing with other Europeans. That task led Hak-luyt to translate Hugo Grotius's *Mare Liberum* (*The Free Sea*), which advocated for the English cause, arguing that no Euro-pean nation held an exclusive right to trade in the Spice Is-lands, despite the claims made by the Portuguese, who hoped to monopolize the business. The business of spices was fast be-coming the business of the nation, and as such its enthusiasts could be found at court, in the streets, and on the docks.

Among those infected by the contagion for profit were Sir Thomas Smythe and Dudley Digges, two prominent members of the city's mercantile community. At the moment when Hud-son embarked in 1610, the fifty-two-year-old Smythe had al-ready represented two districts in Parliament, and was then both the treasurer of the Virginia Company and governor of the East India Company. Digges, another of Hudson's backers, had launched himself on a similar course. Only twenty-eight years old in 1610, he was a generation younger than Smythe but had already become an expert on navigation. A year after Hudson left on his fourth expedition, Digges was arguing not only that the Northwest Passage existed but that it was just a matter of time before some enterprising European found it. Digges soon be-came a shareholder in the East India and Virginia companies, and in 1615 he issued a pamphlet defending the efforts of the East India Company from those who claimed it was not produc-ing profits quickly enough. It was a well-argued piece, con-structed on the evidence of "Custom-books, out of the East-India Companies books, out of Grocers, Warehouse-keepers, Mer-chants books, and conference with men of best experience."

Smythe, Digges, and the other investors poured their money into fitting out the *Discovery* and provisioning Hudson's ship and its twenty-two-man crew, hoping that they had backed a winner. The *Discovery* lacked the impressive size of the *Trades Encrease,* but Hudson had proved himself one of the bravest men on the seas, a captain drawn to explore potentially difficult passages despite their challenges. For those who supported his venture, Hudson was the logical heir to a tradition of maritime adventure that had long lured Englishmen to the sea. To his backers, Hudson's voyage was a wise investment that would lead England to expand its reach and its wealth.

To enhance his chances for success, Hudson brought the mathematician Thomas Wydowse on board the *Discovery*. Having Wydowse along demonstrated Hudson's understanding of the scientific challenges he would face. Scholars associated with England's universities recognized the close links between math and navigation. In this choice Hudson was following the advice of Hakluyt, who had urged royal support for the kind of annual lecture in navigation he had witnessed when he was in Paris in 1584.

Hudson sailed into the Atlantic knowing that earlier English mariners had achieved lasting fame by virtue of their discoveries. From 1577 to 1580, Sir Francis Drake had led a voyage around the world, an achievement that made him the first commander to circumnavigate the earth and survive. (The Portuguese mariner Ferdinand Magellan's crew had managed the feat earlier, but its captain did not survive the effort.) In 1586, Thomas Cavendish, who had commanded one of the English ships that had landed in Roanoke in 1585, left England on a journey to circle the world, intending to ransack Spanish posts along the way. He returned home in 1588, having sailed from Acapulco, which he reached by following Drake's course northward along the west coast of South America, across the Pacific, and then through the Indian Ocean and around the Cape of Good Hope. He tried to repeat the feat three years later, but his ships dispersed and he was lost at sea, though his fame survived. Although Frobisher, Davis, and Weymouth never found the Northwest Passage, their efforts attracted attention in contemporary printed books, including major works like Hakluyt's compilations of the most important narratives of English travelers and small pamphlets describing specific voyages.

Of the great explorers of the day, only Sir Walter Ralegh, Elizabeth's favorite who had hoped to establish an English

settlement in Guiana—in the heart of Spanish claims in northern South America—had failed to attract universal respect for
his explorations. That was hardly surprising; King James, who
ascended to the throne after Elizabeth died in 1603, had
Ralegh locked in the Tower of London for most of the last
years of his life. James's attitude toward Ralegh might have
seemed strange to some, but it fit the new monarch's desire to
improve relations with Spain. Part of his strategy for rapproche-
ment entailed publicly punishing Ralegh for exploring the
Orinoco Basin in 1596, which was then claimed by the Spanish. James eventually released the explorer, who soon organized
what turned out to be his final expedition to the Orinoco. When
he returned, James had him executed to punish him for an English assault on the Spanish town of San Thomé in early 1618,
which Ralegh had justified by contending that the English had
a legal claim to this portion of South America. Killing Ralegh
was, to the monarch, one  way to preserve peace with Spain.

❧

At the start of the *Discovery*'s voyage, Hudson's crew plied what
was by then a well-known route into the North Atlantic. Yet
the commencement of his trip proved eventful as well as omi-
nous. Hudson reported that the ship sailed from St. Katherine's
to Blackwall and then to Lee by April 22. But that day, even
before the vessel had left English waters, Hudson reported that
he ordered a crewman named Coleburne removed from the
ship and sent back to London on a "pink," a small, typically
flat-bottomed boat used for navigating along coastlines or for
fishing. Hudson told Coleburne to take a letter, now apparently
lost, to the merchants who were supporting the expedition to
explain the circumstances of his dismissal. Another member of
the crew noted that the *Discovery* was near Shopey when the
incident occurred. Neither of the reports described what Coleburne had done to prompt the unusual action, which signaled
that this journey might not go as smoothly as Hudson's previ-

ous missions had. The crew was already proving to be more challenging for the captain to manage than the men who had worked for him on previous expeditions.

Hudson's report provides only sketchy details of the early days of the journey. But Abacuk Pricket, whose narrative would become the most detailed report of the expedition, offered sufficient information on the route, noting that after Coleburne's departure, the *Discovery* sailed to Harwich, where it arrived on April 28. Hudson and his men remained in that English port until May 1, and then departed for the Orkney Islands, an archipelago off the coast of Scotland, which they reached (according to Hudson) on May 5.

Hudson's account followed the pattern he had established in his previous reports. He frequently made note of the ship's latitude, using his measurements to suggest that previous cartographic efforts might have been inaccurate. According to his projections, the *Discovery* reached 59°22′N on May 6; this event prompted him to observe that the upper coasts of Scotland, in addition to the Orkneys and Shetland, were not as far north as others had claimed. On the eighth of May, they reached 62°24′N and spotted the Faro Islands. Three days later, they approached the eastern coast of Iceland. Hudson ordered the crew to drop anchor.

By 1610, that volcanic outcropping already figured prominently in the annals of European seafarers. Norse sagas dating to the turn of the first Christian millennium had described Iceland in depth. The Norse who sailed there decided that the island was habitable and established settlements. There were never very many of these outposts and they did not grow very large, because Iceland's unforgiving climate and jagged coasts made it difficult to sustain a large population. But the fact of the colonies themselves proved that it was possible to live in such a frigid region.

The news about Iceland that filtered back to Europe was not very positive. By the time the Flemish cartographer Abraham

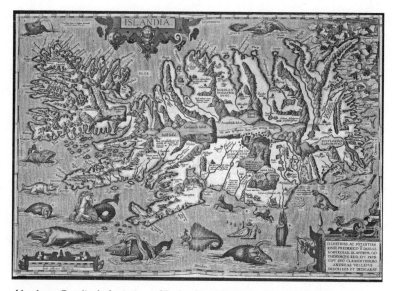

Abraham Ortelius's depiction of Iceland in 1595 prominently displayed the volcano at Hecla, which became a landmark for Europeans sailing in the region. From Ortelius, *Theatrum Orbis Terrarum* (Antwerp, 1595). *Huntington Library*

Ortelius produced his map of the island in the late sixteenth century, the dangers of the place were more evident than its positive attributes. He depicted fierce beasts roaming its coasts and swimming just offshore, and its steep mountains must have seemed formidable obstacles to anyone who thought of staying there.

Pricket's account indicated that Hudson's approach to Iceland squared with how sailors of his era perceived the place. They arrived, he wrote, "in a fog, hearing the Rut of the Sea ashore, but saw not the Land whereupon our Master came to an Anchor." Pricket's observation spoke directly to the sounds of the sea that were long familiar means of measurement to those who spent their lives on ships. Navigational tools, they all knew, could be wrong. But the sea made specific noises, especially when waves broke against a rocky shoreline. Hearing the presence of Iceland before actually seeing it conformed to English sailors' preconceptions of the frosty island—as shrouded in gloom, overrun by fierce creatures, and pummeled by waves capable of shattering the hull of an unlucky ship.

Iceland might have been forbidding to humans, such as those who recorded the Norse sagas, who told tales of woe about its perils, but as many Europeans also recognized, it was a breeding ground for enormous flocks of birds, and its waters hosted a variety of aquatic life. While they lay at anchor, the crew of the *Discovery* took advantage of these natural resources. Hudson, noting that the ship had mostly kept to the southern edges of Iceland, wrote that his men caught a variety of birds, but he did not identify them. Pricket added that the men on board also managed to haul in ling, cod, butt (probably turbot), and other fish that the English could not identify. The men had no desire to remain in this place, but their experience, as they took time off from what they hoped would be a rapid journey into the Northwest Passage, reminded them about the possibilities of surviving at sea. Besides, Iceland had its benefits—as the expedition's mathematician, Thomas Wydowse, wrote to a London printer at the end of May—including its easily hunted population of birds.

Despite the reputation of the North Atlantic as a place buffeted by fierce storms, the crew of the *Discovery* remained in placid waters near Iceland until the end of the month. Only then did a strong wind pick up, which drove them beyond the western shores of the island. They left their harbor on June 1, Hudson recalled, and sailed west along the line of 66°34′N. Their course shifted slightly southward the next day, when they found themselves at 65°30′N, with, as Hudson put it, "little wind Easterly."

Pricket, characteristically, filled in some of the gaps in his captain's account. The gale had pushed them past the isle of Westmonie, where the Danish king maintained a fortress. They continued until they passed "that famous Hill, Mount *Hocla*," an active volcano thrust upward along the mid-Atlantic ridge.

The volcano, Pricket wrote, spewed fire, signaling that foul weather would soon arrive. Yet despite the fire the men encountered ice. As they sailed away, they beheld a large iceberg—"a Main of Ice," as Pricket put it—that adhered to the landmass near Dyre Fjord on the northwestern side of Iceland's northern peninsula. Like much of that region, the area was populated mostly by birds. The men seized the opportunity to go fowling before they set off into the open ocean. But rather than proceed toward Greenland, the *Discovery* entered a natural harbor, which the crew called "Lousie Bay." Exploring the shore, the men discovered a natural hot spring, in which every member of the crew took a bath. The temperature of the water impressed Pricket: "The water was so hot that it would scald a Fowl."

The winds returned by the first of June and the crew set sail again toward Greenland. At first mistaking a massive bank of fog for land, they cruised beyond it. Four days after they left Iceland, a strong wind put them in sight of Greenland, which the crew could discern over the tops of the nearby icebergs. Pricket and the others noticed that this part of Greenland's landscape was dominated by snow-covered round hills that resembled loaves of sugar. The *Discovery* sailed mostly north by northwest, remaining near the coast but keeping a distance from the ever-threatening ice. Soon the ship came upon the aptly named Island of Desolation, a large island off Greenland's western coast. Pricket wrote that the men observed a sizable population of whales there. One day, three of the leviathans approached the ship and the men could not chase them away. The whales came closer, and one even swam under the ship, a prospect that terrified the English sailors, who knew too well the dangers that whales posed to relatively small ships like the *Discovery*. But the whales did not harm the men or the ship, and Pricket offered his praise to God for sparing them from the cold depths.

Given the valuable oil and ambergris that Europeans knew they could extract from the bodies of captured whales, it might seem surprising that these three creatures aroused such fear in the hearts of the English. After all, whaling in the North Atlantic had become a common enterprise, one practiced by the English, Basques, and natives of Biscay. But whalers, and other sailors, had long since learned that the interaction of whales and ships could lead to disaster. They might have dismissed as biologically unlikely the scriptural story of Jonah, but they could not have ignored their well-founded fears of whales or other large creatures. That fear had already sunk deep into the European imagination, promulgated by texts such as the Uppsala archbishop Olaus Magnus's mid-sixteenth-century history of northern peoples (*Historia de gentibus septentrionslibus*). It was one thing to find a whale when a ship was prepared to kill it. For sailors on a ship not large enough to hunt whales, encountering one of the beasts could be fatal.

Whales were not the only creatures that endangered the *Discovery*. Two years before Hudson left on his quest for the Northwest Passage, the London printer William Jaggard had published the naturalist Edward Topsell's *Historie of Serpents*. [The book followed by a year Topsell's study of four-footed animals, also published by Jaggard.] Topsell was the self-appointed heir to the great Swiss bibliophile Conrad Gesner, who in the middle decades of the sixteenth century had produced enormous catalogs of the natural world. Topsell brought that knowledge to the English-reading public. Though it is impossible to know how many people actually read his books, the fact that the same printer published the works only a year apart suggests there was a ready market for details, legendary or factual, about the terrifying creatures who shared the earth with humans.

Topsell's new volume primarily focused on terrestrial creatures, including tortoises, crocodiles, frogs, and snakes. But it included fauna that in seventeenth-century ethnography fell into the category of serpents, including elephants and dragons. The book also contained a description of various kinds of sea serpents. Topsell described most of them as creatures varying in

Edward Topsell, one of England's leading naturalists of the early seventeenth century, cautioned that some sea monsters were sufficiently large to capsize a ship. From Topsell, *Historie of Serpents* (London, 1608).
*Huntington Library*

length from 1 to 4 cubits (about 1.5 to 6 feet). But he added that Magnus had described one serpent of 120 feet long that directly threatened those who sailed in the North Atlantic. Magnus had declared that these sea beasts could be found on the coasts of Norway and that they posed real dangers to sailors because they were known to lift their heads out of the water, grab a man in their jaws, and then pull him into the depths. What's more, they could overturn ships—or wrap their long, sinuous bodies around one and squeeze it into splinters. Topsell illustrated this catastrophic scenario with a print of a serpent encircling itself around a three-masted ship—a vessel in all likelihood larger than *Discovery.*

When these English sailors looked across the bow of their ship at Greenland, they saw a land that belied its name, one that the Norse had bestowed on it centuries earlier because of the lushness of its grasses during its short summer season. To those on board the *Discovery,* Greenland was terrifying—a place as fearsome as Iceland, surrounded by mists and jagged icebergs. The crew did not go ashore and see for themselves how the colonizing Norse had domesticated the land to meet their needs. If they had lingered, they may have seen that

Greenland in June was a less forbidding place than they would have been expecting. During the summer months, when the sun hung in the sky hour after hour, it teemed with life. Birds by the thousands nested there, in numbers so vast that hunting them could have made only the slightest dent in the population. Greenland boasted animals, too, notably its indigenous bears, walrus, and seals. Those creatures provided a source of meat for those who chose to settle there. Greenland tempted the Norse, who even hauled a large bell there to hang in a church at Gardar, perhaps the ultimate sign that Europeans could survive (if not quite thrive) far from home, but their population on the massive island never exceeded 3,500.

Some contemporary writers recognized Greenland's appeal. In the early seventeenth century, the most recent authoritative geographical treatise to appear in English, a translation of work by the renowned Ortelius, offered a remarkably positive assessment of Greenland. The English translation appeared in London in 1606, at exactly the time that Hudson was preparing for his voyages. It was true, Ortelius wrote (in a passage he derived from the writings of the fourteenth-century Venetian explorer Nicolò Zeno), that the winter in Greenland lasted for nine months and that the snow never melted the entire time. But Ortelius wrote glowingly of how, along the island's far eastern shores, a group of Friar Predicants, dedicated to St. Thomas, maintained a successful monastery. Ortelius thought it significant that they had built their spiritual home near an active volcano that did at times "cast out huge flakes of fire." The monks also used nearby hot springs to warm their house and to clean and cook their meat and their bread. They gathered a certain kind of local volcanic stone that proved ideal for construction, providing excellent insulation no matter what the weather. Ortelius reported, too, that the monks had gardens and orchards that remained green for almost the entire year. The monks erected the priory hard by the shore at a spot with a "reasonable capacious and large haven" into which local hot streams drained, giving them fresh running water all through the hard freeze of winter. The area also lured enormous schools of fish that took refuge there from colder waters. The monks and their indigenous neighbors, whose populations tended to be low, always had an ample supply of fish on their tables.

The English who sailed with Hudson saw none of these benefits. They never inspected Greenland's eastern coast, but instead spied only its western shores. There was no sign of European habitation or civilization to be found in Ortelius's map of this region, other than the names that earlier explorers had given to prominent rivers. To the English aboard the *Discovery,* Greenland was like Iceland—a place with a coastline so fierce that it needed to be avoided at all costs. They did not consider Greenland a potential way station on the journey toward the South Sea. They identified it by its terrors. The whales swimming near its shores were only one of the many threats they sought to avoid.

And yet, despite the harrowing circumstances, the *Discovery* suffered no harm or damage during these first six weeks of its voyage. Hudson did not always find the winds that he sought, but the ship made it past the ice, past the rocky shoals, and past the whales. The men suffered no deprivation; their bodies were replenished by the birds and fish they consumed. Aside from Coleburne's departure from the ship only days after they left London, all continued to go well for Hudson's men as they approached the opening, marked by what Pricket called "a great Rippling or over-fall of current" that they believed would lead them to the South Sea.

Despite the shortfalls of his previous three journeys, Hudson had every expectation that he had found the entryway that would lead him to the East Indies. The challenge, he understood, would be to preserve the health of the ship and its crew when the *Discovery* crossed into waters that, as far as he knew, no European had ever entered before.

# The Labyrinth Without End

HUDSON STRAIT TO JAMES BAY,
JUNE 1610 TO JUNE 1611

*On the ninth of June*, 1610, the *Discovery* entered the channel marked "Frobisher's Straightes" on the earlier English explorer's map. Hudson judged the winds ideal because they allowed the crew to sail southwest for almost a week. On the fifteenth, he and his crew reached a barren island that the earlier English mariner John Davis had aptly labeled Desolation, named, as Samuel Purchas later put it, "for the loathsome view of the shore covered with snow, without wood, earth, or grass to be seen, and the irksome noise of the ice."

Hudson calculated that Davis had marked its location incorrectly, writing the kind of note typical of him demonstrating what he believed to be his superior ability to identify geographical sites. But Hudson saw no reason to suggest a less bleak name for the island. The crew spotted "much Ice, and many Riplings or Over-falls, and a strong stream settling from East South-East, to West North-west." The *Discovery* rode those shifting winds (Hudson called them "variable") from June 21 to 23 to the northwest, near ice flows, to the point of 62°29′N. On the

Even in summer, Resolution Island—at the head of modern Hudson Strait—could be locked in ice, as one traveler recognized when he sailed on a journey toward Hudson Bay in 1812. From Thomas M'Keevor, *A Voyage to Hudson's Bay, During the Summer of 1812* (London, 1819). *Huntington Library*

twenty-fourth and twenty-fifth, the crew spotted land to the north—probably Resolution Island—but they lost sight of it, presumably in a fog, as they headed on a mostly westward course that took them to 62°17′N.

Hudson's description of this part of the journey was characteristically brief. But Pricket was, as ever, more voluble. After passing Desolation Island, he wrote, as the ship's master had also reported, that the *Discovery* sailed on a northwestern course, but according to Pricket, the route was not as simple as Hudson implied. Pricket noted that ice threatened the ship until the crew managed to steer southward. But still the ice kept advancing, first in large floes and then in smaller chunks. When they headed northwestward and sailed between icebergs, the men witnessed one of the floes roll over, which served as a warning that they should never again sail so close to them.

But the men had no choice but to plunge farther into this sea of floating danger. They survived a storm, but soon a fierce wind threatened to drive shards of ice through the ship's hull.

The men came upon the only solution that made sense: They would position the *Discovery* near the largest of the icebergs, with the hope that one natural barrier might protect the vessel from others. Still, all was not well. In the midst of this ice-packed sea, some of the men became sick. Pricket wondered if their ailment was actually due to terror of the approaching ice and the possibility of a shipwreck. In any case, the expedition, now in its tenth week, had begun to take a psychological toll even on those who had ample experience in such waters.

❧

The encounter with the capsizing iceberg signaled that the men on the ship had now entered a region whose challenges might surprise them. Hudson and the veterans of his previous journeys had encountered icebergs before, but it is unlikely that any of the other men on the *Discovery* had much experience of them, though the mathematician Wydowse probably knew about icebergs from his reading. If they were to sail through the Northwest Passage, the men on the ship would have to learn how to avoid the kinds of catastrophes that had doomed Europeans like Barentsz.

The farther west they sailed, the more they realized that ice would pose the greatest danger to their progress. At times the journey became harrowing. Pricket reported that the ice was encroaching on the *Discovery* from seemingly every direction— north, northwest, west, southwest. Finally Hudson came to believe that the only way out of the deadly obstacle course was to head due south. That turned out to be a false hope. "[T]he more he strove" to escape the ice, Pricket recalled, "the worse he was, and the more enclosed, till we could go no further." The situation tortured Hudson. He despaired, as he later confessed to Pricket, that the *Discovery* would never be able to escape the ice, and worried that all of his men would die there. If Pricket's claim was true, it suggests that Hudson was already persuaded that this venture would not end as positively as his previous expeditions.

In early July, Hudson gathered the crew, pulled out a map, and informed the men that the *Discovery* was then 100 leagues farther west than any English expedition had gone before in these waters. According to Pricket, the captain offered his men a choice: They could go farther, seeking to fulfill their original goal, or they could turn back. The captain's timing was not accidental. In addition to the dangers they faced at that moment, Hudson knew that the time was drawing close when the advancing winter ice would make a return home too risky to attempt. As Pricket reported it, some of the men wanted to go home, others urged their captain and crewmates to continue onward, and some apparently did not care what decision was made as long as they could immediately escape what seemed like impending death brought by converging floes of ice. But, Pricket added, in an aside that would later come to have more significance, "there were some who then spake words, which were remembered a great while after."

One crewman, unnamed in Pricket's report, purportedly told Hudson that if he had a hundred pounds he would give ninety for the chance to return to London. Philip Staffe, the ship's carpenter, who would become closely aligned with Hudson in the coming weeks (and was presumably already an ally or confidant of the master) retorted that if he had that much money, he wouldn't even give up ten pounds—because he believed that the expedition would be a success and that providence would guide them on their way. The debate dragged on, to no obvious conclusion. "After many words to no purpose," Pricket wrote, the men went back to work, focusing on the task of escaping from immediate danger, quite likely pushing off the nearest of the ice floes to create enough room between the ship and the dangers, and so turn the ship. Eventually they reached open water again, then headed north and northwest on their way out of Ungava Bay, apparently the only logical way to continue on a westward course.

As they continued, they soon found land lying to the southwest, which Hudson named Desire Provokes (modern-day

Akpatok Island), a large island between Hudson Strait and Ungava Bay. As the *Discovery* lay offshore, the men heard the sound, as Pricket put it, "of a great over-fall of a tide" coming from the interior. The men had learned much from their time trapped in these forbidding channels between rocky shores and large shards of ice calved from even larger icebergs. When a storm broke or fog made it impossible to see, they had learned to anchor the *Discovery* as close as possible to a large iceberg. While waiting for better conditions, some of the men would go onto the ice and fill their barrels with the fresh water that they often found in shallow ponds on the surface. That water was "both sweet and good," Pricket commented. The men had learned that lesson from experience, but what they found was real indeed: Water on top of an iceberg in the summer would be potable because icebergs were always composed of fresh water. Any salt they might have contained would have been squeezed out over the years. The ponds formed when the winter snow on top of an iceberg—which made these floating islands appear white—melted in warmer temperatures.

Such newly developed skills showed that the men of the *Discovery* had learned how to survive amid the routine dangers that would have confronted anyone sailing toward Hudson Bay. Though there had been disagreement on board about whether they should turn homeward, there is no evidence that tensions remained after the airing of alternative views. Perhaps the common struggle had made them more unified. If so, in the weeks to come their solidarity would be tested when the physical challenges the crew faced became ever more apparent.

❧

As both Hudson and Pricket acknowledged in their reports, there was more to a voyage of exploration than the labors required to make it from one point of latitude to another—efforts that involved the kind of detail that obsessed Hudson but rarely appeared in Pricket's narrative. The English sailors were aware that they were now in waters not yet navigated by any European. As the geographer Ortelius had put it, Europeans had "sailed around" the entirety of the American landmasses, "except the North tract thereof, whose coasts are not yet discovered." His map of the Americas in his atlas conveniently hid this fact by cutting off the top of the Americas.

Hudson understood that he faced both an opportunity and a challenge. As the man who would become known as the discoverer of this territory (at least in the opinion of Europeans, who would have ignored any notion that the Inuit had long knowledge of the region), he had the ability and the right to name whatever he found. He took that task seriously, as the surviving texts reveal. But those documents also demonstrate that Hudson recognized that he needed the support of his crew, and the debate about the future of the expedition suggested that tensions might have lingered even after each of the men had an opportunity to voice his opinion. Even those who

Abraham Ortelius was deeply immersed in the community of scientists and explorers who together tried to map the Americas in the years preceding Hudson's journey. This map from his atlas suggests the limits of knowledge about the land existing in the northern reaches of the Western Hemisphere. From Ortelius, *Theatrum Orbis Terrarum* (Antwerp, 1593). *Huntington Library*

English sailors frequently reported polar bears leaping off icebergs into the sea, often just before visitors managed to snare them. From Sir John Ross, *A Voyage of Discovery* (London, 1819). *Huntington Library*

voted to go home would have had to acknowledge that Hudson needed his men to have faith in his abilities if the mission was to succeed. But, as would soon be revealed, he had not in fact managed to gain—or maintain—the trust of all of those on board.

The *Discovery's* initial passage had taught its crew crucial lessons. After several weeks, they had come to the conclusion that the ice was most dangerous when they were in an open sea. When the vessel navigated a bay, icebergs tended to remain in place, as if they were floating in a pond. But the bay near Desire Provokes was different; the men saw enormous icebergs— Pricket called them "Mountains of Ice"—floating in water as shallow as 120 fathoms. Yet ice was not always dangerous. When the crew saw a polar bear float by on a small piece, they immediately dropped a boat into the water and chased it. Unfortunately for them, the bear's floe got caught in the tide and took its passenger to a larger iceberg, where the bear debarked and eluded its hunters. The discouraged men returned to the *Discovery*, their effort wasted.

Those who sailed in these northern waters had at least some knowledge of polar bears, and quite likely realized the danger that the beasts represented. According to the naturalist Edward Topsell, "there are Bears, which are called *Amphibia*, because they live both on the land and in the sea, hunting and catching fish like an *Otter* or *Beaver,* and these are white coloured. Topsell, whose views were available before the launch of the *Discovery,* offered details about the kinds of bears that travelers in such regions might meet. "In the Ocean Islands toward the North, there are bears of a great stature, fierce and cruel," which had the ability to break holes in the ice with their massive claws and then grab fish from the water below. This creature is exactly what Hudson's men saw. Had any of them read Topsell's book, they would have known that these bears had enormous black paws and that they spent most of their lives near the water, although sometimes a storm forced them to seek shelter on land. Polar bears, and other beasts able to survive in these bitter climes, would continue to fascinate Europeans for centuries.

The men soon encountered another polar bear on an iceberg, but this time the ice worked in their favor as they watched the bear jump from one small floe to the next, approaching the ship. When the bear got close, she saw the men looking at her, and so she dove into the water, where the fragments of ice would protect her from any weapons the men might hurl in her direction.

The men soon realized that they were not surrounded by ice alone but had, in fact, come upon another unknown island. Hudson ordered the ship into a harbor. The winds had pushed the *Discovery* perilously close to a large, jagged rock, but it had caused no harm, and the crew soon anchored safely, well into the bay. Hudson named this array of islands the Iles of Gods Mercies (near modern Lake Harbour). He sent Pricket and several others to explore it, presumably in a shallop, which would have less chance of catching a rock than the ship would have in those waters. The men surprised a covey of partridges;

Fox, hart, and polar bear each attracted the attention of Europeans exploring northern lands. According to one late seventeenth-century writer, polar bears "eat Men alive when they have an opportunity to master them." From *An Account of Several Late Voyages & Discoveries to the South and North* (London, 1694), quotation at 102. *Huntington Library*

Wydowse shot at them, apparently managing to kill only the oldest. Pricket called the island "a most barren place, having nothing on it but plashes of water and riven Rocks, as if it were subject to Earthquakes." The men believed there might be a large bay or sea lying to its north, but rather than hike in that direction, they gathered some driftwood and headed back to the *Discovery*. Hudson had little to say about the place in his journal, other than to mention that the tide came in from the north, presumably from the large body of open water that Pricket had briefly described.

Try as they might to elude it, ice dogged the crew as they went on. The men struggled to continue west but often found their way blocked. Hudson ordered a series of maneuvers intended to get the *Discovery* into open water. Eventually he succeeded, managing to find a course that took the ship along the northern edge of a series of landmasses. In early August, the *Discovery* passed three capes, or headlands. Hudson named one of them Prince Henry Cape (or Foreland), after Henry Frederick, Prince of Wales. (The heir apparent would die two years later, at age eighteen, likely a victim of typhoid fever.) Once they passed those headlands they saw another cape, jutting even farther north into the sea. Hudson labeled this promontory King

Ice off Cape Wolstenholme, in an undated photograph probably from the early twentieth century. From Canada Department of Marine and Fisheries Report of 1906. *Huntington Library*

James Cape and the next one Queen Anne Cape. Pricket noted that on the far side of King James Cape lay an island-studded bay. He wanted to write more about the coastline here, but because the *Discovery* cruised by during the half-light of a summer Arctic night, he could add no other details. A sudden storm convinced Hudson that he should do all he could to keep the *Discovery* near the mainland that lay on the ship's south side. As the crew struggled with the winds, Hudson took the time to name Mount Charles and Cape Salisbury, then went on to identify new locales on a nearby island, likely modern Nottingham Island, designating them Deepes Cape and Cape Wolstenholme, the latter named for one of the three major investors in the *Discovery*'s journey. The men had not yet seen any humans—people who would have had their own appellations for the notable terrain of their homeland—but Hudson was in the process of putting the mark of the English on the landscape.

Hudson was not content merely to add new place-names while surveying his sightings from the deck of the *Discovery*.

He wanted more facts, and so he sent Pricket ashore along with Staffe, crewmen Henry Greene and Robert Bylot, and perhaps several others. Hudson charged them with finding the western and northwestern coasts of the island. But the trek proved more difficult than he had imagined, with the distance greater than the men had estimated, and thunder roared as lightning crackled nearby. Still, the men scrambled up one hill, going from rock to rock, and eventually reached its peak. There they spotted four or five deer, and soon came within sight of a small herd numbering twelve to sixteen. Unfortunately for them, they could not get close enough to take any with their muskets.

The men saw a steep hill to the west and hiked toward it, but when they reached it the north and east faces were too sheer to climb. They decided to walk to the south and soon came upon a sizable pond that fed a stream so large that Pricket thought it could drive a mill. The territory held other surprises too. They discovered a meadow of lush grasses, a breeding ground for migratory birds that surpassed any the men had yet seen on the expedition. More important, they found ample supplies of sorrel and also what the English called "scurvy grass." That plant, also called spoonwart, contains vitamin C,

Sailors who traveled through northern waters knew they needed a supply of green plants to avoid scurvy. Scurvy grass, illustrated here in a late seventeenth-century English compilation of travel accounts, was among the seasonal greens that prevented the disease. From *An Account of several late Voyages & Discoveries to the South and North* (London, 1694). *Huntington Library*

which battles the disease of scurvy that strikes people who do not regularly consume fruits or green plants. The men of the *Discovery* ate it despite its bitter taste.

Pleased by their findings, the men continued exploring and soon made a more important discovery. "Passing along we saw some round Hills of stone," Pricket wrote, "like the Grass cocks"—using a term for conical piles of dried grass—"which at the first I took to be the work of some Christian." The explorers ventured among these edifices and realized that they were filled with birds hanging from their necks. Human hunters had been here, the first tangible sign that the men had that they were not alone in these Arctic reaches. They had expected to find Inuit, as earlier travelers had, but quite likely had little idea that the locals exerted such control over the environment—especially since Frobisher and his men had deemed the Inuit to be savages lacking any sign of civilization. The men would have lingered on the island, but Hudson had in the meantime steered the *Discovery* close by. He shot his guns when a dense fog began to envelope land and sea alike, signaling the men to return. Once on board the ship, the explorers urged Hudson to remain in the area for a day or two so that they could refresh their stores. But Hudson refused, an action Pricket found unfortunate. "So we left the Fowl, and left our way down to the Southwest," Pricket wrote, as they left behind the land that had been in their sights for so long as well as an ample supply of food.

Two or three days later, as the *Discovery* edged through these waters, Hudson made a crucial change in the expedition's leadership. He decided to demote Robert Juet, who had held a privileged place as the captain's mate, along with the boatswain, as a result of what Pricket said were "words spoken in the first great Bay of Ice." To replace Juet as mate, he promoted Robert Bylot; William Wilson became the new boatswain. The shift in the crew revealed Hudson's lack of faith in his one-time mate. But making the change in the midst of a journey was highly unusual. In the confined rooms of a relatively small sailing ship, everyone would have known that the master's act could poison relations on the vessel. Juet would not soon forget the insult.

On Michaelmas (September 29 on the modern calendar), the ship entered into some kind of a harbor but soon exited, prompting Hudson to name it Michaelmasse Bay. Soon the weather turned against them yet again, forcing the men to remain at anchor for eight days. Finally the winds changed and Hudson ordered the anchor raised. But the command displeased many of the men, who felt Hudson was acting "against the mind of all who knew what belonged thereunto." He wanted to press ahead, but they felt the timing was poor, given the winds. The men were right. "Well, to it we went," Pricket remembered, noting that as they lifted the anchor close to the surface, a wave took it away "and cast us all off for the Capstone, and hurt divers of us." They would have lost the cable, too, had Staffe, the carpenter, not been ready for such a hazard and already had his axe in his hand to cut the cord and thus minimize their loss.

The *Discovery* continued its journey southward into the bay, quite likely following a course that Hudson hoped would bring them into more temperate climes for the fast-approaching winter. By sometime in early autumn, with at least some of the ship's men apparently seething from what they saw as Hudson's mismanagement of the journey, the *Discovery* entered into what Pricket called "a Sea of two colours, one black, and the other white." They were in James Bay; its western waters were very shallow and silt-filled, which explained its light color (and also made it prone to quick freezing). The ship sailed 4 or 5 leagues in water that was, Pricket estimated, about 100 feet deep. Soon they reached another body of land, presumably the eastern shores of the bay, and dropped another anchor. They dispatched a shallop for shoreline investigations. This was no easy feat. The coast was rocky and it proved difficult to land the small craft.

Pricket did not identify those on the shallop, but he did report that they had observed the snowy footprints of a man and a duck in the rocks. They also brought some wood back to the *Discovery*. The ship weighed anchor at midnight, but soon Staffe rushed to tell Hudson that the ship was about to be thrown onto the rocks. Hudson had believed that the *Discovery* had sailed past the most threatening part of the jagged coastline, but he was wrong. Pricket wrote that almost immediately the ship ran onto the rocks and that it remained wedged there for twelve hours. At the next tide, the ship became free. "[W]e got off unhurt," Pricket noted, "though not unscarred." Such an incident would likely have tried the crew's nerves once more—and perhaps renewed their doubts about Hudson's command.

It was now late October. Hudson had either stopped writing in his journal by this point—or, more likely, those pages later became detached from his journal before the manuscript fell into Hakluyt's hands. The gap is unfortunate, because it was at this moment in the journey that Hudson made a fateful decision. Recognizing that there was not enough time before the advance of the ice either to get through the passage that he still presumed existed or to return to England, he instructed Pricket and Staffe to go on shore to find a place to spend the winter. Pricket understood why Hudson had made the decision. The nights had already grown long, the air had turned colder, and regular snowfalls had whitened the coastline. Like his captain, Pricket now recognized that the *Discovery* had "spent three months in a Labyrinth without end."

❧

The men of the *Discovery* had signed on for a journey they believed would take them relatively quickly through the Northwest Passage and to the South Sea. But by the time they reached the southern reaches of James Bay, they had been away from home for six months. All of them knew there was no hope for a return to England before the next summer. That realization would have been disappointing enough, as would the thought that they were not going to make history by sailing through the long-sought-for passage. Rather than swapping yarns on London's docks or at home with relatives, or enjoying what they believed would have been the more temperate climes of the South Sea en route to the Spice Islands, the men instead faced grim months ahead. They were trapped along a rocky shore where, to that point, the only sign of human habitation had been a windblown footprint on a rock and some dead birds hanging in small stone huts, waiting to be consumed by people the crew of the *Discovery* had not yet met.

On November 1, the crew steered the *Discovery* toward what would become its winter home. The worst place to be trapped by ice would have been in the middle of a large expanse of water where the crew would be unable to garner supplies and the grinding of ice sheets could crush a ship's hull. To avoid such a fate, an able captain and crew would try to steer a vessel toward a coastline and perhaps even try to ground the ship gently on a rocky shoreline so that the hull would not suffer too much damage. If they ripped a gaping hole in the hull in the process of securing it, the sailors might not be able to make it seaworthy when the ice melted the following summer. Moreover, because water expands when it freezes, any ship faced certain risks during the winter if ice filled it below decks. But skilled seamen, working with a ship's carpenter, could repair minor damage if the vessel remained intact. No one reported it at the time, but Hudson and his men must have managed the feat perfectly, or nearly so. At any rate, they caused such minor damage to the *Discovery* that the ship was seaworthy when summer returned.

By November 10, James Bay had iced over and the ship could not escape. In all likelihood they were in the deeper waters of the eastern part of the bay—close to the rocky shoreline, but wedged in place so they could not be thrown into any more danger. Now that they were trapped, it made sense to see what they had on the ship that would help them survive the winter that had now arrived.

The men believed that they had sufficient food to last for six months. Pricket thought that perhaps Hudson had some additional food hidden away, a suspicion that others would eventually share. But for the moment the men thought they had supplies to last until spring; they could get more food if they could find a way to return to the breeding ground for the many birds they had seen on the island they had explored on foot. They would need plentiful supplies of protein to survive a long ocean journey either to the west, according to the original plan, or back home. Hudson agreed. He ordered the men to first use up what they had on hand and then look for more. According to Pricket's account, Hudson offered a reward to any of "them that killed either Beast, Fish, or Fowl, as in his Journal you have seen." Pricket's remark at this moment was no accident. His record of what happened that winter was only one account, and he wanted it read along with Hudson's earlier journal to show that he was in agreement with the captain at the start of the long winter.

In the middle of November, John Williams, the ship's gunner, died. Pricket did not explain the circumstances, noting only that "God pardon the Masters [Hudson's] uncharitable dealing with this man." Whatever happened between captain and gunner remains beyond the testimony of the narratives, but its significance is evident. As suggested in his journal, Pricket sensed a shift in the crew's sentiments then, the early signs of a distemper that would fester until it exploded and "brought a scandal upon all that are returned home." No one would escape unscathed.

Williams's death set off what appeared at the time to be a minor squabble over who among the surviving members of the crew would be able to gain possession of what Pricket described as a "gray cloth gown," presumably a warm, loose, flowing coat. Among those who wanted it was Henry Greene, one of the members of the crew whom Hudson knew best. Before the voyage, Greene, a native of Kent, had been a servant living with

Hudson in London. According to Pricket, Greene had been responsible for his own descent into poverty. He had been born of churchgoing and presumably respectable parents—Pricket referred to them simply as "Worshipful"—but he had lived wildly. "[B]y his lewd life and conversation he had lost the good will of all his friends," Pricket wrote, "and had spent all that he had." Hudson had decided he would provide for Greene, and so he gave him a place to live and put food and drink on his table. He took him on the journey because Greene was literate, perhaps sensing that he might be another chronicler of the expedition or at least be able to help make sense of the maps and books that Hudson must have had stored in his cabin.

Greene was also something of a con artist, according to Pricket, who said he had earlier in his life schemed to get 4 pounds worth of clothing (though the result of the effort remains unclear). But Greene was not a regular member of the crew. Pricket noted that he was not "set down in the owners book, nor any wages made for him." He had a special relationship with Hudson, but its extent—and the bitter feelings he felt toward his new master—only belatedly became evident.

Greene had not been an ideal crewman. When he boarded the *Discovery* he was immediately disruptive. Pricket wondered if he should have been put off the boat at Harwich, but he remained part of the crew. When the *Discovery* sailed the coast of Iceland, Greene had fought with the ship's surgeon, an act that terrified the other men, who feared the surgeon would not reboard. Pricket claimed that he told Hudson about what had happened, but that Hudson refused to see any fault in Greene's actions. Instead, Hudson blamed the surgeon, noting that he "had a tongue that would wrong the best friend he had."

Juet also thought little of Greene, at least in Pricket's version. When Juet got drunk one day, 40 leagues after they had passed Iceland, he spun a long tale emphasizing that Hudson "had brought in Greene to crack his credit that should displease him"—that is, he would permanently ruin his reputation if he crossed him. When Hudson heard Juet's story, he was tempted to turn the *Discovery* around and sail back to Iceland, just so he could put Juet on a fishing boat and send him back to England. But calmer minds prevailed and Hudson let the matter rest. The surgeon, the carpenter, Juet, and Greene all remained a volatile combination on the vessel.

At the time of the gunner's death, Greene, in Pricket's opinion, was unobjectionable. He had no obvious religious sentiments, but there was nothing about him that would cause much concern. Greene had stayed in Hudson's good graces, as became evident when he gained possession of the gray gown after pleading with Hudson to let him have it.

But all was not well on board the *Discovery,* and preparing for the long winter brought out new tensions. Hudson ordered Staffe, the carpenter, to go onto the land to build a house, a reasonable request, given the fact the English knew they were going to be trapped in the area for months. But the carpenter refused. He told Hudson that it was too cold and snowy to build a house and retreated to his berth.

Hudson became enraged. Soon, according to Pricket, the captain called Staffe out of his cabin, cursed at him, and threatened to have him hanged. But the carpenter was unmoved. He informed Hudson that he knew best what he could do, and besides, "he was no House Carpenter." That clarification signaled much about the nature of the work needed on and around the *Discovery* that winter. To Hudson's mind, any ship's carpenter could presumably build a house. But the carpenter would have none of it, and treated the request as an insult revealing Hudson's ignorance of the skills that his own men possessed. Pricket noted that after the fracas, everyone soon calmed down, and that some individuals—never named in the narrative— built the house.

But the matter was apparently not quite over. The day after the fight, the carpenter decided he would leave the boat to visit the land. The ship's standing order demanded that no one venture on land alone, so the carpenter took Greene along. One carried a gun and the other a pike. They were ready for any encounter.

They might have been prepared to contend with a polar bear, perhaps, but they were not ready for the wrath of their captain when they reboarded the *Discovery*. Hudson was furious that Greene had gone with the carpenter—so furious that he gave Juet the gray gown. Greene exploded and challenged the captain, since the gown had already been given to him. But Hudson screamed at his crewman "with so many words of disgrace, telling him, that all his friends would not trust him with twenty shillings, and therefore why should he?" Hudson reminded Greene that he would not get paid unless he pleased him, a suggestion that he was only on board the *Discovery* through Hudson's largesse. Then, in a more conciliatory gesture, he added that he would stick to his promise to pay him equally with other members of the crew and to secure a coveted position for him in the prince's guard upon their return to London.

The tension passed, at least as far as Hudson knew. Pricket, who described the incident after the fact, added that from that moment on Greene had nothing but ill will toward Hudson and plotted to discredit the master. But the former servant's psychological turmoil was still private and had no obvious effect on the others. The men had more important things to do, notably figuring out how to survive the most difficult days, weeks, and months they would ever experience.

❦

No account survives chronicling what happened to the men on the *Discovery* during the brutal months from November 1610 to June 1611. Pricket never described the fear that must have gripped them when they heard the ice piling up against the sides of the ship. One later explorer, sailing in a much larger ship, likened the sound to thunder. For men, including Hudson, who had never suffered through the unique experience of being trapped, the ice must have evoked awe and terror.

Though Pricket mentioned none of the trials Hudson and his crew confronted, thirty years later another English ship wintered nearby, and its captain, Thomas James, left a detailed record of what he and his men endured. (He also gave his name to the body of water where the *Discovery* overwintered.) James's journal, published soon after his return to England, suggests that the locale might have been among the worst places in the world for a group of Europeans to wait out the season.

The ice, snow, and bitter cold of southern James Bay were like nothing that Hudson and his crew could have anticipated. All of them by then had experienced sailing amid ice floes and battling winds that might have driven their ship into rocks. Except for occasional mild periods, they also had experience with the fierce cold of the North Atlantic winds. Yet winter here plunged these men into a different category of wind and cold. Snow replaced rain by October, and the waters quickly became so frigid that it began to freeze at the surface, a consequence of the bay's shallowness. The tides at first still moved water under the surface, but James reported that by early December the ice had thickened. When they went onto their ship to retrieve their clothes, they found them encased in ice and had to chisel them out with small iron spikes. One day it was so cold that the men's hands, noses, and cheeks froze "as white as paper." The nearby ground offered no reprieve; the ground had frozen early in the season. By late December, the men were living, as James put it, in a "Wilderness of Snow." By January the ground was frozen to a depth of 10 feet.

When James outfitted his crew for their voyage into the region where Hudson had traveled, he had the advantage of knowing what kinds of skills his men would need and how to provision the ship to avoid any problems. With the benefit of the next generation's greater lore and experience, he was better prepared than Hudson had been. Still, overwintering along the southern edge of James Bay caused troubles that even the most able and informed European would have found vexing.

The first order of business would have been to steer a ship into a place where the relentless pressure of ice would not destroy it during the winter. That would mean harboring it as close to land as possible while avoiding sharp rocks that could pierce the hull. If the crew managed that feat, then perhaps the boat would still be seaworthy when the ice finally receded. The members of James's crew, who feared that they might beach their ship in such shallow waters that it might never escape, punched holes in the hull to sink it in a likely place, with the idea that they could patch it when it was time to raise the vessel. The ship's carpenter nevertheless feared that the damage to the hull from the ice would be so great that the vessel might never be seaworthy again.

The Arctic can upset even the best of plans. James reported that over the winter the constant storms filled the decks of his ship with snow and ice. He feared that when the warmer temperatures arrived and the pressure of the ice subsided, more holes in the hull would be revealed. He understood that extracting a ship from its winter grip could be as difficult as finding a safe harbor for it. To prevent it from sinking, the carpenter and other crewmen would need to plug the holes as they emerged above the water line. In April, James's men began the arduous task of extracting their ship from the ice. Fortunately for them, some of their stores, including barrels of salted pork and beef as well as kegs of beer and cider, had survived the winter under the ice.

The travails faced by a wooden sailing vessel paled in comparison to those of humans who had to endure a winter they could never have imagined. James, in anticipation of the worst winds, had the ship's surgeon cut his hair short and then shaved his beard because he was already being bothered by the icicles that formed every time he took a breath. His men used driftwood and boughs from nearby trees to create three dwellings—a house for the officers, another for the crew (where the food would be prepared), and a storehouse, which was little more than a lean-to formed with their sails. The men hauled their chests from the ship to the land and kept a fire going to keep from freezing to death. Some planned to spend the winter building a small ship, called a pinnace, out of any wood they could gather on land in case the main ship could not be re-floated. In such a circumstance, they would have stripped their original ship of its still serviceable planks to secure their new craft.

The human body is not equipped for long durations of extreme cold. In the early seventeenth century, provisions typically brought along for sailors on English vessels were inadequate for what these men faced. By February, James reported that two-thirds of his men were suffering from one kind of malady or another. They had mouths full of sores, their teeth became loose, their gums swelled "with black rotten flesh, which must every day be cut away." Some could not even eat because the pain was so excruciating. Some men suffered from headaches and pains in their chest, while others could barely walk because of pain or weakness in their legs or backs. They were suffering, though he did not mention it, from scurvy. To survive, they needed a constant supply of firewood, which meant daily trips scouting for wood even though none of them possessed shoes that kept their feet dry. Getting wood was not easy, especially since tools broke easily because of the cold. If they managed to get wood into the house and set it alight, they ran the risk, if the wood was still green, of making a fire so smoky that it was unbearable to remain inside. Even dead wood was often no better, because the felled trees the men found often contained turpentine, which created fires so sooty that it made them look like a group of former chimney sweeps.

Eventually, the men on James's expedition identified three kinds of cold. The first and easiest to bear was characterized by hoarfrost, which accumulated on the men indoors as they slept and covered them by morning when they awoke. Venturing outside for wood or game was a worse kind of cold; any exposed flesh froze almost immediately. Yet even that exposure was better than when someone had to go onto the ship. That relatively short journey exposed a man to the worst that winter had to offer, a cold, as James put it, "so extreme that it was not endurable." No one had sufficient clothing to protect their bodies from these chills, and even movement did not generate enough heat to keep someone going. Men complained that frigid winds froze their eyelashes so that they could not even see. To be exposed to such conditions for more than a short time caused certain death. James's men were less fortunate than Hudson's: Three died during the winter. James's descriptions of the effects of cold lingered in the English imagination for years. A generation after he had returned, the experimental scientist Robert Boyle, a prominent early member of the Royal Society, repeatedly drew on James's account for his own descriptions of the ways that cold threatened the human body.

James and his men had no choice but to wait for the brief Arctic summer to arrive. By early May, migrating geese and cranes had returned, a sign of thaw. Two weeks later, James actually planted some peas in the hope that the men would finally have some green vegetables. By late May, the sun had begun to melt much of the nearby snow, leaving the ground honeycombed, as James put it, "so that the land whereon it lies will not be at all wetted." But even then, temperature fluctuations tortured the men. They complained about the excessive heat, or "hot glooms," which made it impossible for them to be outside in the daytime. Still, each night brought a hard frost. By the end of the month, the temperature had risen, but the first four days of June brought more hail, snow, and fierce winds. To make matters worse, even though the bay was too ice-choked for them to escape, the summer heat had brought on an infinite number of blood-sucking mosquitoes: "[W]e were more tormented with them," James wrote, "then ever we were with the cold weather." The men eventually tore old ship's flags into bits and wrapped them around their heads to protect their faces, but to no avail; the mosquitoes penetrated these improvised coverings and stung them repeatedly, often on their faces. The men scratched at the bites so vigorously that they often tore their own flesh.

James's men set sail in early July, or about two weeks later than the date the *Discovery*'s crew had managed to get their ship back into the water. They were ultimately luckier than the *Discovery*, however. They made it home without any other calamities.

❧

The disputes that occurred on board the *Discovery* did not signal a complete breakdown of either Hudson's authority or the spirit of comity that kept the crew together during the long, dark winter months. As Pricket later recounted, during the first three months of their winter refuge the men had access to perhaps 1,200 white partridges, along with other birds, which they either killed during the winter or perhaps had taken earlier, and they had no trouble landing fish before the bay froze. The last of the partridges flew off when spring began to arrive, but fortunately, ducks, teal, swans, and geese soon appeared, though they were harder to capture. Hudson thought that perhaps he had found their breeding grounds nearby, but that hope turned out to be false. These birds were only in the midst of their migration to lands even farther north—a destination more northerly, in Pricket's opinion, than the *Discovery* had ever gone.

The departure of the birds brought hard times for the men, who now decided to explore the land more thoroughly in search of food. They went, Pricket recalled, into the nearby forests and valleys, looking "for all things that had any shew of substance in them, how vile soever." And vile it was indeed when the crew found themselves trying to get by eating moss. They even ate reptiles: "The Frog (in his engendering time as loathsome as a Toad) was not spared." The mathematician Wydowse brought back the bud of a tree "full of a Turpentine substance." The surgeon cooked the goo into a barely palatable drink "and applied the buds hot to them that were troubled with ache in any part of their bodies." Pricket admitted that the drink eased the pain that had been brought on by the cold.

By midwinter, it had been months since they had seen another human being. They had seen signs of human activity, of course—those lodges with the birds hanging by the neck and the footprint on the shore. But seemingly out of the blue one day in spring—Pricket did not provide the date but noted that it was the time "when the Ice began to break out of the Bays," so it was probably late May or early June—a local man, presumably a Cree, arrived at the *Discovery*. Hudson, who had had extensive, if problematic, experience with the native peoples of the mid-Atlantic coast in 1609, treated the American well. Pricket reported that Hudson welcomed the man, no doubt because he recognized the value of a possible trade partner—a lesson he had learned the year before. This was someone whose knowledge of the region could help provide his crew with fresh food and help restore their health. Hudson asked his men to offer their hatchets and knives, the kind of tools that all of them possessed, but neither Pricket, nor John King, nor Staffe would go along with the plan. Still, Hudson managed to give the man a mirror, buttons, and a knife. The man accepted the goods with thanks and made a sign that he would soon return. Exchanging signs, as Hudson would have known from his reading of other travel narratives, was the only way to communicate ideas at the time.

The Cree man returned the next day, dragging a sled bearing the skins of two deer and two beaver. "He had a scrip [small bag] under his arm," Pricket remembered, and pulled out the things that Hudson had given him the day before. The man laid the knife on top of one beaver skin and the buttons and glass on the other, and offered them to Hudson, who understood that he had to accept the goods to satisfy the man that they were making a fair trade. The man then took the things that Hudson had offered and put them back in his sack. Hudson produced a hatchet and signaled that for him to part with it the man would need to trade both deer skins. At first the Cree was reluctant, but eventually he agreed. He signed, too, that there were people to the north and to the south, and that he would come back again. He never returned.

Pricket did not keep track of dates very well, but he at least provided some clues about the changes that altered the camp when winter released its grip and the first signs of spring appeared. Among those signs was the loosening of the ice along the shore. When the ice receded somewhat, Hudson sent his men out in a shallop to go fishing, even though the *Discovery* remained ice-bound. The first day, the fishing crew included William Wilson, Michael Perse, John Thomas, Adrian Moter, Bennet Mathews, Arnold Ladley, and the rancorous Henry Greene. Pricket rarely displayed the ability to recall who did what on the journey, but in this instance, he was able to supply details, perhaps because this first fishing expedition was the most successful. Using the *Discovery*'s net, they managed to haul in 500 fish on the first day—some trout, others unidentified but as big as herring. The yield cheered the men, giving them hope that their dietary needs could finally be met. But that was not the case. Never again would any fishing party do so well. As often as not, the men returned with no more than a quarter of the first day's haul.

Out in the water, away from Hudson, the men talked among themselves. Pricket, who was not with them, had no way of knowing what they discussed. But as the days passed, he learned that Greene had conspired with William Wilson and unnamed others to steal the net and the shallop, which had been put together by Staffe, and leave the others behind.

They never got the chance. Hudson decided that he would take the shallow drafting boat on his own excursion in search of more of the Americans. He planned to travel to the south and southwest—along the southern edges of James Bay, the homeland of the Crees—in search of their fires. According to

Pricket, Hudson took the shallop and enough food to last for up to nine days. He paddled off to the south, leaving orders that those who remained behind were to gather wood, water, and ballast. Now that the ice was finally thawing, Hudson wanted the men to be ready to sail upon his return.

When Hudson set out to explore and find supplies, some of the men who remained behind—who had sailed with him through the labyrinth, endured the bitter cold of the northern winter, and managed to survive by learning what the land and the water produced one season after another—decided to mutiny against him.

VI.

#

JAMES BAY TO LONDON,
JUNE TO AUGUST 1611

*Henry Hudson had no luck* finding any of the locals around James Bay. He knew they were close by because he could see their fires. They undoubtedly knew he was in their vicinity, but apparently they saw no reason to meet him along the shoreline. Unable to acquire new provisions, he returned to the *Discovery*. The ship remained trapped in the ice, though the frozen barrier was thinning by the day. The men no doubt realized that their moment of liberation was quickly approaching. But freedom for the ship, as Hudson would soon learn, did not mean all would prosper.

On board Hudson found that the food supplies had grown dangerously low. He then made the decision to distribute the last of what seemed to be the remaining supply of bread. Each man received a pound. He also gave each what Pricket termed a "Bill of Return, willing them to have that to shew, if it pleased God, that they came home." These receipts were a kind of insurance policy for the men, like those that Hudson had given to his crew in 1608 when he realized that the *Hopewell* could not make it through the Northeast Passage. But this time he had not made the decision to return to England, though that possibility must now have commanded his attention. Still, even the thought that he would abandon his quest took a psychological toll. Pricket reported that Hudson broke down in tears, perhaps because he realized that he might fail again.

The bread, which Hudson believed was enough to last each man for two weeks, was meager at best, so it comes as no surprise that the men launched the boat with a seine on Friday morning, June 15. They returned on Sunday morning, but did not have much to offer. They had managed to bring back only about eighty "small Fish," as Pricket termed their puny haul—"a poor relief for so many hungry bellies."

The *Discovery* soon edged from its winter imprisonment. The crew dropped anchor in the open waters of the bay, then sailed a bit farther and anchored "in the Sea," according to Pricket, which probably meant they had escaped the shallower waters of the bay. By then, the bread that Hudson had distributed was gone. Greene had eaten his within a few days. The boatswain, Wilson, apparently devoured his ration in a single day, an act that left him sick for two or three days. Confronted by a starving crew, Hudson ordered the distribution of the remaining cheese. He divided it up equally, the moldy and ruined along with some that still could be eaten. Pricket believed that Hudson did so to make a point: If the captain gave them all of the cheese, good and bad, the crew "should see that they had no wrong done them: but every man should have alike the best and worst together." Each received 3½ pounds, an amount Pricket thought should last them for about a week.

On June 17 the *Discovery* began to push toward open water, though its final destination was not yet clear. But the next night the crew encountered more ice. The winds were indifferent, so they decided to stay put for almost a week—still in sight of land, but in open water. Meanwhile, the men were starving. With the ship anchored near the ice, Hudson ordered the boy Nicholas Syms to break up all of the remaining chests on board the *Discovery* to search for food that crewmen might have hidden; he also instructed him to bring up any remaining hoard that had escaped the earlier distribution. Syms soon brought Hudson thirty cakes of bread. Pricket could not understand what had taken the master so long to make the obvious decision to parcel out all of the ship's food among the men. Had he done so earlier, Pricket believed, he might have prevented the escalation of tension on board the ship. Now it was perhaps too late. The fate of the ship, the chronicler thought, was now in higher hands, not Hudson's. "*There are many devices in the heart of a man,*" Pricket wrote, quoting from Proverbs 19:21, "*yet the counsel of the Lord shall stand.*"

Pricket was not feeling well during this incident, so he retired to his cabin. He later claimed that he was in fact "lame," though he did not describe the nature of his wound or ailment. But he did remember in vivid detail what happened next. According to his version of events, on the night of June 21, Greene and Wilson came to inform him that they had a group of like-minded allies who would convince the rest of the crew to turn against Hudson. They would put the master and the ill men onto the shallop and let them take care of themselves. The plotters told Pricket that all of the food on the ship could not provide more than two weeks of nourishment. Besides, the disgruntled were hungry. They had not eaten for three days.

The long months of the journey, the frights they had experienced, and the close confinement during the winter had churned some of the men into a frenzy. They could take the situation no longer. Hudson, they understood, had not yet abandoned his search for the Northwest Passage, and they now knew that pushing on could leave them stranded in unmapped terrain. Few of them could have thought they could survive yet another winter in this frozen land. They had had enough, and their desperation could not be contained. They were "resolute," Pricket recalled, "either to mend or end."

The men had resolved to carry their new strategy to its end, even if it meant they would die during their rebellion or on the gallows when they made it back to London. Pricket could not quite grasp their words. "When I heard this," he later wrote (in a perhaps self-excusing passage), "I told them I marveled to hear so much from them, considering that they were married men, and had wives and children, and that for their sakes they should not commit so foul a thing in the sight of God and man." Pricket said he believed that even if they managed to talk their way out of hanging, they would be banished from England for their treachery.

Greene told Pricket that he understood the gravity of the situation as well as the potential consequences of following Hudson further into unknown and possibly fatal territory. He could bear the thought of remaining under Hudson's command no more. "Henry Greene told me to hold my peace," Pricket recalled, explaining that he (Greene) knew that those who defied Hudson might be executed for their actions when they reached England's shores. But if Greene grasped the deadly risk of rebellion, why did he still persist in the effort? He told Pricket that of the two options facing him, "he would rather be hanged at home than starved abroad."

The next moment proved fateful, both for Pricket himself and for the mutiny on the *Discovery*. Greene and the others had resolved that they should spare Pricket. According to his report, the rebels had only goodwill toward the man who would eventually—though no one could have known it at the time—write the most widely disseminated account of the voyage and its turmoil. They might have also believed that Pricket, a former servant of the expedition's backer, Sir Dudley Digges, could reach out to his former master when the *Discovery* reached London. Perhaps his prior association with Digges would give him the standing to defend the men against the charges they would face. Pricket at first resisted. He wrote that he thanked them for the chance to join them, and told them that he had not joined the expedition only to abandon it. He hoped, he added, that no harm would come to anyone because of his decision, but he would remain with Hudson. Greene responded immediately, Pricket remembered: *"Henry Greene* told me then, that I must take my fortune in the Shallop."

Pricket, for the moment, accepted his expulsion, putting his fate in God's hands. His resolve only further inflamed Greene, who could not understand why anyone would resist his plans. Pricket observed that Greene became more visibly angry and went off "in a rage," swearing that he would slash the throat of anyone who interfered. Greene left Wilson alone in the cabin with Pricket. Pricket would later write that he tried to convince the boatswain to change his mind, but his arguments did no good because Wilson had become convinced that he had to go along with the unfolding plot.

Soon Greene returned and asked Wilson if he had managed to convince Pricket to side with the mutineers. After Wilson told him that Pricket still refused to join the insurrection, Pricket spoke to Greene directly, imploring him to wait three days. He promised that in that period he would work on Hudson to improve conditions. Perhaps he thought he would be able to get Hudson to abandon the journey for the passage and sail directly for home, or planned to work on the master to convince him to distribute food supplies that had not yet been made available to the entire crew. Greene apparently refused, so Pricket asked for two days, then for twelve hours. Greene was either stubborn, as he must have appeared to Pricket, or resolute. Finally Pricket entreated Greene to wait until Monday—not long, since it was already Saturday night—and that then he would take it upon himself to distribute any food supplies that still might be hidden on the ship, even if it meant that Pricket would need to answer for his disobedience to Hudson once the *Discovery* returned to England.

Pricket asserted that it was only at that moment—when Greene refused his offer of intervention—that it occurred to the chronicler that this was no simple dispute about the management of the *Discovery*'s meager barrels of food. At that point, he confronted Greene and the others, accusing them of hiding their true motives. This was not a disagreement over the supplies stored on the *Discovery* or even a legitimate dispute about the future destination of the ship. Instead, Pricket now believed, the rebels intended to extract revenge for whatever slights the mutineers felt they had suffered. They wanted blood, not food.

Greene then lurched forward and grabbed Pricket's Bible, which was lying in front of him, and swore that he had no intention of harming any of the men on the ship. Instead, he saw himself as the savior of the entire expedition. He told Pricket that he was acting in the best interests of everyone on board, and he hoped that others would join him. Wilson immediately seconded him.

Greene left the cabin, and soon Robert Juet, Hudson's mate on his journey to the mid-Atlantic coast of North America, entered to confront him. Pricket hoped that Juet would be reasonable since he was "an ancient man"—meaning he presumably had more wisdom than some of the hotter-tempered young men on the ship. But Juet was even angrier than Greene and vowed he would justify the rebels' actions once they returned to England. Two others, John Thomas and Michael Perse, came and echoed Juet's feelings. (Pricket, writing well after the mutiny, refused to say more about two of them because they died before the *Discovery* reached England—an odd omission, given his willingness to quote other mutineers who were also dead before Pricket told his story.) When Adrian Moter and Bennet Mathews came into the cabin, Pricket asked them if they understood the consequences of their actions. They replied that they knew what they were doing and had already sworn an oath to uphold the insurrection against Hudson. (In the end, neither joined the mutiny.) According to Pricket, the oath pledged each man to do what was best for as many people as possible. *"You shall swear truth to God, your Prince and Country,"* Pricket claimed they said, *"you shall do nothing, but to the glory of God, and the good of the action in hand, and harm to no man.*" Though Pricket did not see how their actions fit their alleged aims, spelling out the oath might have been one way for him to justify remaining on the *Discovery* even though he claimed to have tried to halt the mutiny.

Pricket waited in the cabin, expecting more rebels to enter. There were others, he knew, involved in the plot, but no one else materialized. Having sought his support and at least neutralized him as an advocate for Hudson, the rebels could now make their move. "It was dark," Pricket remembered, and the mutineers were ready "to put this deed of darkness in execution." He tried once more to delay what must have now seemed inevitable, calling out to Greene and Wilson, urging them not to proceed during the night but at least wait until the morning. He hoped that the plotters would go to sleep, and in the hours before dawn come to their senses. He later wrote that he knew then that "wickedness sleepeth not."

Pricket reported that Greene spent the night with Hudson, perhaps making sure that the captain did not try to foil their plans—if, that is, he even suspected them. The other plotters kept watch on the ship's deck, though for what remains unclear, since the only other human they had seen in weeks was the lone native man who had never returned. Perhaps they stood guard lest others of the crew would come to free Hudson once the mutiny was under way. If so, they had little to fear; there were few men strong enough at this point to combat Greene, Wilson, and Juet.

At some point Pricket confronted Greene one more time. Who, besides Hudson, he asked, would be put into the shallop and set adrift? Greene replied that he intended to cast out the carpenter, Staffe, who had been Hudson's closest ally recently, along with John King (the former quartermaster) and all the debilitated men. Pricket challenged the idea that the mutineers should dispatch the carpenter. Wouldn't they need his services later on? But Greene responded that the carpenter had to go because he and King bore some responsibility for Hudson's earlier unwillingness to share all of the food on the *Discovery*.

More damning was Hudson's promotion of the carpenter to the position of mate in place of Robert Bylot as the *Discovery* sailed into its winter confinement. The men thought the change in leadership only portended danger for the mission because, as they told Pricket, the carpenter was illiterate. Why would that matter? As Pricket recreated the conversation, the elevation of such an unlearned man to a place of prominence in the governance of the ship meant that "the Master and his ignorant Mate would carry the Ship whither the Master pleased."

Hudson had apparently already laid claim to all of the navigational tools on the *Discovery,* which meant that even an experienced mate like Juet or a literate Bylot could not make any measurements. Hudson, they asserted, had forbidden any of the men from keeping track of their location and had confiscated the navigational tools—an unlikely allegation, because the master would have never taken any equipment from the mathematician Wydowse. Pricket managed to convince Greene and Wilson to spare the carpenter, and he hoped that he would persuade them to save Hudson. He also held out hope, at least momentarily, that someone would warn Hudson of the fate that awaited him when he emerged from his cabin. Pricket did not mention it, but if Greene and his associates abandoned their plans, then he, too, would avoid the shallop.

❧

Like any ship intended for a long voyage, the *Discovery* had an assigned berth for each of the men. The social geography of the vessel now played a role in the unfolding rebellion, as Pricket realized when he recounted the shipboard arrangements. Bennet Mathews slept in the cook's room, along with the cooper Silvanus Bond, who was lame. The mathematician, Wydowse, now lying ill, had a berth just outside, alongside Syracke Faner, who was also sick. Nearby slept the surgeon and Hudson's son John, and farther along slept Wilson and another crewman, Arnold Ladley. Robert Juet and John Thomas occupied the gun room. The larboard side had the berth of Michael Bute and

Adrian Moore, a man whom Pricket noted "had never been well since we lost our Anchor." Also in the gun room were Michael Perse and Adrian Moter. Just outside lay John King, Robert Bylot, Francis Clemens, and Pricket himself. Henry Greene and Nicholas Syms occupied a part of the midship between the pumps and the capstone. John King, Pricket remembered, stayed up late that night on the poop deck to keep watch on Staffe.

When morning broke, Mathews went up on the deck to fetch water for his kettle. Immediately the rebels shut the hatch beside him, keeping him away from the others. Greene and one of the others pulled Staffe aside to tell him about what was going on. Hudson then emerged from his own cabin, and Wilson ambushed him and tied his hands behind his back. Hudson demanded to know what was going on.

"They told him," Pricket reported, "he should know when he is in the Shallop."

Hudson's remaining allies confronted the plotters. Hudson cried out for the carpenter, to let his friend Staffe know that he was now bound. But no reply came. Arnold Ladley and Michael Bute yelled at Greene and the others, warning them that "their knavery would shew itself."

The mutineers then raised the shallop and forced "the poor, sick, and lame men" out of their cabins and onto the shallow craft.

Finally Hudson called for Pricket, who struggled to get out of his cabin, presumably because he was weak from illness. Pricket later claimed that he tried to reach the captain, but got only as far as the hatch, where he hoped he might be heard. Pricket fell to his knees in front of the rebels and pleaded that "for the love of God, to remember themselves, and to do as they would be done unto."

The rebels told him to hold his tongue and get back into his cabin. They refused to let Pricket speak to Hudson. But when he returned, he heard Hudson's voice through the horn, which normally provided light into the cabin and could also, as in this instance, be used to communicate through the cabin

127

walls. He told Pricket that it was Juet who was behind the trouble and that he would "overthrow us all." Pricket yelled back that Greene was behind the insurrection—or so Pricket would claim in his testimony.

Most of the men that Greene, Wilson, and the others wanted to get rid of were now on the shallop. The mutineers had already decided to keep Pricket on board, but the fate of Staffe, the ship's carpenter, was not yet sealed. The mutineers had wanted to dispatch him, too, because of his loyalty to Hudson, but Pricket had apparently gotten them to reconsider his fate. Yet the carpenter himself had not yet made up his mind whether he wanted to stay or go. He was, in some ways, the only person (other than Pricket) who had control of his own destiny. "Will you be hanged when you get home?" the carpenter asked the rebels. He told them that he would stay on the *Discovery* only if the mutineers forced him to do so. The rebels told him that he should get on board the shallop, because they had no intention of forcing anyone to stay with them. The carpenter agreed to go, and hoped that he would get to keep the contents of his chest, which apparently contained his tools. The rebels put the chest into the shallop.

Staffe came to say goodbye to Pricket, who would claim later that he tried to persuade the carpenter to stay. But Staffe assumed that the mutineers would not accept him back. During the tense moments of the rebellion, Hudson had told Staffe that no one else would be able to guide the *Discovery* home. The carpenter, who still held out hope that all could be reconciled, guessed that the castaways would do their best to follow the ship, though he knew that the shallop would lag far behind. He apparently planned to lead them toward a likely reunion with the *Discovery*. Toward that end he asked Pricket to "leave some token" at the "Capes"—probably Digges Island—to indicate that the *Discovery* had in fact made it close to the place where the crew had watched the fowl nest the previous summer. Pricket added no more details about the carpenter's plan for a possible reunion. The carpenter and Pricket wept when the moment came for them to part. The sick men were now herded onto the shallop, and eventually Arnold Ladley and Michael Bute joined them, either out of loyalty to Hudson or because of the repugnance they felt toward the mutineers.

Even before the shallop was set free of the ship, those who remained on board ransacked the vessel looking for whatever they could find. They acted, Pricket wrote, "as if the Ship had been entered by force, and they had free leave to pillage." They acted, that is, as if they were pirates looting an enemy for uncertain bounty. They broke into chests and rifled through them. Pricket would write that one of the mutineers came up to him to ask what they should do next, whereupon (by his own testimony) Pricket told them they should stop their petty pillaging. His request apparently had no effect. Pricket noted that the one who had approached him did "nothing but shark up and down," a phrase meant to signal the crewman's voracious predation.

Meanwhile, above decks, the fate of those on the shallop had been determined. According to Pricket, the nine on the shallow craft included Hudson and his son along with Staffe, Ladley, Syracke Faner, Wydowse, Adrian Moore, Henry King, and Michael Bute. Staffe had managed to get some necessary tools from the rebels, including some pikes, a gun and powder, some food—Pricket did not specify what kind—and an iron pot. If Greene and the others had intended the unfortunate to die a quick death, they did not act like it. The tools could only have been understood by all as just enough to let the men fend for themselves, at least for a brief time.

The shallop had been tied to the *Discovery*'s stern. The mutineers cut the rope and immediately began to drift away, even though some of the ship's sails remained tethered. The rebels also continued to rifle through the possessions of the departed men. As some had suspected, they found quite a bit of food in the hold that Hudson had apparently secreted away. They found enough meal, beer, butter, peas, and pork to sate their hunger.

Someone on board spotted the shallop trying to catch up to the ship. Hudson and the others had managed to rig a small sail, though it would never be sufficient to gather enough speed to catch up. The mutineers unfurled both the mainsail and the topsail, and the *Discovery* caught the wind. As Pricket described it, they then took off and flew "as from an Enemy."

❦

As from an enemy? Greene and the others had indeed come to believe their captain was their adversary. They believed that Hudson had mismanaged the resources of the *Discovery*. They were angry that he had hidden food stores and refused to distribute them to a crew desperate for nourishment. They also felt that he had made an unconscionable error when he had decided to promote an illiterate carpenter to first mate, a position that brought with it responsibility for negotiating with the master to plot a course. With Staffe as first mate, Hudson would control all the information and tools necessary to chart the ship's course according to his own whim, no matter what the other men wanted—even, they worried, to the point of searching for the Northwest Passage all summer, and perhaps missing the opportunity to return to England before another winter set in. The men who put Hudson and the others into the shallop would need to make a case for Hudson's gross incompetence or malfeasance if they wanted to escape execution—if, that is, they managed to survive a return journey homeward through ice-choked seas.

But neither Pricket's narrative nor the other scant surviving documents suggest that Hudson took such actions to threaten the crew. He could be stubborn, to be sure, and perhaps in those long months trapped in the ice he had barked out orders that annoyed some of the men. They were, after all, confined in dank, close, and freezing quarters far from home, watching their food supplies dwindle and their bodies become increasingly infirm. Such conditions might have made them even more brash and prickly in their response to perceived slights and injustices. But in the June thaw when Hudson apparently prepared to continue his search, the rebels were no longer willing to take a chance on finding the passage. Hudson had become their enemy, and as such, any last vestiges of his authority over them had melted away with the worst of the winter ice. The mutineers got their wish: Hudson's command over them had now come to an end, whatever the consequences for those on the shallop or those who might survive the passage to London.

After the mutineers pushed the shallop away, the *Discovery* began its homeward journey, with Hudson and his men rowing furiously behind them, growing ever more distant as the larger vessel's sails billowed with wind and increased its speeds, until the captain and his boatload of mostly sick men vanished from sight altogether. Within a short period—Pricket did not note the number of days—the remaining crew anchored the *Discovery* off the eastern shore of either James Bay or, more likely, Hudson Bay. Some then went ashore, including Michael Perse, who managed to kill two birds, a paltry catch considering the number of migratory birds that would have been in the area at the time. The men on land found a large and welcome supply of cockle grass. The ship remained there from one evening through the next day. During their stay, Greene approached Pricket and told him that from that point forward he could take possession of Hudson's cabin. Presumably Greene was trying to get on the good side of the man who was keeping a record of the expedition. Pricket at first demurred, suggesting that the place of honor should go to Juet. But Juet had refused to enter into the chamber or touch any of Hudson's maps or his journal. Pricket, by his own account, accepted Greene's offer. He took the key to Hudson's chest, and also took possession of the bread that Hudson had apparently squirreled away for his own use but had not yet consumed.

As the *Discovery* lay off that unnamed and unmarked part of the eastern shore, Pricket recognized just how alone they were—not just from any other native peoples in the area but from their former captain and crewmen. "Here we lay that night, and the best part of the next day," he recalled, "in all which time we saw not the shallop, or ever after."

✑

Those who remained on the *Discovery* did not all agree about the best way to proceed. Juet, quite likely the most experienced seaman on the ship, believed that their best bet lay in initially heading northwest, perhaps because he understood that in the middle of the bay they would be able to avoid any ice that might still be choking the coastlines. Bylot, who had ample experience at sea, disagreed. He argued that the ship should instead sail to the northeast, which is the course they chose. They kept the eastern side of the bay in sight, no doubt to guide their way. They understood that navigation would have been more difficult now that the ship's mathematician was among those on the shallop. But such a strategy was hardly foolproof, as the men soon discovered when they encountered a series of ice floes. "[W]e ran from thin to thick," Pricket recalled, describing how the ice became so dense in front of them that they could not go forward. Worse still, the wind had pushed ice behind the ship, too, effectively trapping the *Discovery* in a midsummer ice field. For the next two weeks, they remained in place amid ice floes too thick for them to avoid. At this point both the food stores and the tempers among the mutineers must have grown even thinner. The ice spread out across the surface of the water and seemed to block any escape route. When Hudson was captain in this sort of situation, they had managed to find open water to the northwest or the southeast. But not now. "[T]his floating Ice contained miles, and half miles in compass," Pricket remembered.

Juet proposed once again that they try to steer the ship toward the northwest, but Bylot remained stubborn. Pricket recalled that the navigator insisted that the ship sail toward the northeast, and the crew complied. Eventually they managed to wrestle the ship free of the ice and continued on a journey that kept them in sight of the mainland. They passed a cluster of four islands, then doubled back and anchored between two of them, lowering a small boat, and a party went ashore to explore and look for supplies for their journey. All they found was cockle grass, which they gathered once again for the ship's storehouse.

Pricket's narrative to this point had dwelled on the mundane details of the events elapsing since the mutiny, suggesting that once the horrible deed had been done, those who remained on the *Discovery* at least got along well enough to focus on whatever challenges they might face on the way homeward. But that mood was not to continue. While the ship was anchored near a cluster of unnamed islands, Greene began to intensify the level of conflict between himself and Pricket. Greene's hostility toward Pricket had been clear, but as the ship lay anchored, the chief mutineer's actions became more threatening. Pricket recalled that Greene "began (very subtly) to draw me to take upon me to search for those things" which Pricket knew Greene had in fact already stolen for himself. He then accused Pricket of treason, arguing that the journal writer had cheated the rest of the men out of thirty "Cakes of bread."

Pricket and the others began to argue among themselves about where they could take their ship and have the best chance to save their own lives. Some men had concluded that returning to England without their captain was going to be too dangerous; they knew what happened to those who threatened an English ship at sea, especially an expedition that had the support of politically powerful investors. In an age when the English were eager to embrace long-distance trade, merchants and policy makers could not tolerate any misbehavior that threatened the security of ships bound for distant locales. Shipboard troubles were nothing new, of course; along the Thames, the English had long displayed the bodies of pirates who had robbed English ships and faced the ultimate punishment once they were caught. Authorities hoped that the public presentation of their corpses would discourage anyone who might have thought about breaking free of customary maritime restraints in an effort to enrich themselves. A man who joined a conspiracy against a ship's captain, if he ever came home again, had a date with the hangman. The men on the *Discovery* might well have remembered that less than three years earlier, on December 22, 1608, the king had authorized the simultaneous hanging of nineteen pirates, whose bodies made a ghastly row at the docks at Wapping in London. James was no more willing to live with pirates than Queen Elizabeth had been; he bragged that the state had executed more pirates during his reign than in the entire previous century.

But the men on the *Discovery* ultimately listened to Greene, who promised them that all would work out. He told them that the ship would not lower its sails in English waters until he had in hand a promise from King James that it could dock safely. The men were dubious—they had, Pricket wrote, "many devices in their heads"—but in the end they recognized that Greene was now in charge and so deserved their loyalty. In an act that would have stunned Hudson, the men now called Greene their captain. The servant had become the master.

Greene, perhaps the only man among Hudson's original crew who had not previously spent much time at sea, might not have been prevaricating when he claimed he could secure their lives. Though James had already staked out a vigorous position against any infractions of English law at sea, some pirates had in fact argued that exceptions due to mitigating circumstances should be allowed. Greene might have heard about the gallows' confessions of the pirates Purser (a.k.a. Thomas Walton), Clinton, and Arnold, who had used their last moments in 1583 to argue that they had always been loyal to the realm and acted like any brave Englishman would have in the face of dangers and opportunities at sea. Their pleas emphasized their loyalty to Queen Elizabeth. Soon after the executions, enterprising printers published testimony for the wider reading public about the pirates' expression of patriotic values. The one surviving brief pamphlet contains confessions of the three pirates in verse.

The 1583 gallows confessions caught the imagination of the English playwrights Thomas Haywood and William Rowley, who produced a dramatic recreation of the pirates' last days. In the script, two of the pirates muse about their command of the waters. "[W]e reign'd as Lords, nay Kings at Sea," the actor playing Purser declares, "the ocean was our realm." Clinton agrees: "[T]he seas had been to us a glorious monument, where now the fates have cast us on the shelf to hang 'twixt air and water." The play was performed in London at some point between 1607 and 1609—in the years, that is, just preceding the voyage of the *Discovery*. Is it possible that Greene had seen it and been inspired by it to believe that perhaps the circumstances on board the *Discovery* would be serious enough to justify clemency from the king? The idea was perhaps not so outlandish. After all, if Hudson had been acting in ways contrary to the best interests of those on board the ship, then he in effect had been working against the interests of his prominent supporters and of the entire realm. Pricket accepted the argument that the mutineers had rebelled because they believed that Hudson had been hoarding food, but the voyage's chronicler never delved into any underlying motivations or justifications.

In any case, according to Pricket, the *Discovery* continued its course steadily to the northeast, soon passing what Hudson had the year before named the Rummies Islands. The channel between the islands and the shore was shallow, but Bylot kept the ship within sight of the mainland. Not surprisingly, the vessel's hull soon ran onto a large submerged rock—an impediment sufficiently serious that Pricket realized they might never escape it. But once again providence (in Pricket's opinion) intervened, and the ship shouldered free without much harm.

Bylot's course was far from ideal. The men on the ship had hoped to sail near the capes they had passed before, a place where they might gather provisions for the crossing. Such a course would have brought them back into the breeding grounds of the millions of birds that they had seen flying in massive flocks toward the northern edges of Hudson Bay. But Bylot steered them farther north, telling the crew that he thought they would find the best route there. Pricket intervened to say he believed they were approaching Cape Wolstenholme; he recognized the rocky shore and shallow water as the same that Hudson had steered through on his way to the bay the previous year. But Juet entered the discussion at this point, contending that they had not reached that point yet. He probably dismissed Pricket's views as those of a landsman, since Pricket never had any real experience at sea until Hudson decided to bring him along on this expedition.

In the end, Juet prevailed. The *Discovery* continued on its course until it anchored amid a cluster of small islands choking a narrow channel between two large lands. Some of the men explored the land on the north and returned only with what Pricket termed "the great *Horn*, but nothing else"—possibly the horn of a narwhal, which many English at the time believed could be ground down to make medicines. (Frobisher's men had returned with such a specimen a generation earlier.) Those who landed to the south had better luck: They at least found a large supply of cockle grass. The discovery could not have come at a better time, since Pricket believed that the declining stores on the ship made it unlikely that the men would survive much longer without replenishing their food supply. Within days, they arrived at the capes, where the famished crewmen landed—as Pricket put it—"with joy," since they anticipated killing and eating all the birds they wanted. It was a sensible expectation. According to one modern estimate, at least 2 million thick-billed murres (*Uria lomvia*), a member of the auk family, breed in the area during these summer weeks.

Pricket remembered that it was on July 27 that those on board sent the small boat ashore with a fowling party. But getting on the land was not as easy as they expected. The winds were fierce that day. The *Discovery* remained in place only because it was anchored. The poor men on the small boat struggled against the waves, which beat them back repeatedly and eventually drove them toward cliffs far from the breeding grounds they sought. Fortunately for the men, the cliffs were home to a large population of gulls. They managed to kill thirty and returned that night to the ship. The next day the crew steered the vessel closer to the fowling grounds, but again they had no luck. They could not find the breeding spot and eventually had to turn back for fear that the winds would propel the ship into the rocks.

On the twenty-eighth, the men set the small boat on a course for Digges Cape, again in search of some of the area's abundant supply of migratory birds. But as they neared the breeding grounds, they saw seven kayaks approaching them. The local Inuit, upon seeing the English, brought their boats together and began to row straight for the newcomers. The natives made a series of signs to the English, indicating their apparent friendliness. Soon enough, the locals had left one Inuk man with the English on the small boat and taken one of the English in exchange, a strategy they had apparently followed because they wondered about trusting these visitors. Pricket recalled that the Inuit then escorted the Englishman to a nearby cove where the Inuit had pitched their tents close to the birds' abundant nests. They led him inside and waited for the English to return with their own comrade.

When the English arrived with the native at the breeding grounds, they asked him how the Inuit hunted the birds. The man quickly obliged them. He showed them how they made a snare out of a long pole, then slipped the end around a bird's neck and pulled down. It was a quick and efficient method, one no doubt honed through generations. The English were unimpressed by what he had shown them. Rather than rely on indigenous technology, they instead resorted to their own weaponry. They blasted their guns into the flocks. Each shot killed up to eight birds.

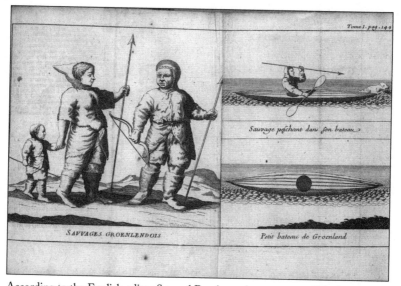

According to the English editor Samuel Purchas, who was responsible for printing Pricket's narrative and other testimony documenting Hudson's voyages, the Inuit who approached the English were "big-boned, broad-faced, flat-nosed, and small-footed, like the Tartars," but were well-dressed with handsome clothes, gloves, and shoes. They were also skilled with their kayaks, as Europeans knew from various visual depictions of the indigenous peoples of the North Atlantic. Image from Jean Bernard, *Recueil de Voyages* (Rouen, 1716); text from Samuel Purchas, *Purchas his Pilgrimage* (London, 1626), 818.

Soon the English paddled to the local village to get their own man back and to drop off their Inuk guide. When the English arrived, the Inuit greeted them with apparent joy; they leaped and danced and beat their chests and offered "divers things" to the visitors. The English traded a knife and two glass buttons for walrus tusks, then retrieved their man and returned to the *Discovery*, "much rejoicing at this chance," as Pricket put it, "as if they had met with the most simple and kind people of the World."

Greene was ecstatic and trusting in the wake of their encounter with the Inuit, convinced that the English had found a friendly group and that there would be no reason to stand guard. Pricket, who wrote after the fact, claimed he knew better. Greene had reckoned "to receive great matters from these people," but as Pricket realized, "he received more then he looked for." He soon became "a good example for all men: that make no conscience of doing evil, and that we take heed of the Savage people, how simple soever they seem to be."

The next day, the twenty-ninth of July, the crew—now under the unquestioned command of Greene—dispatched the small boat to the shore. Though Pricket was, by his own description, infirm, he joined the party with the idea that he could help load things onto and off the boat. So he rowed toward land with Greene, Wilson, John Thomas, Michael Perse, and Adrian Moter. As they approached the shoreline the English noticed that the Inuit, having pulled their boats onto the beach, were "dancing and leaping" in the nearby hills. The party from the *Discovery* tied their boat to a rock and waited. Soon the natives walked down to them, each bearing something to be traded. But Greene would not allow for any bartering because, as he told his fellows, the Inuit "should have nothing, till he had Venison, for that they had so promised him by signs."

Along the shore the English and the Inuit communicated as best as they could with hand signals. Pricket noted that the locals had signaled their many dogs, and then, after pointing toward the mountains and the sun, had begun clapping. In the meantime the English had scattered around the beach. Greene, Wilson, and Thomas remained near the boat while Perse and Moter had clambered into the rocks hoping to pick sorrel. Pricket, who had stayed on the boat, realized that none of his compatriots were armed except for Greene, who held "a piece of a Pike in his hand." The Inuit appeared similarly unarmed, which put the English at ease.

Soon Greene and Wilson got down to business. They pulled out mirrors, bells, and a mouth organ known as a Jew's harp. While the locals gathered around to look, one of them slipped away toward Pricket and showed him a bottle, possibly to distract him. Pricket, on edge, tried to sign to the man that he should head back to the shore. But the Inuk did not understand Pricket, or else chose to ignore him so that he could remain near the boat. At the same time, another Inuk sneaked behind the boat. Then, without any warning, one of these men, or perhaps a third, lunged at Pricket's chest with a knife.

Pricket reflexively threw up his right arm to block the thrust, but the knife caught his arm and then struck him under his right breast ("pappe"). The Inuk swung again, this time catching Pricket in the left arm, and stabbed him again in the right thigh. For some reason, he tried to cut off Pricket's left pinky. But Pricket managed to grab hold of a string attached to the knife, preventing the man from stabbing him again, then blunted the assault by grabbing the man's hands. The Englishman then remembered that he was carrying a dagger. He drew it and slashed the man's body and throat.

Even as these men assaulted Pricket, the other Inuit were attacking the Englishmen on shore. Thomas and Wilson, according to Pricket, "had their bowels cut, and Michael Perse and Henry Greene being mortally wounded, came tumbling into the Boat together." Moter, who had been gathering sorrel, saw the scene from a distance. He immediately rushed to the shore and jumped into the water to swim to the boat, where Perse somehow managed to help drag him in. Perse still had enough strength to grab a hatchet, which he used against an oncoming Inuk, whom Pricket wrote was sent "sprawling into the Sea."

The attack continued. Greene, according to Pricket, cried "*Coragio,* and layeth about him with his Truncheon." The Inuit grabbed their bows and started to shoot arrows at the English. They pierced Greene, who died on the spot, and hit Perse and the others repeatedly, even as the men tried to free the boat to row back to the *Discovery*. Pricket himself took an arrow in the back, which further disabled him. Perse and Moter managed to get the craft on its way toward the ship. The locals, who had run to their kayaks to give chase, decided to let them go.

On the way back to the *Discovery* Perse fainted, but Moter managed to get the shallop close to the ship. The rest of the crew took them in. Greene, already dead, was cast into the water. The other men were all still alive, but not for long. "[T]hey died all there that day," Pricket later wrote, "William Wilson swearing and cursing in most fearful manner; Michael Perse lived two days after, and then died."

When he wrote his account of the assault, Pricket used it to make a larger point. "Thus you have the Tragical end of Henry Greene and his Mates," as he put it, "whom they called Captain, these four being the only lusty men in all the ship." Those responsible for the uprising against a legitimate captain had faced justice for their actions. Pricket, a man who liked to position himself (at least in his narrative) as morally superior to those around him, thus once again drew distinctions between himself and those who had organized the mutiny.

❧

The *Discovery* had departed from St. Katherine's fourteen months before with twenty-two men and two boys on board. After the mutiny and the assault, only nine remained. They amounted to what Pricket aptly called a "poor number." It was now up to these survivors to make their way home.

In the weeks following the deaths of Greene and most of the rest of the mutineers, the *Discovery* reentered the waters of the straits that would eventually take them back into the better mapped territory of the North Atlantic. But their troubles were not yet all behind them. The men still needed to feed themselves, and they often found it difficult to locate a place to anchor where they might be able to paddle over to land to forage for food. Fortunately for them, it was summer, when the annual avian migrations brought countless seabirds to the region. Yet each time they lowered their shallop into the open water to pursue the birds, everyone knew the risks. Losing more men now would be disastrous. With an even smaller crew, it would have been much more difficult to get the *Discovery* across the Atlantic, especially if the men on board were starving. Still, some of the men managed to kill 200 birds "with great labour on the South Cape." Their haul on board, the ship headed eastward.

But once again the winds proved difficult. They had made it, by Pricket's estimate, 6 or 7 leagues (about 18 to 21 miles) from the capes when a fierce easterly wind blew them back there. Seizing the opportunity, the men killed another 100 fowl. Then the winds switched, coming from the west and driving them toward Queens Fore-land, about midway between Hudson Bay and Davis Strait, where they anchored. They retraced their path eastward—past the Iles of Gods Mercies until they were driven toward the islands in the mouth of the straits. But still they had problems, including a fog so thick that they almost steered the *Discovery* against the rocks. The master of the ship at that moment—probably Juet or Bylot, though Pricket did not identify him—finally found a place to anchor amid the rocks so they could wait for better sailing conditions.

The ship's supply of food again drew thin. "[W]e had put ourselves to hard allowance," Pricket remembered, "as half a foul a day with the pottage: for yet we had some meal left, and nothing else." They tried to find new ways to extract nutrients from the birds. Juet realized that they could burn the feathers off the skin, which made for additional food. Pricket claimed that the men tossed nothing into the sea and even ate what in better times they would have thought of as garbage.

By then, of course, the men had a clear idea about the direction back to Europe, even if they would sail east hungry. They steered a course east southeast, then south and then east again. The *Discovery* passed near Desolation, and the crew then set off for Ireland. But once again the weather altered their plans. A fierce headwind blew straight into the ship's path, stalling their progress. Juet suggested that they tack toward Newfoundland, which by then had become a reliable English

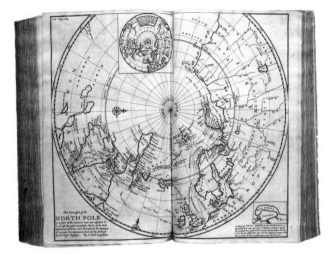

This early eighteenth-century map identifies most of the crucial locales visited (and named) by Hudson, including Hold with Hope, the Iles of Gods Mercies, Queens Fore-land, and Digges Island, as well as James Bay, the place where Hudson wintered. From John Harris, *Navigantium atque itinerantium bibliotheca: or a compleat collection of voyages and travels* (London, 1705). *Huntington Library*

whaling and cod-fishing station. He told them they could find relief "if our Country-men were there," as Pricket remembered it, "and if they were gone before we came, yet should we find great store of bread and fish left ashore by them." Juet was perhaps the only man on the *Discovery* who recognized the benefits of taking this option. The English had been visiting Newfoundland since the early 1580s when Sir Humphrey Gilbert had dreamed about creating a colony there. But to reach the region's lush pastures and the settlement of English sailors meant risking the ship's bottom. It would be difficult to avoid the jagged shoals that had sunk some others who had tried before.

Then the winds shifted again, opening alternative routes. Pricket confronted Juet. Wouldn't it make sense, he claimed he told the new master, to take the ship toward a well-known locale where they knew they could find sustenance rather than taking their chances in Newfoundland? The logic worked, and the *Discovery* headed eastward once again. "Towards Ireland now we stood," Pricket wrote, "with prosperous winds for many days together."

The winds had turned in their favor, but pushing once again into open seas did nothing to solve their food shortage. The men had consumed all of their meal, Pricket remembered, and the remains of the birds had become dry. Juet showed the others how to burn off the feathers to eat the skin "so they became a great dish of meat, and as for the garbage, it was not thrown away." They survived on salt broth for their midday meal and the birds for their daily supper. Eventually, Mathews, the ship's original cook, melted the candles to make grease to fry the last bones of the consumed sea birds. He cooked them until they were crisp, added vinegar, and served them to the survivors. The meal must have seemed unappealing to men who had only recently harvested hundreds of fresh birds, but Pricket again claimed that it made "a good dish of meat."

Juet at one point thought that the *Discovery* was a mere 16 or 17 leagues—perhaps about 50 miles—from Ireland. But without any way to measure longitude, he miscalculated, as the crew soon found out; they were at least ten times farther away, perhaps 200 leagues or so. By now they had been at sea so long that the men had grown debilitated. Most of them sat on the deck because few had the strength to stand. Juet himself never realized quite how far they were from Ireland. He died, apparently from starvation, before the ship managed to dock on Ireland's west coast.

The men "were in despair," Pricket wrote, but soon enough—following the route that Juet had marked—they spotted the harbor at Galway. On September 6 they encountered a fishing boat from the village Foway in Cornwall. That ship, captained by a man named John Waymouth, led the *Discovery* into Bear Haven, a natural channel whose deep, calm waters, easy access to land, and proximity to prolific Northeast Atlantic fishing grounds had long drawn European fishing crews.

The crew of the *Discovery* stayed in Bear Haven for a few days and entered into negotiations with the local Irish. They soon learned that no one would offer them food or drink. The Irish suggested that the crew try to cut a deal with the fishermen who had directed them to the port. But their attempt to do this proved fruitless. The fishermen refused to deal with the *Discovery* men because the survivors of Hudson's expedition had no money. Pricket and the others eventually turned to Waymouth, who lent them enough money to purchase beer, beef, and bread. In exchange, the men on the *Discovery* gave Waymouth an anchor and their best cable.

And yet the *Discovery* was still not quite ready for its final push toward London. They needed more than nutrition. To get safely home they needed at least a skeletal crew that could handle the ship, presumably because the survivors at this point were too weak to finish the task. A Captain Taylor soon intervened and, like Waymouth, provided the survivors with assistance to keep them on their journey. Taylor helped recruit the men needed to lead the *Discovery* to London. When some resisted, he threatened to either impress them or have them hanged, a sign of his apparent prominence. That proved to be sufficient incentive to get the men back into bargaining with Pricket and the others. The unnamed sailors agreed to guide the ship to either Plymouth or Dartmouth, with the pilot earning more than the others. They agreed after Waymouth promised that they would be paid.

In the end, enough men came on board to guide the *Discovery* homeward. They sailed from Bear Haven to Plymouth, anchoring in front of the castle there. Favorable winds next took the ship to the Downs, then to Gravesend. Most of the men got off the ship there. Bylot, the master of the *Discovery* at that point, traveled with Pricket to London, where the two of them went to see Sir Thomas Smythe, the most prominent of the original investors in the venture.

Pricket did not provide the date when he and Bylot finally reached London, but their return occurred about sixteen months after Hudson had led the *Discovery* out of the city. If Pricket believed that his travails had at last come to an end, it would prove a naïve assumption. He no longer had to worry about an iceberg cutting through the hull of a ship, an Inuk thrusting a knife into his arm, surviving on a diet of fried bones, or a mutineer putting him off onto a small craft that had no chance of surviving an ocean crossing. But as he would soon learn, the disappearance at sea of an English mariner—especially one whose journey had received support from powerful and prominent patrons—was not a matter that could be left to mystery. Smythe and his partners would demand to know what had happened on the shores of James Bay. London's mercantile community and its explorers would want to know if they had found the Northwest Passage. Those charged with insuring that all went well on English vessels would investigate the breakdown of relations on board the ship and how a dispute could have escalated to a full-blown mutiny.

Only eight men of the original twenty-three arrived in England: Robert Bylot; the boat's surgeon, Edward Wilson; the new boatswain, Francis Clemens; the cooper Silvanus Bond; Adrian Moter; Bennet Mathews; the boy Nicholas Syms; and of course Pricket.

The *Discovery* itself was back in London. But as it turned out, the ship had tales to tell as well. Soon men would go on board and examine it. They would find bloodstains. They wanted to know what had happened to Hudson's possessions. They asked questions. And they wondered—mostly about whether Abacuk Pricket, the venture's unlikely chronicler, a man named for a biblical prophet, was telling the truth about what he had seen.

# VII.

# *Interrogations*

❦

*Overseas commerce had become* such a big business in London by the sixteenth century that many people involved in it recognized that they needed institutions to regulate what happened to English ships on the open sea. The issue was not new, of course. English fishermen, who had long been working in the Atlantic, had created a basic code of behavior that would govern both masters of ships and those who signed up to work on them. Much of what took place on these ships remained beyond the firm understanding of the landlubbers who never ventured far into the sea.

But the situation began to change in the early sixteenth century. In 1513 a group of men calling themselves the "masters, rulers, and mariners" of the king's navy approached Henry VIII and proposed that he create an institution that could manage trade and traffic along the Thames. They were concerned, their petition claimed, with the growing number of young men rushing to command their own ships to take advantage of new commercial opportunities. These newcomers had no interest in learning the science of navigation, were squeezing the ancient mariners out of the business, and, lacking basic nautical skills, endangered everyone who sailed the river. The petitioners also claimed that lack of supervision of those who traveled the Thames created possibilities for England's enemies—Scots, Flemish, French, and "other Strangers borne not being your natural subjects"—to gain valuable knowledge of the capital. Henry issued letters patent the next year to Trinity House of Deptford, giving it the power to regulate commerce and promote the science of navigation. It was also to maintain an alms house.

On October 24, 1611, the masters of Trinity House took up the challenge of trying to determine what had happened to Henry Hudson near the shores of James Bay. For the next five years, English authorities would repeatedly try to piece together the circumstances surrounding the apparent mutiny. Year after year, observers offered theories of what they believed had happened there. The investors in Hudson's journey exerted their influence, too, though apparently behind the scenes.

Some of those backers also would decide that the route Hudson attempted in search of the Northwest Passage could not be abandoned and hoped that answers about the fate of the shallop might still be discovered. Consequently, they outfitted other expeditions, including two on the *Discovery* itself. Hundreds of Englishmen would eventually sail into the frigid waters around Greenland, Fretum Davis, and Hudson Strait. The most prominent among them, notably Sir Thomas Button and Sir William Baffin, would gain fame for their efforts. Each expedition that set off into the cold sought either the Northwest Passage or to explore unknown territory. Each journey would add yet another chapter to the growing book of knowledge about the North Atlantic, and especially about the formidable waters that framed the northern reaches of the Western Hemisphere. None would discover exactly what happened to Hudson and the others cast off onto the shallop—though many of the incidents and encounters would offer indirect clues about their fate.

❦

This seventeenth-century painting of Deptford depicts the docks of the East India Company as well as the port's crowded waters. *National Maritime Museum, Greenwich*

The town of Deptford, situated just west of Greenwich, was, in the seventeenth century, 4 miles from the border of London. Many in England knew of its ancient church and the depth of the Thames there, which gave the settlement its name (deep ford). One eighteenth-century observer noted that it had not been much more than "a mean fishing-village" before King Henry VIII established a royal dock there, which became the base for the construction of ships for the royal navy (until it moved its operations to the deeper waters at Woolwich in 1512). On April 4, 1581, Henry's daughter Elizabeth, then queen, dined with Sir Francis Drake on his *Golden Hind,* which had docked at Deptford after it returned from its three-year circumnavigation. Twelve years later, the town gained its share of infamy when the playwright Christopher Marlowe was murdered there. In 1607, the East India Company decided to build its ships in Deptford's dockyards. The company's policy signaled the further rise of Deptford under King James I. The town attracted those interested in long-distance commerce—including Hudson's primary backer, Sir Thomas Smythe, who built a great house there.

It is impossible to overstate the importance of the Thames to London and its environs. Starting at its headwaters in Oxfordshire, the river ran through the university town, followed "a marvelous quiet course to London," as the surveyor John Stow put it at the end of the sixteenth century, "and thence breaketh into the French Ocean," by which he meant the English Channel. The depth and breadth of the river made it ideal for transporting travelers and their wares to London, "the principal store house, and staple of all Commodities within this Realm." At least 2,000 small craft conveyed people and goods in and around the city, together employing, in Stow's estimate, 3,000 men. It is no wonder that the first efforts to regulate movement by water within England aimed to protect commerce along the river.

By the beginning of the seventeenth century, the masters of Trinity House had accumulated substantial power. They took it upon themselves to improve navigation along the Thames by administering its beacons, lighthouses, and buoys. They decided which poor former seamen, or the wives and widows of seamen, could get licenses to beg in London. They provided weapons for merchants to protect themselves and their wares while traveling in dangerous waters and gave advice about matters ranging from the construction of ships to providing for defense at sea. They also became the primary arbiters of any disputes that had taken place at sea. It was in that capacity that the masters found themselves conducting an examination of the survivors of the *Discovery*'s ill-fated journey of 1610–1611. It would prove to be only the first of a series of inquiries that ultimately shed light on the fate of Henry Hudson.

❧

Well before their investigation into the *Discovery*, the masters of Trinity House had resolved disputes that had taken place on ships sailing hundreds or even thousands of miles away. In 1610, they settled an argument between a merchant and some men who had sailed to Virginia, and they had determined the wages owed to crewmen—or, more likely, their survivors—who had worked on two East India Company ships but who had either been taken captive or were lost at sea. They also took a hand in trying to improve the lives of those who had suffered abroad, including a gunner who had been taken captive by the Turks but had then been rescued as well as other men, hauled off their ships by pirates, who had returned destitute. They also offered geographical opinions. In 1611, they issued a certificate decreeing that the western edge of the "Levant sea" began at the Straits of Gibraltar, "anciently called the Straits of Marocke, and so continueth itself eastwards thence into all the gulfs, ports, and places, within that Middle Earth sea."

The masters also served as an advisory board on matters relating to the seas. On February 9, 1610—two months before the *Discovery* embarked—they received a proposal forwarded to them by the Privy Council to establish a small settlement in Newfoundland. The petition was from the merchants of Bristol and London, who knew about the area from the fishing trade and believed that the time had come to do more than travel back and forth in the quest for cod. The petitioners argued that Newfoundland should be settled because it was at a latitude of 47° north, which put it on a parallel with Bordeaux (and thus lay south of England). Newfoundland was an ideal place for a settlement, they claimed, since it boasted extensive forests, rivers teeming with fish, and game animals (including deer and fowl) that could be easily harvested. Accounts of its natural resources had circulated in pamphlet form since the 1570s and appeared again in the compilations of Hakluyt. Furthermore, it took only three weeks to get there from either England or Ireland (depending on the winds), which meant that "the island is as near to England as it is to Spain."

To advance their commercial objectives, the petitioners believed that the English government should provide financial support to establish a small settlement in Newfoundland, "especially since they would not be molested because savages have not been seen there." Such a settlement could service the 200 ships and perhaps 6,000 individuals who traveled to New-foundland each year for the fishery. Besides, if the English did not establish themselves there, other Europeans might. The French had tried and failed a generation earlier, but they or others could return. Reports of the fertility of Newfoundland's soil, the possibility that residents could engage in whaling (like Biscayans already did nearby), and the opportunity to produce goods to be used in the maritime industry—pitch, turpentine, masts, train oil—made it an obvious place for an outpost. The petitioners added that it could become a valuable way station for those traveling to Virginia. The masters agreed and advised the Privy Council that it would make sense to establish the outpost as long as it did not interfere with the freedom to fish that English mariners already enjoyed there.

The masters often had to adjudicate matters that transpired far from England's shores. In early October 1610, Sir Thomas Smythe had asked them to determine what wages the East India Company owed to the crew of the *Hector*, which had been captured by the Portuguese, along with its valuable cargo. The men on board did not offer any resistance, claiming that it was their gunner's responsibility to protect the ship. But as it happened, the gunner had already expended his ammunition before the attack, possibly by firing off his guns to salute the ascension of a new captain. The ship had fallen prey to the Portuguese because at the moment they arrived it lacked the means to defend itself. Some of the men died in captivity, others were still being held prisoner, some now worked for the Portuguese, and a few had managed to make it back to England.

What wages, Smuthe asked the masters, did the company owe those who had returned? Should they receive what was due to them up to the point of their capture, or the date when the ship itself came to England, or when the individuals themselves came home? The masters ruled that the company needed to pay the men from the time of their service until the ship's return to

England. If the prisoners ever came home, the company would decide what to do, but any who took up service for the Portuguese were only due their compensation until the moment they defected from the company. With such rulings, the masters solidified their position as the preeminent authorities on any questions about English ships in distant waters. They would be the first to investigate the events on board the *Discovery* the previous June.

❧

On October 24, 1611, the masters took depositions from the survivors of Hudson's expedition. Robert Bylot told them that it had taken five weeks for Hudson and the crew to reach Cape Salisbury, but the passage back through the same area had taken a mere sixteen days. He went on to say that the mutiny had taken place on June 23, when nine men were put into the shallop. Of the rest, two had died during the journey—meaning the gunner and Juet—and four others had died in the assault by the Inuit.

Others testified the same day. Pricket avowed that Greene and William Wilson had hatched the plot while they were fishing. He claimed that Bylot—who must have been the object of some suspicion since the revolt had benefited him directly—did not know of the mutiny beforehand, but he was convinced that Juet had played a role. Silvanus Bond had few details to offer. He thought that Wilson had hatched the plot, and also hinted that Bylot might have known about it. The surgeon, Edward Wilson, told the masters that he, like others, had no knowledge of what was going on until he saw Hudson pinioned near his cabin. The other three deponents—Francis Clemens, Bennet Mathews, and Adrian Moter—testified that "the master was put out of the ship by the consent of all that were in health, in regard that there victuals were much wasted by him." They added that some had opposed Hudson personally, and that the organizers of the insurrection were those who had died before the ship's return to London. The deponents maintained that Hudson gave more food to his favorites than to other men, who had to survive on a meager diet. They believed that the captain's practice was wasteful as well as unfair.

After taking the depositions, the masters recorded their conclusions about the mutiny: Hudson and the others condemned to the shallop had been put there by the healthy men on the ship—including, they implied, the men who had returned to England, none of whom, of course, wanted to be implicated in any criminal action. The masters summarized the mutiny simply, laying the blame squarely on Henry Greene and William Wilson, who had benefited from the guidance of Juet. They noted that Pricket had cleared Bylot of any involvement in the organization of the mutiny. All of those they deposed, they noted, blamed Hudson with hiding food in a small hatch, known as a scuttle, which ran between his cabin and the ship's hold. According to the deponents, he used his special access to the stored food to feed his favorites (including the surgeon) but kept the rest of the crew at their normal allowance, which made the others angry and more prone to violence.

The masters of Trinity House apparently accepted the word of these survivors that those who rebelled had done so to prevent men on the ship from starving. Their summary of the evidence suggests that they believed the mutineers did not plan the fate of each member of the crew in advance but instead made quick decisions in the midst of the furious moments that doomed Hudson and his party.

Rather than deliberate any further over the actions of the men, the masters instead reconstructed what they believed was the route of the *Discovery*. They wanted to know as much as possible about the journey itself and whether the route followed by the ship might have led to the South Sea. Their effort here revealed that these men did more than adjudicate maritime disputes. They also tried to advance knowledge about far-off shipping possibilities. Much of their surviving report recapitulated the notations in Hudson's journal and avoided the kind of commentary that characterized Pricket's narrative (which he might not have written yet). The masters sought knowledge that could only come from firsthand observations, such as the likelihood of ships on future expeditions making it through certain passages, and the locations of possible landfalls along the route. They paid particular attention to the directions of channels. The report noted that "[o]n the western side of Fretum Davis," for example, "they enter an indraught the 26th of June, the sea to set S.W., the land trending from N. to W."

Like everyone who wanted to know more about the North Atlantic, the masters became obsessed with the ice. The authors of the report frequently mentioned the crew's struggle to avoid the most dangerous areas. The masters were particularly interested in using the survivors' recollection of the exact presence of ice to establish where it might block a future ship's passage. Much of this part of the report focused on the course the *Discovery* had followed, both on its way into James Bay and on its homeward voyage. The surviving record suggests that the deponents occasionally provided details of specific incidents, such as the crew spotting a whale playing in open water on August 7 during their return journey, but it was the ice that proved the greatest constant. The movement of what the survivors called "islands of ice" caught the attention of the masters because they were attempting to ascertain the logic, if any, that drove dangerous floes through these channels.

The second part of the report offered what the masters called "Grounds for Conjecture." Here they strove to determine the geography of this little-understood region. Some of the points seemed clear. "The straits lie from Fretum Davis West and East," the masters began, "a mere at least 200 le[agues] long, and 30 or 40 broad at most, sometimes very narrow." They added that the southern coast was "full of bays and pestered with ice, the Northern shorter and free" of such encumbrances.

The masters were seeking to add details to the store of knowledge that the English were accumulating about the American Arctic, which meant it was crucial to report that the western end of the strait opened to the north northwest and "the Great Billow" arrived before Salisbury Island and that the bay extended about 600 miles southward from where it met the strait. The masters reported that the tide came into the bay from north by west, but it set more directly to the west, thereby blocking the current that came from the east, "and always bears the Ice into the West as the Whale played." But although they could extract some information from the crewmen, the masters could not gather enough detail to answer some of their questions, which they left in their report as a series of mysteries. Was the bay fed from the western ocean? Could that ocean be found northwest of Salisbury's headland and the strait? And, most important of all, could that ocean be the South Sea?

On October 26, two days after they had taken depositions from the survivors, the masters offered their final opinion. They understood that their charge was to determine what, exactly, the crew of the *Discovery* had found on their journey to the northwest. They had listened most closely to Robert Bylot, who had led the *Discovery* homeward and was, the masters added, "the only man of that Company that can speak of Navigation." All of the evidence they heard convinced them that the *Discovery* had never traveled far enough to the west to find the Pacific. Such a judgment would have been received with disappointment by those who had sacrificed so much for the journey. But the masters concluded that the large bay was in all likelihood fed from the Atlantic Ocean, not the South Sea. They had agreed on that point because of the reports that the current almost always drove primarily from the east and because "the Islands of ice" drove away from Cape Salisbury toward the west northwest. They accepted prevailing wisdom that the Northwest Passage existed, but they believed that "the Passage is to be found between the West and N. West, and not more Northerly."

The Trinity House records contain no more about the autumn 1611 investigation of the *Discovery*. Instead, the masters' papers reveal their continuing efforts to arbitrate matters of pay-

*Interrogations*

ments and recompense far from England. In the spring of 1611, Sir Thomas Smythe, who was then the treasurer of the Virginia Company, sent a plea asking the masters to make their scheduled payment to support the venture. The company agreed to pay its obligation, but first asserted that it would receive a proper share of any gold, silver, or other precious metals mined there, or any pearls and other treasure acquired in the course of getting there. In the following years, the masters would attend to the kinds of issues that had always fallen under their jurisdiction— making efforts to improve navigation along the Thames and other English rivers; adjudicating financial disputes; trying to resolve whether foreign ships had the right to transport herring; and declaring the loss of the crew and goods from the ill-fated *Sea Flower,* which had sunk in a storm near Lisbon. In 1618, they even received a petition from Peter Frobisher, heir of the famed explorer of the North Atlantic, who wanted to erect a lighthouse at either Ravenspurre or Kelsey-upon-Humber and charge each ship that passed by. No record survives to indicate whether the masters were still interested in the fate of Hudson or the survivors of the *Discovery.* The goals of the nation's merchants, it seems, were more important than establishing the possible guilt of the survivors of the 1610–1611 expedition.

❧

But even if the masters of Trinity House were not going to do a thorough inquiry into the mutiny, the mystery of what had happened on the *Discovery* intensified—thanks in part to surprising new evidence that cast fresh light on the interactions on board the ship. A search of the vessel had turned up a note that the mathematician Wydowse had secreted in his desk. Since Wydowse was among those who had been lowered onto the shallop with Hudson, the document represented the last words of someone who had presumably died soon after the mutiny.

Wydowse's note focused on the tensions on the ship that predated the mutiny itself—thus explaining the actions that had led Hudson to demote Robert Juet. According to Wydowse, on

157

September 10, 1610, Hudson summoned the men together to confront charges leveled by Juet that the commander had abused his authority. Apparently he heard even more than he had expected. Wydowse wrote that Hudson had listened to "many and great abuses, and mutinous matters" muttered by Juet, the kind of insubordination that could threaten a voyage if a captain ignored it. Hudson decided, again according to Wydowse, to punish those he deemed responsible and to "cut off farther occasions of the like mutinies."

Wydowse kept track of those who came forward to repeat Juet's angry claims. The first was Mathews, "our Trumpet," who reported that by the time the English first saw Iceland Juet had warned there would be "man-slaughter, and prove bloody to some." His words implied that discord had beset the ship very early in its route west. One unnamed witness alleged that after the ship had left Iceland Juet had hoped to turn the *Discovery* around and head back to England—an idea that Hudson himself had managed to quell. The carpenter, Staffe, and Arnold Ladley swore on a Bible in front of Hudson that Juet had persuaded them to keep their muskets loaded and a sword near at hand, because it was obvious that they would be attacked before they completed their mission, though Juet did not identify the likely foe.

Accusations continued to fly, and Wydowse recorded them. When the *Discovery* was pinned in the ice, Juet had, according to an unnamed member of the crew, "used words tending to mutiny, discouragement, and slander of the action, which easily took effect in those that were timorous." Had Hudson not intervened then, these dissenters could have "overthrown the Voyage." Even though the *Discovery* was then in a deep bay, one that Hudson wanted to explore, Juet—for reasons that he alone understood—tried to cajole the men "into a fray of extremity, by wintering in cold." He even made fun of Hudson's idea that they would soon be through the passage and able to see Bantam—on the western edge of Java, near Batavia—"by Candlemasse" (February 2).

"For these and other base slanders," Wydowse wrote, Hudson dismissed Juet from his position as mate. He awarded the position to Bylot, whom Wydowse noted had been "honestly respecting the good of the action." Hudson decided he had to take further action to solidify his command of the ship. He promoted William Wilson to boatswain, replacing Francis Clemens, who had, in Wydowse's opinion, also treated Hudson poorly and undermined the mission. Moter became the new boatswain's mate. Hudson ordered that Bylot would receive Juet's wages, and the surplus wages that were to go to the boatswain were to be divided between William Wilson and John King, a quartermaster whose work to that point had advanced Hudson's goals. Hudson also told those who had acted against him that all was not yet lost. If they behaved properly in the future, he would do all he could for them and also be willing to put behind the insults they had made to his authority.

This note eventually fell into the hands of the High Court of Admiralty and would figure in the final inquiry into the mutiny. The masters of Trinity House did not mention whether they had seen it too.

❦

After the masters took their testimony and finished their inquiry, the survivors were not yet free of suspicion. In a series of Latin and Dutch pamphlets in 1612 and 1613, the Dutch geographer Hessel Gerritsz summarized what he believed had happened to Hudson. Gerritsz was not much of a fan of Hudson. He believed that the 1602 expedition of the English explorer George Weymouth had proved that the Northwest Passage, if it existed, could not be found in the territory that Hudson looked for it. Weymouth's notes from that mission came into the possession of Gerritsz's countryman (and fellow geographer) Plancius, who had told Hudson about their findings before he left on his journey in 1609. Hudson had begun that journey heading back toward the Northeast Passage but changed course and headed for the mid-Atlantic coast instead.

Gerritsz thought that the mission had been a waste of time. "Hudson achieved in 1609 nothing memorable, even by this new way," he wrote in 1612. "All he did in the west in 1609 was to exchange his merchandise for furs in New France," he sniffed the next year, dismissing Hudson's dealings in Canada. But even when he dismissed Hudson's efforts, Gerritsz wrote as if he assumed the mutineers were in prison. At least as late as the summer of 1613, when the last of Gerritsz's books appeared, observers on the continent believed that the men had been jailed for their crime.

Yet when Gerritsz's small Latin book appeared in 1612, it contained one crucial new document: a map that delineated the territory where the *Discovery* had sailed during 1610 and 1611. It identified the crucial places mentioned in the narratives, including Hold with Hope, the Iles of Gods Mercies, Queene Anne's Fore-land, Salisbury's Island, and Digges Island. It also labeled the large inland sea with the title "Mare Magnum ab Mo. Hudsons primum inventum"—the large sea first found by Hudson. The cartographer added a crucial detail in the lower left-hand corner of the map, at approximately the location of modern James Bay (which was not yet named). It stated simply "The bay where Hudson did winter." Europeans now had a precise visual understanding of where the expedition had spent its most desperate months.

News about the *Discovery* mutiny had also reached Frankfurt, one of the publishing capitals of Europe at the time. It was there in 1590 that the printer Theodor de Bry had engraved a series of images based on watercolors of Native Americans at Roanoke painted by the English artist John White in 1590. Those images, and many others that came out of de Bry's workshop over the course of the 1590s, made his studio one of the most important centers for the distribution of information about European explorations to the east and west. De Bry's heirs joined the business and kept it going after his death in 1598.

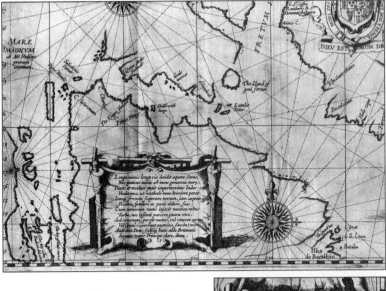

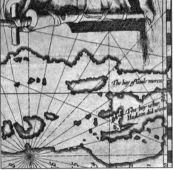

This map *(above)* from Hessel Gerritsz's 1612 pamphlet provided the first solid evidence of Hudson's probable route and the place where the *Discovery* had spent the fateful winter of 1610–1611 *(detail right)*. From *Descriptio ac delineatio Geographica Detectionis Freti* (Amsterdam, 1612). *Huntington Library*

In 1613, Johannes Theodor de Bry published a thin book in Latin that included a series of images of northern journeys toward China and Japan. (The family workshop printed books only in Latin and German after 1590.) He included a brief note about Hudson. Like Gerritsz, de Bry did not have much respect for the English mariner. He flatly declared that Hudson had "done nothing worthy of memory" when he worked for the Dutch in 1609, suggesting that the English should not have decided to employ him the following year. De Bry repeated the story then being disseminated about Hudson's meeting with the solitary American man during the 1610–1611 expedition, adding the spurious detail that the man possessed what de Bry called a "dagger" that apparently came from Mexico or Japan, "for which reason Hudson suspected that he was not far off from Mexican lands." He also claimed the English sailors had mistreated this man, which had caused him to stay away. With no new trading partners, the explorers soon strained their supplies and had to find a way to survive. Eventually, some of the men, angry that the venture had lasted longer than they had agreed to serve, turned on Hudson. "They returned home in the month of September," de Bry noted, "where they were shut into prison for their crime." De Bry had this information in hand before the spring of 1612, when he claimed that the Prince of Wales (along with English merchants) had ordered a new expedition into the region to find Hudson and to continue the exploration of the area. "Happily," he concluded, these explorers would bring back the story of Hudson's fate, "and it is expected hour by hour."

News of the rebellion on the decks of the *Discovery* reached England's reading public in 1613. That year, in his first compilation of travel accounts, Samuel Purchas wrote that Hudson had made great discoveries but had been lost "by means of his mutinous and (as is supposed) murderous companions." The next year he provided more details, based on what he had learned from Hakluyt (who supplied Purchas with many of the accounts he had read about long-distance travels) and Sir Dudley Digges. Purchas recognized that Hudson's 1607 efforts had brought him closer to the North Pole than any other European, and he told the story of how, on Hudson's expedition the next year looking for the Northeast Passage, some of his men had spotted a mermaid—the kind of detail that he knew would keep a reader's attention. Purchas dismissed the significance of the 1609 voyage that charted the mid-Atlantic region of America and what would later be called the Hudson River, and then turned his attention to Hudson's "last and fatal voyage."

Purchas had already learned much about the expedition. He knew about Hudson's sighting of the smoldering Mount Hecla on Iceland, the thermal spring near Lousie Bay, the journey around Desolation, and the naming of sites such as the Iles of Gods Mercies and King James Cape. Purchas added that Hudson named new places for his sponsors, including Cape Wolstenholme and Digges Island. And, more significant, he captured what must have been the highlight of the journey for Hudson: his entry into "a spacious Sea, wherein he sailed above 100 leagues South, confidently proud that he had won the passage."

Purchas also detailed the fateful winter of 1610–1611. Hudson had managed to steer the *Discovery* into a protected cape in early November, where, as it turned out, the men on board found ample supplies of birds and fish. They also found a pleasant-smelling tree with green and yellow leaves that they boiled to produce an oil that worked effectively as a salve and, when drunk, seemed to cure the "diseases which the coldness of the climate bred in them." He mentioned the visit of the Cree man who had come and traded with the English. But any hope of success faded after the ice melted and Greene and William Wilson led the mutiny that put the master and eight others on the shallop. Purchas singled out Staffe for praise because he alone among the rest of the crew volunteered to remain with Hudson.

Purchas reveled in the details of the assault on the chief mutineers. Though he presumably would have ordinarily eschewed praising any murder of English subjects, this situation was different. When the locals launched their "cunning ambush" on Greene, they quickly shot this "mutinous Ringleader into the heart where first those monsters of treachery and bloody cruelty . . . had been conceived." Purchas described the deaths of the other rebels with similar contempt. William Wilson, Greene's "brother in evil, had the like bloody inheritance, dying swearing, and cussing." "Every where," Purchas con-cluded, "can divine justice find executioners."

Purchas also related the Inuit attack on Pricket (which the chronicler of the voyage fended off with "a small Scottish dag-ger") and the return of the mostly starved men to England. De-spite the failure to find the Northwest Passage and the loss of Hudson, Purchas added that patrons of the venture had backed another expedition, this time led by Sir Thomas Button. Al-though Button did not find the Northwest Passage, high hopes remained in England. In March 1614, the month Purchas fin-ished his work, sponsors were fitting out "the good and lucky Ship called the *Discovery*" and one other vessel for an expedi-tion. Hardy English sailors would soon set off to enhance the glory of the realm, another example of what Purchas called the "undaunted spirits amongst us" who—like others who had pre-ceded them—would make "Resolute, gallant, glorious attempts" in their effort "to tame Nature, where she is most unbridled, in those Northeasterly, Northwesterly, and Northerly borders."

Purchas never mentioned the exact whereabouts of the sur-vivors of the *Discovery*'s previous expedition—an odd omission given that at least two of them had already been involved in other journeys towards the northwest.

# Dead Ends

*If, as Hessel Gerritsz had claimed*, the survivors of Hudson's expedition had been jailed, they did not remain confined for long. By 1612, Pricket and Bylot found themselves in a familiar position: back on board the *Discovery*, now under the command of Thomas Button, on the venture to which Purchas had referred, aimed again for Hudson Bay. Remarkably, Pricket again became a chronicler of the voyage, relaying his findings to Luke Foxe, himself a sea captain, who would publish the account in 1635 after he explored Hudson Bay. Other mariners also left reports about expeditions into the waters sailed by Hudson. Among them was William Baffin, who became the most famous English explorer of the first half of the 1610s and, as it turns out, the man who might be able to write the definitive word about what had happened to Henry Hudson.

From 1612 to 1616, the English sent many ships into the North Atlantic, including Hudson Bay. Their purpose was twofold. Some of those on board wanted to find out what had happened to Hudson. Others, embracing Hudson's quest, went looking for the Northwest Passage. Pricket and Bylot, for their part, might have had a third reason to brave those ice-choked waters again. By joining parties to find any traces of their former commander, they might effectively throw off any suspicion that they had anything to do with the mutiny. They knew better than anyone that this could be a risky strategy, so they were either very committed to finding Hudson or eager to find the passage to the South Sea. Or, perhaps, they feared that the suspicions about their possible involvement in the rebellion of 1611 would not subside unless they did all they could to find Hudson.

❧

On July 26, 1612, King James granted a charter to the Company of the Merchants Discoverers of the North-West Passage. But even before this company's ship left the docks, other expeditions had sailed off in that direction. According to Pricket, two vessels—the flagship *Resolution* (under the command of Sir Thomas Button) and the *Discovery* (led by John Ingram)—left London in May 1612. They entered Hudson Strait and found themselves surrounded by ice floes. But they persisted, as Hudson had earlier, and made their way to Digges Island, where they remained for eight days. While they waited, Button ordered the crew to assemble a pinnace they had brought with them in pieces. They set off again, landed at a place the English named Carys Swansnest (probably the southern parts of modern Southampton Island), and then sailed southwest until they found land again at 60°40′N. They named this spot Hopes-Check. There the English endured a brutal storm, which prompted Button to head south on August 13 to find a harbor where the men could repair the ships. By then it was too late to either go much farther or return home that year.

Winter arrived, bringing with it the all-encircling ice and the kinds of storms that Pricket, Bylot, and other survivors of Arctic exploration knew too well. The men settled themselves along a small creek on the north side of a river at 57°10′N, which they named Port Nelson after one of the ship's masters who had died that winter. They protected their small vessels with piles of earth and firs, hoping to keep them intact in the face of the inevitable assault of rain, snow, ice, and flooding. They kept three fires burning all winter long as they waited for the ice to release its grip, and the men managed to take over 21,000 birds over the next several months. But despite their efforts, the season proved fatal: Button "lost many men," according to Foxe's account.

Foxe offered no further testimony from Pricket, but the captain had managed to obtain reports from others on the venture, notably from a captain named William Hawbridge (or Hawkeridge) and Button himself. Remarkably, Hawbridge's testimony echoed one part of Pricket's account of the return of the *Discovery* in 1611. He reported that Button's ships had anchored between Cape Wolstenholme and Digges Island. Some of his men went on shore to hunt guillemot (called "willicks" in the report) but were set upon by seventy to eighty Inuit men. One of Button's men managed to fire off his musket, killing one of the attackers and injuring others. The Inuit retreated; the English thought they had been shocked by the noise of the musket. Soon after, however, when Button sent his pinnace back to the land to collect fresh water, the Inuit ambushed the boat, killing five men. Only one managed to escape. Hawbridge added a chilling detail about the location of the attack: "[H]ere it was where the villains *Greene* and *Juet* were slain, after they had exposed Master *Hudson*."

From there, as Pricket had reported, the ships made their way to Carys Swansnest, then to Hopes-Check, before they settled in for the winter at Port Nelson. They remained until the ice broke way in late April, "after which they killed daily with their Net abundance of Fish, as big as Mackerels." Button, for his part, was keen to get accurate measurements of distance and to gather knowledge about the places his men explored. He was especially eager to travel far enough to encounter, as he put it, "the Flood coming from the Westward," because that would signal they had found the opening to the Northwest Passage and water flowing from the Pacific.

Foxe never saw Button's actual journal, if it survived, so he had to reconstruct it from his interviews. Fortunately, he was able to get his hands on the journal of Sir Thomas Roe, who was also present on the journey and whose notes picked up the story of the exploration at the point when the travelers reached Hopes-Check after they had escaped the ice.

At one point in August—Roe did not provide the exact date—the English saw five polar bears. The men then decided they should explore the land nearby, especially because they needed fresh water. So Roe (or perhaps Button himself, though the journal is not clear) sent a well-armed man onto the shore. He found water quickly, but discovered more than that. Nearby he found two abandoned dwellings—"old houses broken," as Roe put it, "and fallen down to the ground, wherein the skulls and bones of dead men." The man who had been sent out, apparently joined by others from the ship, began to dig around to see what else they could find. Before long they came upon what Roe called "Images and toys," which the men had extracted from underneath the old houses "with some dozen of small Morse [walrus] teeth."

The discoverer of these dwellings believed that the abandoned shacks were all that was left of the improvised lodging of a small group of Inuit who landed there after the wreck of their canoe (which the English found nearby). They had tried to build a secure shelter for themselves, "but the extremity being so strong for them," they could not survive the winter. They might have even burnt their own boat for warmth. The man who had found the place guessed that it was the brutal cold that had killed them. Only the extremes of an Arctic winter would prompt anyone to leave such valuables behind, he thought, especially the carvings intended to propitiate local gods. The tusks were valuable, too: The English knew that the locals spent long hours hunting walrus—not only for their tusks but also for the oil that could be extracted from their blubber.

Neither Roe nor Foxe explained why the discovery of this site, of all that they had seen, merited such extensive attention in their narrative. But it would have been difficult for anyone at the time to have heard this news without thinking of Hudson and the others cast out on the shallop. Their fate, not yet known to the English, would very likely have been identical to that of these unknown Inuit, who had perished of winter exposure even though they knew the region much better than any English explorer possibly could.

Yet for all that the two captains and their crew witnessed, none of them ever came close to finding out what had happened to Hudson. Pricket believed that, contrary to the claims made by Roe, the ships had not crossed through Hudson Strait. In fact, he later claimed the ships returned to England in only sixteen days—a span of time suggesting that they had not gone nearly as far as the earlier journey of the *Discovery*.

Even if the voyage of 1612–1613 did not find the Northwest Passage—or resolve the question of what had happened to Hudson—the investors who had supported Hudson and Button remained convinced about the promise and potential profit of such a route to the South Sea. Finding the Northwest Passage remained among the highest priorities for the community of English merchants, who avidly consumed any and all details about explorations into and through the North Atlantic. Some of those merchants no doubt sponsored William Gibbon's voyage in the *Discovery* into the same territory in 1614. But as Foxe wrote, there was little purpose in describing Gibbon's expedition in much depth, because those who led it failed to bring back anything new. The captain and his crew managed to get the ship as far as the mouth of Hudson Strait, which could have led them into Hudson Bay, but the ice drove them into a place they called Gibbons Hole. They stayed there for twenty weeks, unable to get through the ice. Rather than push their luck, they returned before winter could trap them. They came back to England without greater hope for a Northwest Passage, and without news of the long-lost Henry Hudson.

❧

The *Discovery* was not the only English ship bound for the Northwest Passage in 1612. On April 10, the 140-ton *Patience*, with forty men and boys on board, and the 60-ton *Heart's Edge*, carrying twenty more, both embarked for America. This two-vessel mission had a familiar sponsor: the Merchants Adventurers of London, which included Thomas Smythe, Walter Cope, and Dudley Digges among its leaders and ardent advocates. Only a few months earlier John Chamberlain had observed that Digges was obsessed by the possibility of finding the Northwest Passage.

On the twenty-sixth, the two ships passed the Orkney Islands. They then tacked south of Iceland and headed toward Friesland, where, as chronicler John Gatonbe noted in his journal, they hoped at the end of the first week in May to pick up the current that would take them all the way into the Northwest Passage. They knew that all the others who had sought it had failed, but that was not enough to halt their plans.

By May 14 they found themselves as far as Cape Farewell on the southern coast of Greenland, but they could not land because there was too much ice. Two days later, the men lowered a shallop into the water and pursued a pack of twenty seals lying on the ice; they managed to catch one, but the others dove into the water and escaped. Their measurements that day suggested that they were 115 leagues, or less than 350 miles, from the coast of North America.

By May 18, the ships had headed northwest and arrived near Desolation. Like other travelers who had been in the region, they encountered foul weather, including a snow squall. The next day, Gatonbe wrote in his journal, they found a current that led from Desolation toward America, and specifically toward the area the English now called Hudson Straits—"being so called by his men," as Gatonbe put it, "they leaving him behind in that country, which was his death in the year 1611." They continued northwestward, following the coast of Greenland to a place they called Cape Comfort, where some of the men used the shallop to kill four seals. They also managed to bring two live seals on board, "we having good sport betwixt them and our mastiff-dogs." Such cruelty was common among European sailors in the sixteenth and seventeenth centuries, some of whom laughed after slashing marine creatures and watching them die slowly.

Over the next several days, the ships edged up the coast, seeking a safe harbor where they could land. But even in late May, these waters were choked with ice, which frequently impeded their progress. On May 22, Gatonbe wrote that the English "turn'd amongst the ice, meeting with many islands of ice which were very high like great mountains." Four days later, two Inuit paddled over to the ships in their kayaks, but no record survives revealing why they came or what the English thought about the visit. The next day the English anchored in a place they called the Harbor of Hope. It had been five weeks and two days since they had departed.

The sailors spent the next two months—from late May until early August—along or near the western coast of Greenland. They explored its rivers and hunted for bears, foxes, wolves, and deer, though, more often than not, they failed to catch anything. They had frequent meetings with Inuit, who visited repeatedly to trade peaceably with them. The English tried to learn how to deal with the locals. When one group arrived, Gatonbe described the scene of the Inuit "rowing to and fro to our ships, holding up their hands to the sun, and clapping them on their breasts, and crying *Elyot,* which is as much to say in *English, Are we friends?* thus saluting us in this manner every time they came to us, and we offering the same courtesy to them." It was quite a contrast from the kind of deadly ambush that Greene, Pricket, and the other men of the *Discovery* had experienced earlier. The English recognized the benefits of trading with the Inuit, who were much better at harvesting meals from the seas and land; they also often brought what the English routinely called "unicorn horn," by which they meant a narwhal tusk. The Inuit wanted iron, which the English routinely provided to them, often in the form of nails.

Yet while the natives and the new arrivals often got along, there were also incidents of brutal violence rivaling anything Hudson's men had encountered (or engendered). A group of Inuit on one occasion stole an unguarded musket, which prompted the English to hunt them down to get it back—an effort that led to the death of one Inuk (possibly, though not definitely, the thief). Upon hearing of the death of one of their own, the Inuit sent an elderly man, presumed by the English to be a leader, to find out why the English had committed such an outrage. Hoping to make amends, the English gave him a coat made of yellow cotton with red ornamentation. The man was not pleased; he put on the coat but then dove into the water and swam for shore. Gatonbe and his mates saw other Inuit then ceremoniously cut the coat from the man's back, "so little did they regard it."

These English were at that moment among the many European explorers who realized that when they ventured across the Atlantic it was often impossible to determine when relations with locals might go well and when they might sour. Over the course of that summer, the Inuit and the English continued to trade with each other, and the natives provided the newcomers with much of what they consumed. The Englishmen were impressed at the ability of the Inuit to capture a seal at sea, and these natives hauled in far more fish than the English. They brought the English "salmon-trout, nuskfish [perhaps a muskellunge, also known as a *muskie*], codfish, and butfish," Gatonbe wrote, "a little quantity service for our victuals." Eventually, the English salted some of the fish, no doubt realizing that they would need sustenance for their return home. The newcomers had hoped to find whales in the area, believing that if they killed one or two they could turn a profit on their venture, but they never succeeded.

During the course of their stay, the English had divided themselves into several groups. Some stayed with the two ships; others had boarded shallops and pinnaces, put together during the voyage by the carpenters who traveled with the journey, to explore the rocky and ice-choked coastline. Some journeyed up local rivers. Everywhere, they were outnumbered by the Inuit. They often believed that they were among friends, but sometimes they erred in such judgments. During a trading session on July 23, one of the Inuit launched his spear into the chest of James Hall, the leader of the expedition, killing him for no apparent reason—at least no reason the English could fathom. There were twenty of the English there at the time, but they faced more than 150 Inuit, and, since they did not have their muskets ready, they feared they would all be killed. But the Inuit allowed them to leave, and so the English sailed mournfully toward their companions, bringing news of the tragedy. Hall was the second man on the expedition to die; the crew had buried the first, James Pulley, after he was killed by Inuit spears on June 6.

The death of a commander, as all of the English knew, threatened the future of any expedition. But in this case the explorers were lucky. Andrew Barker, master of the second ship, was, according to Gatonbe, "better, wiser, more ancient, and more worthy of the place." Before the voyage, he had played a leading role in the shipping industry in Hull and had been a master and warden of Trinity House. He would be the ideal spokesman for the men when they returned, as they now planned, to London before winter came. By the end of July they were ready to go. As they sailed down the river and into the sea in the early days of August, none of the Inuit approached them. Gatonbe believed they kept their distance because they feared the English would attack them to avenge Hall's death.

During their return, they passed the place of Pulley's death and set their route homeward. Gatonbe noted that they entered a place of temperate air, "and hot weather, the like we had not felt the time we were in *Greenland.*" They charted a path that they thought would bring them in sight of Friesland, but they never saw it. In early September they ran into a severe storm and the ships lost sight of each other. The men realized they could do nothing about it and hoped they could "get to our country so soon as we could." By August 12, they had entered St. Andrew's Bay in Scotland, and a week later they sailed up the Thames to the docks at St. Katherine's, where Hudson had launched the *Discovery* two years earlier. The men, as Gatonbe wrote, gave their thanks to God "for our safe arrival in our own country, who had deliver'd us from the cruelty of the savages, the dangers of the blind rocks in this unknown country, and the noisome cold weather in this waste wilderness, where there are huge mountains without wood, valleys without corn or grass, and the sea with small store of fish." The place was not empty, of course. As Gatonbe put it, "snow and ice there are good store in the sea and in the land."

Neither Gatonbe nor anyone else on that 1612 voyage got much farther than the west coast of Greenland. But among the members of the expedition was William Baffin, who was on the first of a series of what would become annual journeys into the region. Those expeditions would prove crucial to the English, who still wondered what had happened on Hudson's expedition, and specifically whether the survivors who had come back to London could have been implicated in the mutiny.

❧

The surviving part of Baffin's record of the journey of 1612 begins with an entry on July 12, deep into the voyage and during the period when the English had already established themselves in the Harbor of Hope. Baffin filled his journal with the kind of observations that had become ubiquitous in such accounts. He took note of the movement of the ships, and, of course, the weather. He kept his eye on a compass. He joined a hunting party that went in search of deer and found instead an enormous footprint, which Baffin believed belonged to a giant elk. The track was larger than that of an ox.

Baffin was struck by the murder of Hall, an act that demanded an explanation. Why would the Inuit kill this man when it seemed they had more to gain from trading with him? Baffin believed that these Inuit tended to treat others well, though they did avenge any assault against them. He thought that they had singled out Hall because he had been on an earlier voyage to the area with a Danish expedition, and during their time there they had captured five of the Inuit and killed many more. The man who killed Hall, Baffin had heard, "was either brother, or some near kinsman to some of them that were carried away." That would explain the deliberate nature of the attack, which happened—at least in the English version—without any obvious provocation.

In the days that followed Hall's death, the English continued to explore the area. One band of scouts had found a mine begun by the Danes, and the English hauled some of the rock back to their ship. Baffin believed it unlikely that there was anything of value there because the expedition's assayer reported that the shiny rocks had no precious minerals in them. Baffin thus avoided repeating Frobisher's error of the mid-1570s, and the humiliation that had attended it. In late July, as the English prepared to turn for home, they found a large, abandoned Inuit boat, which measured 32 feet long and 5 feet across. It was made primarily of wood, and covered in deer skins held in place by whalebone ribs. The English also came upon abandoned winter village sites, but no Inuit. Baffin reported that Barker and the voyage's supercargo had concluded that the locals, who had stopped trading with the English after the death of Hall, were unlikely to return. Without their continued trade to add extra value to the voyage, the leaders recognized that the time had come to sail to London. Much of the rest of Baffin's journal contains observations about their route.

Baffin, unlike many chroniclers of such voyages (including Gatonbe), believed it crucial to describe Greenland's environment, its natives, and also the likelihood of a passage to the South Sea and a route to China and Tartary, the term used by Europeans to refer to central Asia, from that vicinity. His observations about Greenland itself were not surprising. He reported that it was a rugged place where snow covered the northern face of the mountains all year long. The one valuable plant they found in abundance was angelica, which they noticed the Inuit consuming. Given the widespread use of angelica in England at the time to ward off poison and plague, and the fact that some believed it eased digestion, Baffin knew that news of its existence in western Greenland would be welcome. Despite the fact that the landscape was not very appealing to the English, Baffin recognized that deer and foxes roamed there, along with white, long-haired hares, and the Inuit kept dogs that resembled wolves.

The Inuit, for their part, impressed Baffin. He praised their ability to craft kayaks that never leaked and that were so fast "that it is almost incredible: for no ship in the World is able to keep way with them, although she have never so good a gale of wind." Every Inuit man and woman possessed a kayak, and they were so light that a man could carry several at a time. The locals had mastered the art of fishing and sealing from their kayaks, and proved equally adept at hunting walrus. They fished mostly during the summer, but they often dried their gutted fish and seals on the rocks for the upcoming winter. They also had the longer kinds of boats that Baffin had reported seeing earlier, which he believed they used whenever they relocated to follow fish migrations. In the summer, they used seal skins to make tents, and in the winter they created stronger shelters by burrowing partly in the ground. They ate their food raw, even though they made fires for heat. His observation about the consumption of raw flesh mirrored reports from Frobisher's voyages, and was an indication to English readers that the Inuit remained savages.

Baffin recognized that the Inuit had developed religious and mortuary customs that were quite elaborate. They worshipped the sun and expected that their visitors would do the same, or at least acknowledge its authority. When the locals shouted *"Ilyot,"* they expected the English to be familiar with the ritual. They made this form of greeting "very often," Baffin wrote about the ritual that Gatonbe had also witnessed, "and will not come near you, until you do the like; and then they will come without any fear at all." When an Inuk man died, the survivors would carry his body, still fully dressed, to the top of a hill and fashion an above-ground tomb made of local stones. The structures protected the corpse from foxes and other carnivores. The air was typically so cold that corpses never smelled. They also erected a second tomb nearby and placed a man's spear, bow and arrow, and provisions within it—the kind of grave goods that often accompanied Americans on their journey to the next world.

The English on the 1612 expedition wondered whether the Inuit might be cannibals. All Europeans had lived in fear of man-eaters; in one volume of his *America* series, Theodor de Bry had included six different scenes of cannibalism among the thirty or so pictures he provided to illustrate accounts of Brazil. Though some enlightened figures, such as the French essayist Michel de Montaigne, tried to view cannibals as no worse than many brutal Europeans, most travelers feared the idea of confronting them. But Baffin did not believe that the Inuit of Greenland were cannibals. After all, they had ample opportunity to kill some of the unprotected members of the expedition who remained behind on the ships when most of the men went exploring on land. But rather than kill them, the Inuit instead wanted to trade with them. Even so, it made better sense to go among them bearing weapons, Baffin concluded.

Baffin finished his 1612 journal without speculating about the possible existence of the Northwest Passage. Perhaps he made those observations, but if so, they were lost before the journal fell into the hands of Richard Hakluyt, who transferred it to Purchas. As it turned out, Baffin would soon have other opportunities to discover whether Hudson had been on a noble quest or a fool's errand.

✒

During the early 1610s the English mounted multiple expeditions into the North Atlantic. On April 11, 1611, a group of four English ships, with the patronage again of Sir Thomas Smythe, embarked from London headed for destinations including Russia, Novaya Zemlya, Greenland, and the North Pole. The English were not alone. In 1612, English sailors encountered Dutch explorers and Basque whalers. Baffin returned to the sea as well. In 1613 he was on an expedition bound for Spitzbergen and encountered ships from New Rochelle, Bordeaux, Dunkirk, and Biscay. All the Europeans had the same idea: They had sailed northward to hunt whales, seals, and walrus. The English, according to Baffin, were less successful in their acquisitions than the others, though he offered no sustained commentary or regret. Though most explorers brought home written accounts only, Baffin came home with Robert Fotherby's pen-and-ink illustrations, which soon circulated in two printed versions and showed Europeans how to hunt whale and walrus.

Baffin, proving himself as indomitable an explorer as Hudson, returned to Greenland again in 1614, this time in a flotilla of eleven English ships. The men on this expedition took ceremonial possession of territory by raising the standard of King James and removing, as Fotherby put it, "a piece of Earth, as a sign of lawful possession" on behalf of the "Company of Merchants, called the Merchants of New Trades and Discourse." Fotherby returned the next year in an expedition again sponsored by Smythe (but without Baffin). To prepare for the journey, he read the manuscript of Hudson's own account of finding Hold with Hope. But Hudson's measurements must have been wrong,

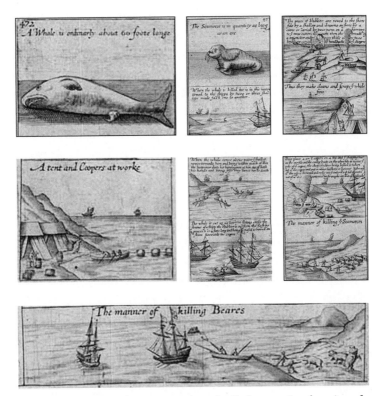

By the early seventeenth century, as these details from a printed version of a pen-and-ink original reveals, Europeans understood how to hunt whales, bears, and walrus. From Edward Pellham, *God's Power and Providence: shewed, in the miraculous preservation and deliverance of eight Englishmen, left by mischance in Green-land anno 1630, nine moneths and twelve dayes* (London, 1631). *Huntington Library*

Fotherby concluded. "I should have seen this Land, if credit might be given to *Hudsons* Journal," he wrote, "but I saw not any." He named Sir Thomas Smiths Island and Mount Hakluyt in the northern reaches of modern Baffin Bay and turned for home.

On April 16, 1615, Robert Bylot, the survivor of Hudson's final voyage who by now was a veteran of three expeditions into the North Atlantic, guided the *Discovery* from its berth at St. Katherine's toward its next attempt to sail through the Northwest Passage. Baffin was on board as Bylot's mate (and the voyage's chronicler), along with fourteen other men and two boys. They spotted the coast of Greenland on May 6, soon ran into a storm, and found themselves coping with massive icebergs. Baffin estimated that the giant chunks of ice rose more than 200 feet above the ocean's surface. Ice bedeviled them for days as Bylot and Baffin debated the best course for the *Discovery*. The master determined that it made more sense to head for Fretum Davis than to Hudson Strait, though the debate was in many ways premature, since at the time they could not find a way through to open water. Over the next eight weeks, the crew explored the area, traded with and observed local Inuit, and named a small archipelago the "Savage Iles."

Baffin spent much of his time tracking the progress of the expedition and performing calculations to improve Europeans' understanding of geography. He hoped that his estimates and others' observations about Japan, Nova Albion, the Straits of Magellan, and other places might produce "a truer Geography than we have." Even more commonly in his writings he was concerned, like every other Arctic navigator, with the ice, which tortured this expedition just as it had the others, even in midsummer. There seemed to be no escape at times. Traveling westward in early July, the crew named one place Mill Island "by reason of grinding the Ice," and several days later they needed to reorient their direction because ice again blocked their way. Eventually they docked at a place they labeled Cape Comfort for the relative ease of entrance into its harbor. Yet even then there was no escape, and thick ice soon returned to impede them. They were then at what turned out to be the farthest spot north—and the farthest from London—on their journey, at a latitude of 65°26′ north and, by Baffin's calculations, 86°10′ west of London. But, as always, the ice proved too menacing, so they opted to sail homeward. Their search for the

Northwest Passage, like those of every mariner before them, had come to an end in failure.

Baffin still believed that a passage existed, but he thought it was to be found via Davis Straight, not the route pioneered by Hudson. If the English could sail around the coast of Greenland into Fretum Davis to 80°N, the land should disappear. A crew could then sail south and west to the 60th parallel. From there, he conjectured, it would be a relatively easy matter to reach "the land of Yedzo," an English variant of Edo (modern Tokyo), the seat of power of the Tokugawa. If the sailors made it that far, they had been told to bring home one of the Japanese—presumably as final proof that the Northwest Passage existed.

Despite yet another failure in 1615, English merchants and adventurers were not ready to give up the quest for a quick passage to the East Indies. In late March 1616, seventeen men and boys once again boarded the *Discovery* for a trip in search of the Northwest Passage. Once again, Wolstenholme, Smythe, and Digges were among the sponsors. And once again Robert Bylot led the journey, with Baffin as the pilot. They tried a new route, established trade with local Inuit, and named new locales for their patrons.

But by mid-July they realized that this journey would be no different from the earlier ones. Baffin and the others were now deeper into Arctic waters than they had ever been before, and the sailing grew more difficult. In Sir James Lancaster's Sound, according to Baffin's report, "our hope of passage began to be less every day then other." The shift was due to the reappearance of their nemesis, the ice. They spent almost two weeks trying to get free of it so they could return on their journey to the west. But by July 27, when they hoped to anchor so they could test the tides, the ice had led them to 65°45′N and the realization that there was no passage to be found here.

Once again, an English expedition—one better equipped than Hudson's had been, and with greater store of knowledge to go on—had failed to find the Northwest Passage. Seeing that they had "made an end of our discovery," Bylot ordered the ship toward Greenland, where he hoped the men could regain their strength after the arduous push westward and where the ship could also restock its supplies. One man had died and several were so weak they could not work. They anchored at a place they called Caukin Sound, where an exploratory party found scurvy grass, which the men boiled in beer, as well as sorrel and orpine. Within eight or nine days the entire crew was healthy again, and remained so until their return to England. They docked in Dover on the morning of August 3, bringing to an end yet another abortive search for the Northwest Passage.

❧

By the time that 1616 voyage ended, Baffin had become one of England's greatest authorities on the North Atlantic. In an undated letter to John Wolstenholme, one of his sponsors, Baffin described the advantages to be had for the English in the region. The area was so full of whales that they would be easy to catch for any properly prepared ship, especially since these behemoths were so unfamiliar with humans that they rarely tried to escape them. The English could harvest walrus tusks and the horns from what Baffin called the "Sea Unicorn" (the narwhal). Of course, all would need to bear in mind that the ice remained a perpetual threat. Ice would block some venues as late as mid-July, which would allow perhaps only six weeks of relatively safe sailing before the return of winter.

But in spite of what Baffin, Hudson, and other explorers had learned, no expedition would find the Northwest Passage—of that Baffin was sure. "[T]here is no passage in the North of Davis Straights," he informed Wolstenholme, "we having coasted all or near the Circumference thereof, and find it to be no other than a great Bay." Try as the Europeans might, there was simply no open route to the Pacific. Hudson's expedition had led to a dead end, and no other explorer had figured out the trick despite the efforts of "the best sort of men" who had been "Writing and publishing to the World," a reference to Hakluyt and others like him who were convinced that the passage must exist. Davis had erred in thinking that he had perhaps found the opening near Hope Sanderson around 72°12′N, because the tides "keep no certain course" there, nor were they large enough to suggest an opening to a large sea. Again, the movement of the ice was significant. Baffin believed that the English now had discovered the source of the icebergs, which calved off from northern ice shelves and sailed southward into Hudson Strait and toward Newfoundland.

In making that observation, Baffin had brought to a close the inquiry that had opened at Trinity House in 1611 when the *Discovery* had returned with its skeletal crew. The masters of that venerable institution had tried to figure out if Hudson had found the longed-for passage. The journeys that followed continued the same quest, usually with the same set of merchant sponsors. Baffin, traveling with Bylot and other veterans of Arctic explorations, had seen enough. He had made five trips to the region, studied the reports of others, and battled enough ice to know for certain that the Northwest Passage, if it existed at all (which he doubted), could not be found.

Baffin never found any sign of Hudson, whose fate now seemed beyond doubt. With the captain dead and the quest for a northern route to the East Indies thwarted, all that remained to complete Hudson's story was to ascertain what exactly had happened on the decks of the *Discovery* five years earlier, when the ice released its winter grip near the eastern shore of James Bay. It was a matter that would need to be settled in a London courthouse.

# IX.

# The Trial

LONDON, 1617 TO 1618

*Vessels docking on the Thames* after a journey from the East Indies smelled of cinnamon, cloves, tobacco, nutmeg, and peppers, a vivid contrast to the stench that often rose from the river or from London itself, where butchers dragging offal through the streets were only the most notorious individuals fouling the air. By the middle of the 1610s, ships returning from Virginia carried tobacco, a plant popular for its alleged medicinal benefits and the pleasures it delivered to smokers. Often sailors brought news about places that the realm's subjects had never heard about before, or told tales of raids on English ships that killed or enslaved members of the crew.

When the *Discovery* sailed up the Thames in 1611 it brought dark evidence of a different kind of shipboard tragedy: bloodstains on its decks, the bloody clothing of those who did not return, stories about a mutiny, tales of an attack by Inuit, and the remarkable and arguably convenient fact that the seven men and one boy aboard all claimed they had nothing to do with the journey's travails. The survivors exonerated themselves and blamed the troubles on those who had died before the ship had made it as far as Ireland. They testified to the masters of Trinity House about what they had seen, and soon all of them were free, though suspicions about the roles they had played lingered.

The disaster in James Bay did not deter the English from pursuing opportunities on the high seas, including in the North Atlantic and the Arctic. Yet even as London's merchants had many reasons to hope that the Northwest Passage could be found, in the mid-1610s their interests increasingly were diverted beyond the discovery of any single route to distant markets. To increase trade, Britain's commercial leaders wanted to advance their knowledge on every front. They sought new geographical data that charted faster routes to desirable commodities and more information about people and places with whom they would trade. In 1614, the printer Felix Kyngston, at the urging of Hakluyt, published a series of "dialogues" intended to instruct the English in the Malay language and the phrases they would need in their dealings in the Spice Islands. But the English also needed stability at home and on the seas if they were to build a commercial empire. They could not tolerate investing their resources into ventures that dissolved in acrimony and violence. The bloodstains on the *Discovery* suggested that the struggle for control of the ship must have been fierce. If the interests of public order, the law of the sea, and the imperative of commerce were to be served, the mystery of the *Discovery* mutiny had to be solved.

In 1617, the High Court of Admiralty reopened the case of the *Discovery* and the fate of its 1610–1611 expedition. It was a time of heightened concern about the safety of English ships sailing abroad because of threats posed by Barbary pirates. Anxieties about journeys via Africa and South Asia to the East Indies may have also prompted the court to make a final judgment about what had happened to Hudson. The court considered charges against Bylot, Pricket, the surgeon Edward Wilson, Adrian Matter (a.k.a. Moter), Silvanus Bond, and Nicholas Syms. They were to stand trial for their roles in binding Hudson and placing him, along with eight others, "into a shallop, without food, drink, fire, clothing or any necessaries, and then maliciously abandoning them, so that they came to their death and miserably perished." The court could not charge them as accessories to a mutiny because there was at the time no law against mutiny in England or on English ships, which had been since the 1530s considered an extension of English property. The men who returned on the *Discovery* were to go on trial for murder.

The only surviving records from the proceedings are a series of depositions and the verdict itself. The testimony, taken by the court's agents six years after the return of the *Discovery*, reveals the suspicions that had been swirling around London since the ship had come home without Hudson. Now the court wanted to find answers that had eluded the masters of Trinity House and the various chroniclers of the expedition. What, exactly, had happened to the man whose patrons had believed would find fame and wealth by discovering the Northwest Passage?

No trial takes place in a vacuum. Every legal procedure reflects the existing laws of the state and the judgments made by those with the authority to analyze the evidence. In early seventeenth-century England, the officials of the High Court of Admiralty, where the realm's merchants wanted cases to be tried because of its special expertise in commercial ventures, were especially concerned with the threats that pirates posed to English ships. That preoccupation shaped the logic of the questions they asked the survivors of Hudson's last journey. It also helped to determine the verdict.

❧

With the explosion in maritime trade had come a plague of piracy. The expansion of English shipping by the early years of the seventeenth century brought sailors from the realm into waters where they ran the risk of being raided. Piracy had long been a scourge for sailors. One English monarch after another had issued proclamations condemning it, and courts had tried their best to identify and punish anyone who engaged in raids on English ships. As early as 1490, King Henry VII had issued a proclamation declaring that piracy was unacceptable not only against English ships but also against the ships of his allies, including Rome, Austria, Spain, and Portugal. He forbade any pirate from entering any port in the realm. Moreover, it was forbidden to sell goods taken from their legitimate owners, and anyone who did so needed to make restitution to those who had been robbed. Failure to follow such guidance would lead to imprisonment and possible further punishment. Of course, officials of the state at times authorized independent raids on the ships of other realms, though the English referred to such acts as "privateering," not "piracy." Either a pirate or a privateer might seize the property and even the ship of an enemy. In English law, the pirate was a criminal who needed to be punished; a successful privateer, by contrast, might come home to a great welcome. For a nation committed to maritime trade, illegal pirates stood in the way of the expansion of commerce and could also interfere with delicate matters of state.

By the time the trial of the *Discovery* survivors opened in London, the prevailing law about piracy had been on the books for more than eighty years. Passed in 1536 during the reign of King Henry VIII, the act linked pirates to "Robbers of the sea." That phrasing is crucial. The law, if it could be enforced, might preserve the lives of those on ships, but its goal was to protect property, not humans. In sixteenth- and seventeenth-century England, a conviction for piracy meant the death penalty, the standard punishment for serious thefts. The act also denied the benefit of clergy, which meant that even first-time offenders could not claim they had taken holy orders and thus escape punishment (or have the case heard in an ecclesiastical court). Queen Elizabeth upheld the principle of this act in 1575 when she included pirates and sea robbers among the population of criminals—such as murderers, counterfeiters, and rapists—not eligible for the general pardon she issued that year.

But pirates were hard to capture and convict. Like the traitors, murderers, thieves, and others who preyed on their victims at sea, pirates often escaped punishment. English common law demanded that before someone could be executed for a crime, either he or she had to confess, which pirates would "never do without torture or pains," or witnesses needed to step forward and provide testimony. But the chance for eyewitness testimony was slim; pirates, the English knew, frequently killed anyone who had seen them in action. Sailors were typically difficult to track down anyway, further limiting the potential pool of witnesses following a raid. Once they returned from a voyage, they did not tend to wait around the docks for long. Instead they would find work on a ship soon to depart and head back out to sea.

The law reflected growing understanding of what life on ships was like and the dangers that sailors faced. Statutes recognized that there were times when it might be necessary to take food, ropes, sails, or anchors from another vessel during a moment of distress. In such instances, the seizure of goods was justifiable, but only when those on the raided ship had enough supplies to spare and, crucially, the ship commandeering the supplies reimbursed the ship owners, either on the spot or in the form of a note promising future payment. Anyone who seized goods close to Europe—defined by the law as on the eastern side of the Straits of Morocco—had to repay their debt within four months. Those who were farther away had a year to make good on their promises.

Henry VIII's law against piracy clarified an important legal point. The English could punish thieves and other felons when they committed their crimes on land controlled by the state, but now they had jurisdiction as well over the high seas. To get around an issue that no court at the time could unequivocally establish, the statute effectively defined an English ship as the equivalent of a piece of English land. As the law specified, anyone convicted of such a crime on board ship could face the death penalty or the loss of property just as if they had committed the felonies on land. The act did more than clarify a point of law. In some ways, it gave authority and legitimacy to what would eventually become the British Empire. By expanding the areas where the state could claim jurisdiction, the statute declared that the realm itself existed wherever its ships sailed.

In the years that followed, the English passed a series of regulations aimed at controlling such matters on the high seas. In 1539, only three years after the new piracy statute appeared on the books, Henry VIII declared that anyone who guided an English ship out of port without first obtaining a license from local authorities faced the death penalty, ordering all mayors, sheriffs, and others in positions of authority to enforce the law. Those who did not would face "his majesty's most high indignation and displeasure, and answer to his highness at their uttermost perils."

The law against piracy was among an extensive series of edicts under Henry VIII intended to regulate what happened on vessels on the high seas. In 1545, the king authorized the death penalty for any sailor on a royal ship who disembarked without the captain's permission. Anyone who provided assistance to the deserter risked imprisonment, confiscation of property, and other unspecified penalties. Four years later, Henry VIII singled out several Irish pirates and declared that whoever brought them in, dead or alive, would receive a reward ranging from 300 to 1,000 crowns (the amount depending on which of these particular pirates they had captured or killed). Yet such orders did little to halt acts of piracy on the seas. In February 1549, responding to the growth in such crimes, Henry VIII declared that anyone who aided, hid, or defended a pirate either at sea or in a port would be liable to the same punishment as the pirate himself: confiscation of property and death. To encourage his subjects' vigilance, the king also promised to reward anyone who helped to catch those who succored pirates.

Over the course of the sixteenth century, pirates remained an affliction for the English, even as the expansion in European shipping in general and English ventures in particular created a new problem for the realm. As Queen Elizabeth recognized in August 1559, during the first full year of her reign, forests in England were becoming thinner, in part because they were being cut down to meet the demand for naval supplies. Though her subjects used wood for other reasons, including building houses and fences and heating their homes, in this age before coal fires became common much domestic wood went to shipyards. But it was not only the English who wanted to build vessels able to travel great distances. Recognizing the environmental limits that she faced and acknowledging the fear of competitors, Elizabeth banned the sale of ships to anyone born or living outside her realm.

Like her predecessors, Elizabeth remained haunted by the specter of pirates plundering England's ships. In July 1564, she issued a proclamation intending to safeguard peace upon the seas. To preserve "good and perfect peace with all princes and countries," she ordered that all English ships remove the arms they carried unless they first made a pledge not to interfere with ships of allied nations. Further, and more significantly, she demanded that no English ship provide any form of support to pirates. The only action a law-abiding crew should take with such outlaws was to arrest them. In 1573 the state executed three pirates at Wapping (after a trial at Southwarke); it exonerated two others, even though they had been convicted.

The queen long remained concerned that English acts of piracy against the ships of her allies could harm delicate international diplomatic relations. In 1591, three years after the English defeated the Spanish Armada but in an age still rife with anxiety about national security, she issued a proclamation commanding that any privateer who returned home with a prize from another nation's ship first report to the Court of Admiralty so that it could ensure that nothing had been seized from an ally. Anyone found to have distributed seized property before reporting to the court would be punished, and anyone who had booty from an ally's ship and tried to hide it would be liable to the same penalty as a pirate—namely, confiscation of goods and the death penalty. The act also specified that the privateers had to capture two or three of the ship's leaders, such as its master and pilot, and take them to the nearest English port to give testimony about the incident leading to their seizure. If local officials (who served on vice-admiralty courts in some ports) deemed the prize legal, they took an inventory of it. Only then could the privateers distribute the property they had seized. Such management of privateers had an added benefit for the realm: The court could use the inventory to levy a tax on the goods brought into English ports.

Later that year, Elizabeth heard reports of privateers based in London steering their bounty from Spanish ships to other ports, hoping they could sell off some of their prize before the booty could be examined by an admiralty court. Though she had no problem with taking goods from enemy Iberians, she recognized that such actions constituted an injustice to her subjects and to her. As a result, she issued a new proclamation prohibiting the unloading of valuable goods—"any foreign coin, bullion of gold or silver, jewels, pearls, stones, musk, wrought or raw silk, cochineal, indigo, or any other merchandises, commodities, or things whatsoever"—before a proper inventory could be taken. Anyone who failed to steer their ships into a legitimate port would face felony charges of piracy. Ten days later, after hearing that such actions were being committed by vessels coming from ports other than London, she expanded the statute to apply to any English ship.

Yet despite her repeated proclamations, English sailors continued to engage in acts that Elizabeth and her advisers deemed piracy. In 1602, more than a decade after she had issued her stringent rules governing foreign prizes brought into English ports, she declared that piracy was among the "crimes most hateful to her mind and scandalous to her peaceable government." To suppress it, she issued a detailed proclamation aimed at potential pirates and at the realm's officials who had to police them. She was particularly concerned about seizures made by English ships near the Barbary Coast of northwestern Africa and in the waters near Greece and Italy. To discourage such acts, she demanded that no one living in any English territory purchase any goods from such regions unless they could be sure the sales were lawful. Anyone who knowingly bought goods taken illegally—which could mean goods sold by privateers before an admiralty court could complete an inventory—ran the risk of having their possessions still in England confiscated. The penalty for pirates was even higher: They would be executed, and their property, including their lands, would be confiscated by the state.

Troubles caused by pirates grew after the accession of King James I—and so did public tales of their crimes. London's always-enterprising publishers had sensed a market for tales of violence on the seas. Chroniclers of English adventures abroad, including Hakluyt, told tales of the capture of their countrymen by Muslims in or near the Mediterranean who gave their captives the choice of conversion or death, claims that confirmed English views of the dangers posed by Islam. More disturbing to the English were the actions of home-grown pirates. In 1609, a shipmaster named Andrew Barker wrote a small pamphlet describing what he had experienced as the victim of a notorious English pirate named John Ward. The danger he revealed went beyond the loss of a single ship. Barker believed that English sailors who became pirates found work with the realm's enemies, especially the Turks, who lacked the nautical experience to effectively command large ships. When a skilled English sailor became a pirate, his betrayal had consequences for the English state. Christendom itself was at risk when such men took control of ships bearing 200 to 300 men and carrying as many as forty cannon. Barker declared that for London-based ships, losses from pirate raids in the previous year had totaled £200,000, an amount, he said, "incredible to report" but nonetheless true. A sailor who made the decision to become a pirate and work in the service of an enemy could never again be considered a loyal subject of the realm, as "nothing but poisonous effects" would follow from his actions. Barker provided an inventory of ships taken by Ward or his allies based in Tunis, cataloging seizures that had led to the loss of vessels and cargoes containing pilchards, currants from Zant, Alicante wines from Spain, and oil from Taloun. But the danger to goods paled in comparison to what the men on some of these ships faced: They might be taken captive and enslaved.

Ward was a particularly dangerous pirate whose exploits proved to be ideal fodder for the peddlers of pamphlets in London. He was a threat not only to those whose ships he attacked, but even to the men on his own vessels. Wine flowed freely on his ship, but rumor had it that if a man killed another while in a drunken state, he was to be lashed to the corpse and both of them thrown overboard. Such claims made Ward into a kind of dark celebrity and the fitting subject of a play. *Newes from Sea, of two notorious Pyrats*, publicly performed in London in 1612, told the tale of "A Christian turn'd Turke."

Ward was exceptional only in the extent of his actions that reached the attention of the public. Other English sailors also became seduced into a life of piracy. Some turned against king, country, and even Christendom itself. In 1609, Londoners

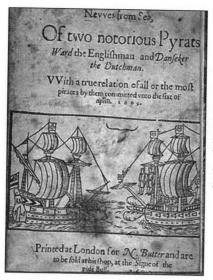

Pirates captured the imagination of readers, and occasionally printers provided illustrations to accompany narratives of maritime depredations. This picture from a 1609 London pamphlet describing the actions of the pirate John Ward shows two of his victims hanged. From *Newes from Sea, of two notorious Pyrats* (London, 1612). *Huntington Library*

could read a small pamphlet featuring testimony of Englishmen who had become pirates, often in league with Islamic foes of the Christian states. They had beset Venetians and Florentines as well as the English, taking up residence at Tunis and, as one annalist put it, "other places of the Turks' Dominions." If the English caught them, their deaths were swift; nineteen died in the gallows at Wapping in December 1608. Once convicted on the basis of their own confession or eyewitness testimony—available because some pirates released their prisoners, who made it back to London to tell what happened—execution followed quickly. Subjects of the English monarch learned that there would be no mercy for anyone who had become a pirate.

The High Court of Admiralty first took an interest in Hudson's last journey soon after the depositions at Trinity House concluded. In late January 1612, the judge Richard Trevor heard the sworn testimony of the surgeon Edward Wilson. Trevor presumably already had in hand what he had learned from the masters of Trinity House. That tribunal had established that the mutiny had taken place because of Hudson's policies relating to the distribution of food. In Wilson's new testimony, he declared that the twenty-two men on the ship had to share "but two quarts of meal" each day, while Hudson "had bread and cheese and aquavit" in his cabin, which he shared with his favorites. The situation aggrieved those not in Hudson's good graces, causing what Wilson called "grudge and mutiny" directed toward both Hudson and those who received the additional foodstuffs. The tension boiled over, Edward Wilson claimed, when William Wilson, the boatswain, confronted the carpenter, Staffe, to find out why Hudson was treating some better than others. According to the surgeon, Wilson told Greene what Staffe said, which prompted the emerging leaders of the rebellion to restrain both Hudson and the quartermaster John King and force them into the shallop. Staffe offered to go with Hudson at this point. The mutineers then put the other six into the shallop. They went voluntarily, the surgeon testified, in the belief that they were not being cast out of the boat for good but would be held to the side while the others searched for hidden caches of food. But that was not the case. The mutineers provided the men with their clothes, but not the rest of their goods, which they later sold to remaining members of the crew in front of the main mast—using the same procedure that the crew of an English ship would perform after the death of a crew member. It was a very orderly process, said the surgeon, with an inventory taken of each man's goods and the costs to be deducted out of their wages when they came home.

Trevor asked Edward Wilson if he could identify those responsible for the rebellion. He responded that he had already given a sworn deposition that he had not known who had plotted the mutiny before it unfolded. But he did add new details. He had first learned about the insurrection when he looked out from his own cabin and saw Hudson pinioned by the other men. At that point the surgeon offered to come out to help distribute food, but those who had tied Hudson told him that he should stay put. He added that neither Silvanus Bond, nor Francis Clemens, nor Nicholas Syms had any part in Hudson's capture.

Before the deposition concluded, Trevor asked Wilson questions that related less to the insurrection itself than to other issues raised by the aborted journey. This part of the interrogation indicated once more the competitive and commercial concerns of the English about Hudson's agenda. Was it true, Trevor wondered, that the Dutch intended to search for the Northwest Passage, and, if so, did they have any maps that could guide them? Wilson answered that he had heard that the Dutch were indeed interested in finding the route, but that he had provided no cards to them. But "some gentlemen and merchants of London" who were interested in the passage had been sharing charts that could have come to the attention of the

Dutch. Trevor pressed Wilson for the extent of his knowledge. Did the passage exist? the judge asked. Wilson replied with what was at that moment the prevailing English geographical wisdom. Flood tides in the bay came from the west and ebb tides from the east, and it was possible that there were channels where ice would not block the way west.

Trevor at last asked the question on everyone's mind in the months following the *Discovery's* return: What happened to Hudson and the men on the shallop? Wilson responded that the banished men had raised a sail and tried to follow the main ship. But then, when the men remaining on the ship raised their main sails, "they could not follow them then," and the men on the shallop headed for shore. The men on the *Discovery* soon "lost sight of them and never heard of them since." He could add no other details. Having heard this testimony, the High Court of Admiralty apparently chose to ask no more questions—of anyone.

❧

For the next five years, neither the High Court of Admiralty nor the masters of Trinity House demonstrated any obvious interest in what had happened to Hudson and the men left behind in James Bay. Investors with an interest in northern voyages funded new expeditions, and quite likely hoped that these explorers might turn up evidence establishing the fate of the men. Baffin's return in the autumn of 1616 signaled an end, for the moment, to English efforts to find the Northwest Passage. The most experienced seaman of his time had come to the conclusion that such a route could not be found.

If the ambition to find the passage had abated among London's investment community, their alarm over piracy grew. Sometime before March 9, 1617, a group of merchants who represented firms involved in long-distance trade—including the East India Company and the Muscovy Company—petitioned the king to crack down on a recent spate of piracies plaguing

English ships sailing near Tunis and Tangiers. Those raids had disrupted trade, caused losses to the companies, and impoverished the sailors aboard the ships as well as their wives and children. The Privy Council asked Sir Thomas Smythe to gather together merchants from nine companies to make recommendations to the king. King James took a personal interest in the suppression of piracy, a point he made obvious to continental observers whenever he could; early in his reign he had threatened to hang pirates with his own hands.

At almost the same moment—perhaps coincidentally, perhaps as a result of renewed concern about lawlessness on the seas—the High Court of Admiralty turned its attention again to the mutiny on the *Discovery*. The surviving transcript consists only of the deponents' answers and lacks the court's questions. But the answers reveal much about the nature of the court's interests and the evidence that its judges had in their possession.

The extant records suggest that the High Court began with Pricket, whom they deposed on February 7, 1617. The court records now identified him as a haberdasher living in London, yet another turn in a life that had earlier gone from relative affluence to servitude to service on the *Discovery* to inveterate traveler and chronicler. He began by listing the men he knew to be on the shallop. His account conformed to what he had written in his narrative of the journey, which—if he had already written it—might have been available to the members of the court. The plot had been hatched by men upset over the distribution of food who feared they would starve if Hudson did not give them more, he said. The entire episode saddened him because Hudson and Staffe were, he proclaimed, "the best friends he had in the ship."

Pricket went on to tell the court that five weeks after the uprising, the English had landed at Digges Island to trade with the Inuit, but they "were betrayed and fell upon by the Savages," and that these mutineers had each sustained mortal blows. The four did manage to make it back to the *Discovery*, but Greene died just as their small craft had reached the main ship. Two of the others had been disemboweled, which explained why there so was so much blood "upon the clothes and other things brought home" on the *Discovery*. That blood, he emphasized, belonged only to those who had been wounded by the Inuit "and no other." He did not want the court to think that Hudson and his allies had been murdered during the uprising. Unlike the others, he admitted that tensions on the ship had predated the final encounter. Yet, despite the fact that there had been disputes, "no mutiny was in question" until those last hours before the rebels forced Hudson and the others into the shallop.

Even Pricket, whose published narrative suggested that he retained a firm command on the sequence of events on the journey, could not answer some of the questions. Yes, it was true that the survivors broke into Hudson's chest and stole his goods, selling some of them (to unnamed parties) and wearing some of his clothes. It was also true that they had taken these items to England with them—but, he avowed, only because none of the men in the shallop had wanted them. He had no idea whether the carpenter could still be alive, since he had not seen him since that fateful morning. He did not think that any of them had been injured during the actual mutiny. There were no shots fired, though he did hear that William Wilson had pinned Hudson's arms, presumably to halt any resistance he might have offered.

In the answer to one question, Pricket responded that some of the mutineers had wanted to become pirates. Greene and the others, he testified, had met to discuss the possibility, which he thought "they would have done, if they had not been slain." But that possible scheme was not the reason for the mutiny, which had to do with the unjust distribution of food. In response to one question Pricket added that the men had never gotten rabbits or partridges before the mutiny.

Pricket's responses to the questions conformed to most of the answers given by the other surviving crewmen, except in one instance: In response to one inquiry he said to his inquisitors that "he for his part told the Masters of the Trinity House the truth of the business as he said." He added that he had never heard that the masters had said that the survivors "deserved to be hanged" for what had happened amid the ice floes on the banks of James Bay. Given the paucity of the testimony, it is impossible to know whether Pricket was being sincere or simply trying to convince the court that the masters had not come to such a conclusion.

When Pricket was done, it was Robert Bylot's turn. He had piloted the *Discovery* back into the North Atlantic in the years after Hudson's final expedition and was now identified in the court records as living in St. Katherine's—the point of departure for Hudson's last journey. Bylot's answers echoed Pricket's. The men of the *Discovery* had become frustrated by their inability to find the Northwest Passage, he reported, and the shortage of food aggravated the situation. Bylot claimed that Henry Greene, along with four associates—John Thomas, William Wilson, Robert Juet, and Michael Perse—were convinced that the captain had secreted away food for his own use and decided to take matters into their own hands. When the five herded Hudson and eight or nine others onto the shallop, Perse had thought the plotters were only confining the men for a short while so that they could search the ship for food. But Greene and the others then refused to let the men back onto the ship. "[S]o the said Hudson & the rest in the Shallop went away to the Southward," Bylot reported, "& the ship came to the Eastward, and the one never saw the other since." He claimed that none of the men remaining on the *Discovery* could have known what happened after the two vessels parted.

The court wanted to know what happened after the uprising. Here Bylot responded that as the *Discovery* headed toward home, the men in charge decided to land at Digges Island.

Soon after their arrival, Bylot said, Greene and five other men went on shore to find food, but the locals turned against them. Two of the men "had their guts cut out, and all the rest wounded but one." Perhaps that one was Pricket, though in his narrative he claimed that he was wounded too. As it turned out, the four died shortly after they had made it back to the *Discovery*. Their wounds bled profusely, which explained the stains on their clothes and beds, Bylot told the court. His testimony about the bloodstains thus corroborated Pricket's account.

Like Pricket's testimony, Bylot's answers suggest that the court wanted to know whether the rebellion had been planned or was spontaneous. Bylot told them that there had been unhappy men on the ship—a point the court presumably already knew from Wydowse's note, which was likely in the court's possession during the deposition.

But there had been no talk of mutiny, Bylot told them, until just before Greene and his allies put Hudson and the others onto the shallop. In other words, if an earlier conspiracy existed, he did not know anything about it. Bylot went further on this point, claiming that when he first heard about the plan the night before Greene and the others executed it, he and Pricket had tried to change Greene's mind. But the chief conspirator refused to budge, telling Bylot (and Pricket) that Hudson "was resolved to overthrow all, and therefore he and his friends would shift for themselves." Bylot repeatedly told the court there was no set plan. Greene and the others had acted as they did because of the shortage of food.

The court pressed Bylot for more details. What had happened to the clothes owned by Hudson and the others? Bylot replied that the men remaining on board either sold what was left or took the items for themselves. Bylot implied that Hudson and his men had taken some things with them, but that the rest remained on board during the return to London. No, he told them, he had not taken Hudson's ring. He had seen the ring on the captain's finger, but he had no idea what had happened to it during the mutiny and after. And no, he added, the men "were not victualled with any abundance of rabbit or partridges" during the voyage.

Some of Bylot's answers reveal that the court was trying to understand the actions of each of the men on the *Discovery*. Responding to a question about the carpenter, Bylot reported that he had volunteered to go into the shallop "without any compulsion," which, if it was true, might help to exculpate Bylot and the other survivors by showing they did not play an active role in the rebellion. Bylot did not know whether Staffe was still alive.

But if Bylot had few answers about Hudson's possessions or the fate of his close associate, he did provide one detail after another about the unfolding plot—beyond what Pricket had told the court. To his knowledge, there was no watchword that signaled the start of the rebellion; Greene simply chose the moment for the mutiny to begin, and then gave orders to Hudson and the others to get into the shallop, which they obeyed. Had those who remained on board shot at the shallop and its small crew? No, Bylot told the court. "No man either drunk or sober can report, that the said Hudson and his associates or any of them were shot at, after they were in the Shallop," he argued, because "there was no such thing done." Like Pricket, Bylot also believed that Greene and two or three of the other rebels would have become pirates if they had survived.

The court tried to find out if Bylot had altered his story over the years. He denied doing so. He told them that he told Sir Thomas Smythe "the manner how Hudson & the rest went from them," but what Smythe may have reported to the lost men's wives was beyond his knowledge. He told the court, too, that he had made the same explanation to the masters of Trinity House. The three men who had the greatest financial stake in the voyage—Digges, Wolstenholme, and Smythe—were, Bylot claimed, "well informed of all that proceeded."

Near the end of his deposition, the court apparently produced Wydowse's note and showed it to Bylot. Was the report in these pages accurate? Bylot claimed that he could not recognize the man's handwriting and had no knowledge of what could be in the note. The mathematician had apparently hidden the note in his desk.

The next deponent, Bennet Mathews, testified in March 1617 that during the mutiny he had been so ill that he figured he would be put into the shallop with the others. But for reasons he did not understand, he had been spared. Apparently he witnessed much of what happened during the insurrection, and said that while Hudson had been tied up, the other men voluntarily boarded the shallop. Indeed, each also had then gone back to the ship to gather their belongings before returning to it. Though Mathews had been ill, he was still sure that the crew put only nine men on the shallop. He added that during the return of the *Discovery*, four men had been "slain by the Cannibals."

Mathews, like the others, added small details to the story. He reported that the carpenter had refused to stay on board the *Discovery*. Staffe had promised that if the others prevented him from joining Hudson, he would "leap out of the ship, on the next piece of Ice that came by the ship." In accord with what Bylot and Pricket had said, Mathews did not know whether the carpenter was alive or dead. All three men were shrewd enough to leave open the possibility that Hudson and his men could have lived—which would make each of them even less likely to be guilty of murder.

As for the remaining physical evidence, Mathews had the same explanation as the first two deponents, claiming that the clothes of Greene and the other wounded men became bloody because the "Cannibals cut up their bellies"; the gaping injuries had stained the ship and everything nearby when the survivors tried to save the wounded. Mathews added that Wydowse could have saved his own life but had earlier refused to give up the keys to his chest when the ship's supplies ran low, suggesting that he had been keeping food from the others. Like Bylot, Mathews also said that as far as he knew, none of the mutineers had signaled each other at the start of the rebellion.

But unlike Pricket and Bylot, Mathews claimed he knew "of no determination that any of them had to turn pirates."

Mathews must have been asked about the treatment of those put into the shallop, specifically any assaults they had suffered. He insisted that all of the men were alive when the little boat "departed from them"—that is, when those on it paddled off on their own from the sides of *Discovery*. He added, echoing Bylot's phrasing, that "no man either drunk or sober ever confessed that any of the said persons were slain."

When Francis Clemens came before the court on May 13, 1617, his testimony supported what Bylot had already told them. Clemens was forty years old then and possibly beyond any thought of returning to the sea. Like the others, he remembered many details of what had happened in James Bay. During that winter, his nails had frozen off; he maintained that he had been so ill that he could not have known much about any plans to depose Hudson—nor did he possess any information about what happened to those who were pushed off in the shallop.

The court must have realized that the details Clemens offered corresponded exactly to the reports of the previous witnesses. After Greene took over the ship, the *Discovery* had landed at Digges Island, where the mutineers went in search of food. Greene, Wilson, Thomas, and Perse all died as a result of the attack by the Inuit, but not before they bled all over the clothes found on the ship; Juet had died later at sea. He, too, said he did not know whether Staffe was still alive.

That Clemens claimed to be ill and out of action before and during the mutiny limited his effectiveness as a witness. He did know that Hudson had rearranged the posts of some of the crew, which meant moving some men from one cabin to another. But the captain's actions had not led to any talk of a mutiny, or at least none that he had heard. He was, he reminded the court, sick and lying in his own cabin when the uprising began, and if someone had cried out a watchword, he did not hear it. His illness prevented him from either stopping the uprising or taking part in it. But he was sure that none of those who had organized it had any thought "that they would turn pirate to his knowledge." Clemens did add one revealing detail: "[H]e confesseth that Henry Hudson was pinioned when he was put into the shallop." Apparently his illness did not keep him in his cabin during the most dramatic moment of the uprising.

The last to testify was Edward Wilson, the surgeon who had spoken to the High Court five years earlier. Wilson answered questions in early August 1617. His testimony was briefer than that of the others and offered nothing new. He said that he was asleep when the mutiny unfolded and had no prior knowledge of any plans to remove Hudson or the others. The court apparently showed him Wydowse's note, but he, too, claimed he could not recognize the handwriting.

The depositions provide only these witnesses' accounts, not any other evidence or the judges' deliberations. The judges' attention to the mathematician's note suggests that they took that evidence seriously, perhaps because it was the only record they had—other than Hudson's incomplete journal—of views from the victims of the mutiny. Apparently the survivors' testimony did not convince the High Court of Admiralty of their innocence. Within a year, four of them would face charges that they had murdered Hudson. Only Bylot escaped a trial.

❧

Every trial occurs in a specific historical context. In the *Discovery* murder trial, the memories of the witnesses would have dimmed over six years, and no matter how truthful they wished to be, they would presumably skew their testimony in their own favor. Even those who could recollect what happened would be influenced by what they heard on the streets or down by the wharves. The talk of London in the middle 1610s was not usually about whether Hudson had been murdered, or even about the existence of the Northwest Passage he sought to find— though certainly some of the sailors awaiting their next berth might have tossed around tales of the dangers of northern seas. Times, interests, and orientations had changed in the seven years since Hudson had begun his final expedition. Now it was more likely that men hanging around the docks were talking about Virginia tobacco, which was then arriving in ever-larger amounts, even as the English continued to debate the virtues and vices of the sot weed. Perhaps some mariners traded stories about the Pilgrims, who had just boarded ships bound for Amsterdam, where they hoped to practice their religion freely and find work in that bustling city's woolen industry. Three years later, some of those same religious dissidents would board ships again, this time bound for a transatlantic passage that would take them to territory that Hudson had scouted on Cape Cod, in a settlement they would name Plymouth.

Long-distance and local shipping was a central concern of England's authorities. The Privy Council, which provided advice to the realm's monarchs and had great power in the early seventeenth century, repeatedly tried to regulate shipping and commerce during the mid-1610s. The council often worked closely with the masters of Trinity House. In 1613, for example, the councillors passed legislation increasing the duties paid by mariners entering Newcastle Harbor, with the understanding that the fees would go to Trinity House, which would then use them to erect and maintain lighthouses to guide ships past the treacherous waters at the head of the Tyne. In July of that year, the council wrote to the mayor of Newcastle directing him to address the complaints of the masters, who had detailed conditions along the banks of the Tyne and in the river itself—including ash and cinder from salt pans and rubbish from nearby grindstones flowing into the river, incorrectly constructed wharves, and ballast tossed into the river by careless mariners—that needed to be improved in order for shipping to thrive. Two years later, the Privy Council, responding to complaints of merchants who felt that regulations on shipping in London hurt their prospects, worked with the masters of Trinity House to

set duties for specific goods in the hope that this would facilitate commerce in the realm.

The frequent attention that the councillors gave to matters
relating to shipping demonstrates that the same commercial impulses that had supported the voyages of the *Discovery* had remained intense since Hudson's departure in 1610. London's
residents, especially its merchants and those who wanted to expand the overseas territory controlled by the realm, were more
eager than ever to learn from those who came back from long
voyages and to use their findings to refine and expand their
trade opportunities. Not every ship returning to an English
berth contained a marvel such as cinnamon or tobacco, and not
every departing vessel headed off with a man or woman seeking
religious freedom. But Londoners still paid attention, eager to
absorb the tales, innovations, and news that came with every
voyage.

Eventually, stories about expeditions into the North Atlantic allowed the mariners to create a glossary of terms to describe the varieties of ice they encountered. An iceberg came to
mean a "mountain of ice," according to one later northern explorer, whereas a "field" identified "a piece of ice so large that
its extent cannot be seen," and a "floe" was "a piece of ice of
considerable size, but the extent of which can be distin-
guished." Every conceivable kind of ice came to have its own
name, including "bay ice," newly formed ice whose color resembled that of the sea; a "tongue," which described a shaft of
ice that lay below the water's surface, but posed an obvious risk
for any ship that got too close; and a "calf," ice that broke apart
from either an iceberg or a field and rose "with violence to the
surface of the water." According to English usage, the *Discovery*
had become "beset," which meant that it was "surrounded with
ice, so as to be obliged to remain immoveable."

It fell to the judges of the High Court of Admiralty, not the
merchants and seasonal laborers who crowded the shops and
docks, to render a verdict on what happened to Hudson in

RAFTED ICE IN ROES WELCOME, JUNE, 1904.

Mariners were obsessed with ice around Hudson Bay because it was almost ubiqui-tous and lasted for months, as this photograph from Roes Welcome from June 1904 reveals. From Canada Department of Marine and Fisheries, *Report of 1906*. *Huntington Library*

1611. It could not have been an easy task. Did the survivors tell the truth to the court? They had had ample time to get their stories in line, and it is possible that Pricket had already written his narrative. Perhaps he was in the process not of remembering but of embellishing his tale in the hopes that his story would exculpate him—and that he could get it published, thereby maybe earning some income and a guarantee of immortality. (Hakluyt had died in March 1616, within weeks of Pricket's deposition to the court, but Purchas had already published two editions of his collection recounting English travel narratives, and Pricket might well have known by now that the minister-publisher would be interested in printing his tale.) From a dis-tance of four centuries, the questions are more obvious than the answers. Was Pricket's narrative an accurate report of deeds done by desperate men in fear of their own lives, or did it serve as an alibi for mutiny and murder? If the men under the command of such an experienced and well-financed captain as Hudson had engaged in such an insurrection, what dangers might threaten other captains and their wealthy patrons? And how could the actions of men be constrained, or even accurately discovered, in territory nominally under the control of the crown but thousands of miles away?

The masters of Trinity House, for their part, had been busy during the months when the High Court of Admiralty was taking depositions from the survivors of Hudson's journey. In January 1617, a poor and elderly man named Nicholas Rudes of Dunwich in Suffolk had come before them seeking assistance to ransom his son William, a mariner who had been taken captive by the Turks (the masters agreed to help). On February 12, only five days after Bylot had given his deposition to the High Court of Admiralty, the masters had sent several men to Winterton, near Newcastle, to take new soundings and provide markers, if necessary, a journey prompted by recent foul weather. Two days later, a royal statute gave the masters the authority to provide buoys and all other markers across the realm, another sign of the political and legal might of Trinity House. On March 1, a poor widow named Mary Clarke sought assistance because her husband, Henry, had been captured (and apparently murdered) when Turkish pirates seized the London-based *Mary Constant*. She asked specifically for funds to redeem her son Martin, whom the pirates had sold into slavery.

News of such events no doubt swirled among Londoners and other subjects of the king who imagined a future abroad. On July 24, 1618, Pricket, Wilson, Mathews, and Clemens appeared in court in Southwark. They were not alone. The court that day also tried men for robbing other ships, and, in one instance, for murder. It found five of the men in the other cases guilty. The court summoned them to the bar and asked each if there was any reason why he should not be condemned to die.

Neither the men nor anyone else objected to the sentence, and the men were ordered back to prison, where they would wait until they were taken to be hanged at Wapping.

The four survivors from the 1610–1611 journey were tried for "feloniously pinnioning and putting of Henry Hudson, master of the 'Discovery' out of the same ship with VIII more of his company into a shallop" without sufficient provisions, "whereby they died." Each of them pled not guilty. They were more fortunate than the pirates tried the same day. The court acquitted them.

No one other than the survivors could have known what happened in James Bay seven years earlier. The court did not try either Bylot or Syms, for reasons that remain unclear. Perhaps Bylot's later service as a commander of English ships in the North Atlantic made him immune from suspicion or too valuable to those who financed his journeys. Perhaps Syms never came into court because he was only a boy at the time of the uprising and thus not culpable for what had happened.

But as far as the public was concerned, the controversy had been resolved. Barbary pirates might threaten English ships heading toward the Mediterranean or the East Indies, but no one knew for sure whether domestic pirates had launched the insurrection on the *Discovery*'s decks. The testimony offered in a London courtroom now stood as the accepted version of Hudson's tragic fate.

# X.

# *Tides*

*T**he masters of Trinity House*, the judges of the High Court of Admiralty, and other contemporary observers shared one common belief: Henry Hudson died soon after the mutiny on board the *Discovery* in June 1611. As Samuel Purchas put it in 1625, Hudson's "last and fatal voyage was 1610." But what befell the captain of the *Discovery*?

It is impossible to know with any certainty what happened to Hudson and the other men in the shallop after the *Discovery*, finally free of the ice that had held it in place for months, sailed toward England. English authorities, notably the High Court of Admiralty, believed that the men were dead, which meant that the rebels could be charged with murder. The court assumed that no Englishman, or even a small group, could survive for long in such a cold, icy, and unforgiving region. They based that conclusion on their knowledge of the North Atlantic and its regional environment and what they had learned about the indigenous peoples of these northern territories, most notably from the multiple accounts of the Frobisher voyages of the mid-1570s, the accounts of Hudson's earlier ventures, the new reports by Baffin and others from the mid-1610s, and even the depositions from the 1610–1611 journey of the *Discovery*.

And perhaps they were right. Who could live for long during an Arctic winter? The English would have guessed that if the weather did not finish them, the natives would. The survivors of Hudson's last journey had told of incidents in which the locals would at first welcome those who came to trade with them and then turn on them, lashing out unexpectedly to strike down their victims. The English feared that these enemies from the north might even eat the dead—the survivors of the *Discovery* had, after all, called the local people cannibals, a common aspersion voiced by Europeans about Americans at the time. Moreover, if Hudson or any of the others even reached the shore, surely one of the English expeditions to the region in the following years might have found some sign of them. But so far, there did not seem to be a trace of the shallop or the men who had been abandoned to fend for themselves.

Still, despite early seventeenth-century speculations, there is no reason to believe that Hudson and the others died so quickly. More likely, they survived for some time. Like five men Frobisher had left behind in 1576, Hudson and his allies may have even contemplated sailing homeward. Their fate remained a subject of fascination, especially for later English mariners who sailed into those same frigid seas.

Henry Hudson was not a man who would have accepted what the English later saw as a death penalty. His journeys proved that he was a survivor. He knew how to adapt to climatic conditions and how to get his men to alter their behavior so that they could survive potentially deadly circumstances. He knew the power of the ice, but it never destroyed him (as it did Barentsz). He understood how to extract food from the land and the sea, how to ward off scurvy, and how to survive destructive storms. He grasped the rules for trading with indigenous Americans, with whom he could communicate by signs, if not by words. And he was not alone. Among his companions was his son John, on the edge of adulthood and already well-seasoned by four summers at sea. However despondent he might have become in the summer of 1611 and beyond, it seems inconceivable that Hudson would have surrendered to death.

Later travelers to the region focused on issues that had always preoccupied English explorers, especially the ubiquity of the ice and the ways that currents flowed in the North Atlantic. Hudson had always tried to understand how tides worked. Other explorers would become gripped by the same obsession. Eventually they would turn up signs about what had happened to the men on the shallop.

❧

Hudson's men spent the winter of 1610 to 1611 in an area that has long been home to the James Bay Cree. The citizens of this indigenous nation believe that they have lived there since ancient times and that they had no known contact with Europeans until the *Discovery* arrived in late 1610. According to the Cree oral historian James Wesley, who in 1985 spoke about the first meeting between his people and Europeans, that initial encounter was peaceful. The Crees at first hid when they saw an approaching sailboat, presumably the *Discovery,* but two of them came to meet some of the visitors who paddled to the shore. Eventually some of the Americans boarded the main ship. "When they arrived on the ship, they saw many strangers," Wesley reported. "From the expression on the strangers' faces, they could tell they were welcome aboard." The English offered the Crees tobacco, which the visitors were smoking in pipes, and an unloaded gun. One late eighteenth-century English observer wrote that local Crees told of "the arrival and wintering of the unfortunate Captain Henry Hudson, as handed down to them by the tradition of their ancestors," but he added no other details.

The Crees had much to teach the Europeans about surviving in such an unforgiving climate. Perhaps they could have taught Hudson as well, especially about the local environment.

Agriculture was impossible in this part of the Canadian Shield, where retreating glaciers 8,000 or so years ago stripped existing topsoil and left behind only rocky ground. Those who inhabited the region confronted nature's brutality every winter. Fierce winds racing up to 30 miles per hour across the water made the average temperature of approximately −4 to −9 Fahrenheit (or negative 20 to 23 Celsius) feel like 30 to 40 degrees below zero. As was common across eastern North America before Europeans arrived, indigenous peoples who relied on tracking animals tended to live in small communities during the winter.

Yet despite the harrowing circumstances, the territory supported those who knew how to hunt and fish there. During the summer, millions of migrating birds flew north to breed. The Crees had words in their language for approximately 200 different bird species found around Hudson Bay. Eagles, owls, loons, ducks, gulls, teal, sandpipers, partridge, osprey, sparrows, chickadees, swans, terns, plovers, turnstones, woodpeckers, sandpipers, geese, grouse, pigeons, curlews, sparrows, cranes, ptarmigan, falcons, guillemots, cranes, and swans all nested in the area. The waters teemed with whitefish, trout, sturgeon, perch, and Arctic char; on land, the available game included beaver, caribou, moose, wolverines, porcupines, foxes, wolves, lynx, skunks, martens, fishers, muskrat, otters, rabbits, weasels, and polar bears. Seals and walrus basking on the ice added to the potential harvest. Anyone skilled with a gun, pike, or seine would not starve. It would be the region's bounty that later convinced the managers of the Hudson's Bay Company to establish trading posts around the southern reaches of the Hudson and James bays and on nearby tributary rivers. The land visited by the *Discovery* that winter would become not just a potential egress to the East. It would offer its own bounty.

The local Crees supplemented animal and marine sources of protein by gathering what they could find during the brief summer months. A short summer produced abundant berries and fast-growing grasses that could be woven for baskets. The growing season might be fleeting, but there was no shortage of available food. A single beached whale, according to one modern account, could provide enough food for a village for most of a year.

But success did not depend on such lucky circumstances. Inuit *qaujimajatuqangit* (ancestral knowledge) and Cree *tipaachimowina* (historical narratives) reveal long-practiced expertise in the hunt for a wide variety of animals on land or sea; they also disclose the secrets of gathering berries, seaweed, and shellfish. In the eighteenth century, European observers who traveled to Hudson Bay cataloged its extraordinary fauna and saw firsthand the natural riches of the region—resources that the native peoples had known how to utilize for dozens of generations.

In Henry Hudson's time, the English only occasionally understood the extent of this natural abundance and how to use it to survive and thrive. The journals of those who traveled in this region in the seventeenth century testify to the sense of isolation that overwhelmed these newcomers. To them, especially during the winter, the landscape seemed almost shapeless and always menacing. They wrote frequently about ice because it was ubiquitous, as the snow must have been during the winter of 1610–1611 when Hudson's crew sat trapped in a small house near the *Discovery*. Nothing in their traditions or their earlier lives could have compared to what they experienced. They knew the dark of winters, of course, but not the brutal winds that whipped across the Canadian landscape, blinding the unwary with bursts of snow. The silence of Pricket's journal during the months before the June thaw testifies not only to the probable boredom that he and others felt but also to the inability to find words to describe such a season in what was to them a vast, inhuman wilderness where gales blinded the very tracks of their boots, seeking to erase their presence with every storm and snowfall. Or perhaps Pricket simply could not hold a quill or find paper dry enough to record his thoughts.

But what seemed ungodly bleak to the English was an environment that made sense to the Crees. Like the Inuit, the other masters of the northern reaches of this part of the world, the Crees inhabited a landscape that was in many ways predictable and often comforting. Indigenous people knew where to find local resources, such as rich clam banks or fields with lush spring grasses or the streams where migrating fish congregated after their journey upriver to their breeding grounds. Geese and ducks arrived in late spring in flocks so large that in flight they must have blocked the sun. They nested on small islands and near the shores of the bay, shrieking a cacophony never heard in the region at other times of the year. All of those who grew up here knew the best places to trap a bird, or the shallow inlets that invited seals and walrus, or the grassy slopes that drew caribou. This land afforded all that a healthy man, woman, or child would need to survive.

By June 1611, Hudson and the others on the shallop had already acquired substantial information about the region and its resources. They knew about the migrating birds, which Pricket had described in his journal. They had consumed the grasses that sprang so quickly after a thaw and which they knew would help ward off scurvy. They understood how to fish and had honed some clumsy skill at hunting. As Pricket had written, men on board the *Discovery* had even tried to kill polar bears, although the beasts proved elusive amid the ice floes. Hudson had been abandoned with a small crew that included men whom Greene and the other mutineers had deemed too ill or injured to deserve any of the ship's dwindling food supply. At the moment of the uprising, Pricket identified six infirm men: Bennet Mathews, Silvanus Bond (who remained on the *Discovery*), Syracke Faner, and Thomas Wydowse, as well as Michael Bute and Adrian Moore who, Pricket noted, had been ill since the *Discovery* lost its anchor. But his report and the later depositions given to the High Court of Admiralty reveal that Hudson and the carpenter, Staffe, at least, were in excellent shape. There is no mention of the health of John King or Hudson's son John. Maybe, indeed, Hudson's small party had the strength and skill to survive in the wilderness—for a while at least.

Staffe's talents likely fit the most pressing needs of the men on the shallop. Brought on board in anticipation of damage and wear and tear to the ship that were best repaired under the supervision of an experienced carpenter—and also to help with the construction of the shallops, which lay in pieces during the transatlantic journey—he would have known how to build a shelter (even though he had haughtily declared the previous fall that he was better suited for work on boats than houses). There was ample driftwood on the shores of James Bay, and the men had at least eight weeks to set themselves up before the first chill winds of winter blew across the water. By then they could have emulated the Crees or Inuit, who had, as Pricket reported, strung up the carcasses of hundreds of migratory birds to eat during the upcoming dark months. The icy winds provided a natural form of refrigeration and eliminated the need to salt the meat, which made it healthier to eat than any flesh preserved on board an English ship. Even after the birds departed for the winter, there was still ample game to be found.

Apart from the advance of disease among some of the men, and the ever-impending winter, the immediate risk to the stranded English would have been an attack by the Crees or some other indigenous group. Europeans and Americans had not yet learned each other's languages in this region and had to communicate by signs. That meant that a simple miscommunication could be construed as an insult or a threat. Perhaps it was just that kind of error that had led to the assault on Greene and the other mutineers on Digges Island.

But in the early seventeenth century, an attack by Americans on a band of stranded Europeans was unlikely. The Crees had no obvious reason to harm the Englishmen. They treated most newcomers as potential suppliers of goods that they did not own and did not know how to make. If the Crees behaved like other Algonquians who met English ships in Newfoundland in the early seventeenth century, with whom the indigenous inhabitants of the James Bay region probably had contact, then they would have wanted iron nails and other manufactured goods. Eliminating the newcomers would have been pointless, especially since these Europeans were relatively harmless— unlike others who had arrived farther south, who had unwittingly unleashed deadly contagions among Indians—or, as on Hudson's 1609 journey, had fought with some of the peoples they had met.

Henry Hudson may have hoped and even expected that if he could just manage to endure another winter in James Bay, a new expedition would come to rescue him, returning him to England where he could bear witness against those who had usurped his command. Perhaps he even hoped to meet with his investors and prepare for yet another foray toward the Northwest Passage. If so, he was sadly mistaken. After 1611, Europeans did not return to James Bay until the 1630s, when the English explorers Thomas James and Luke Foxe traveled there, and no one else sailed there until perhaps 1670, when yet another group of English travelers visited. By then the Hudson's Bay Company, a transcontinental enterprise that soon acquired political authority—at least in the eyes of Europeans—over a vast territory that included all of James Bay and the surrounding lands, was in the process of taking shape. The company's agents had been drawn to the region because of its extraordinary population of fur-bearing animals. As they quickly found out, the locals embraced the opportunity to trade with them. Like other Americans, the Crees wanted to add new goods to their households even as they were determined to maintain their traditional material culture.

In the aftermath of the voyages of the 1610s and the claim by Baffin and others that the Northwest Passage could not be found in the area, Hudson Bay became a less obvious target for English travelers. Though the Danish explorer Jens Munk explored the western shores of Hudson Bay in 1619–1620, his expedition had little bearing on English understanding of the region—except for unfounded rumors that swirled in London suggesting that he had found the way to the Pacific with the assistance of an unnamed English pilot. But after a hiatus of twenty years, the area again attracted Hudson's countrymen. In 1631, a group of Bristol merchants sponsored a mission toward the Northwest Passage led by Thomas James, which departed on May 3. Two days later, Luke Foxe of Hull, with the financial backing of London's mercantile community and King Charles I, left from Deptford bound for the same waters. Though the two voyages traversed similar routes, they encountered each other only once. Foxe, who sailed to Hudson Bay and back again within a single season, explored its western shores and concluded that no opening to the passage could be found there. He never led his pinnace, called the *Charles,* into James Bay. Four years after his return, he published his account, *North-West Fox, or Fox from the North-west Passage,* and soon after the book's appearance he died poverty-stricken in England. He had managed to arrange for both a transatlantic crossing and the publication of a book, which required negotiations with a printer who needed to be convinced there would be an audience for it. But he fared less well financially, as was often the case with the large population of Englishmen who spent years at sea.

James decided to stay in the region until the following spring. Like Hudson, he had to winter in James Bay. Though he survived, some members of his crew perished during the months when they were waiting for the ice pack to release its hold on their ship. Unlike the *Discovery's* mutineers who had steered their ship directly toward home twenty years earlier, James turned westward in the summer of 1632 in a second attempt to find the way to the Pacific. He of course failed to find it, but he managed to guide the leaking 70-ton *Henrietta Maria* back to Bristol by late October. A year later, an enterprising

London publisher offered *The Strange and Dangerous Voyage of Captain Thomas James,* a book briefer than Foxe's but perhaps more successful at capturing the attention of the reading public. Unlike Foxe, James received acclaim after his return, perhaps because of the qualities he demonstrated in Canada during his journey, and became a commander of royal ships near Bristol. He died around 1635, though no record survives of the circumstances of his death and there is no indication of whether his ordeal in those frigid American waters had brought him more than a new title.

Foxe and James both looked for signs of Hudson and his men. Foxe, a historian of sorts who included details from earlier expeditions in his book, had studied the reports carried home by Hudson's crew and used this information to organize his own expedition. He stocked his 80-ton ship with enough food to last eighteen months, employing a baker, a butcher, and a brewer to prepare stores that held beef, beer, bread, ling (a fish typically salted or dried to preserve it), cheese, butter, peas, oatmeal, sugar, fruit, and rice, not to mention sack and aquavit. He had on board a well-supplied surgeon and a team of others who kept the *Charles* more shipshape than anything Hudson could have imagined. He also made his men swear an oath in which they promised not to disrupt the mission or to steal food from one another.

But no amount of preparation could guarantee that an English sailor could survive in these icy waters. Foxe might have known what to expect from his reading, which included tracts describing Frobisher's journeys, and he recognized the potential profits to be made along the way by harvesting whale oil, narwhal horns, and walrus tusks. Yet he looked in vain for any sign of the passage, and at one point declared that it simply could not exist along the west side of Hudson Bay between 55°10′N and 64°30′N, the territory he had explored that filled in the geographical gap between reports sent to London by Hudson and Button.

In June 1631, as they entered Hudson Bay, Foxe's men spotted smoke along the shoreline. As it turned out, they had found signs of James's crew. Several weeks later, Foxe's men found remnants of an earlier English expedition, which Foxe would recognize as refuse from Button's 1612–1613 journey. In late August, Foxe met James near Cape Henrietta Maria, but by then he had decided to sail homeward, disappointed and disconsolate. In his account of his explorations, he claimed that he had spent the previous five years without "Salary, wages or rewards." As he wrote in the margins of his book, he had "Laboured in vain."

That same August, James, who had taken along copies of the collections by Hakluyt and Purchas and was well informed about the challenges of the frozen north, decided that his men would spend the winter in the region. They sailed southward and on October 6 entered James Bay. Winter came on soon after. They posted a letter on a cross at Charlton Island, perhaps with the idea that even if they did not survive, someone else would eventually know what had happened to them. They had reached the same latitude as Hudson.

As James and his crew prepared for the imminent winter, he kept a close eye out for indications of Hudson. At one point, on Danby Island, his men found two stakes driven into the ground and the remains of an ancient fire. James pulled the stakes up. They were about the width of his arm, with a pointed end that seemed like it had been chopped by an iron tool, perhaps a hatchet, and then driven into the ground. James admitted that he could not determine why someone would drive stakes into the ground close to the water unless it was to serve as some kind of marker for boats—something that an Englishman might make but which would have been unlikely for indigenous use.

Finding the stakes made James eager to speak with some of the Crees, "for without doubt they could have given notice of some Christians, with whom they had some commerce."

James's find convinced him that some European had to have been there earlier—either to cut the stakes or to trade the tools to make them. It is possible that the stakes had been left by Hudson and the others on the shallop. Though he did not mention it as such, perhaps James had found evidence of Hudson's presence.

❧

Almost forty years after James spent the winter there, another English expedition traveled into Hudson Bay and then southward into James Bay. Like the crew of the *Discovery*, these men had to wait out the winter near the shores of the bay. A surviving account of their journey, left by a man named Thomas Gorst, suggests what an English crew living in that region would have experienced and possibly what had happened to Hudson.

Gorst was part of a two-ship expedition led by Zachariah Guillam (on the *Rupert*) and Robert Newland (on the *Wyvenhoe*) that set off from Ratcliffe on May 31, 1670, bound for Hudson Bay. In mid-August the *Rupert*, which numbered Gorst among its crew, sailed past Cape Wolstenholme and Digges Island. At some unspecified point the two ships parted company, though with plans to regroup later. By the end of that month, Gorst reported that the *Rupert* was near Point Comfort and reckoned they had sailed 2,930 miles since the Scilly Islands. They docked nearby and immediately hunted fowl, harvesting a bounty among the migrating birds that were near the end of their breeding season. The next morning, two of the locals, who apparently were already known to the ships' captains, came to visit. A day later, the English received six canoe loads of women, men, and children. Gorst did not mention whether the Americans traded with the English.

By the second week of September, the English had begun their preparations for the long winter ahead. They sailed up the Rupert River and anchored in front of the newly constructed Charles Fort. On the eighth, a hunting party brought back eight geese. One of the locals raced into the woods to tell his fellow hunters about the arrival of the English. The crew members unloaded their goods onto the shore and continued to hunt, taking twenty-seven more geese on September 10. They brought in birds as long as they could. The ship's carpenter busily cut wood to build a house for the officers. At that moment, a group of Americans, presumably Crees, arrived, eager to trade.

While the English were building their winter houses, the Crees were also busy establishing lodges. The English were gathering thatch for their roofs, but Gorst was more interested in what the locals were doing. "The Indians set up their Wigwams or Huts which is almost in the manner of a Tent," he wrote in his journal, adding that they covered the frames with the skins of moose and deer and left a hole at the top to vent smoke from their fires. He noted that they made beds out of spruce and pine boughs, which resembled English ferns, and that they used their beaver coats for blankets and even rugs. He described some of the tents as holding as many as sixteen men, women, and children. The arrangement reminded Gorst of the way the Irish lived, except that the Americans lacked hogs and cattle, "although indeed these poor wretches are scarce fit for any better society."

Gorst reflected the prejudices of his times with such comments, but he was also an astute observer of how the Crees lived. He wrote that in late September some of them brought back fish that were 6 feet long and looked like pikes. "There is also fresh Sturgeon very good & Salmon trout plenty enough," he added. Despite the fresh fish, the Americans mostly ate dried beaver and moose meat. They had no bread, but they knew how to extract much from the body of any animal. "The bones of those beasts they use to bruise & boil & the fat arising thence they skim off & keep like butter, which they call cockamo," to be used as a sauce. In previous years they had used the skins of these animals as receptacles for cooking their meat, Gorst noted, "but now they find the better convenience of our English kettles."

Still, the Americans did not need imported goods to get by. Gorst wrote that they wove birch bark so well that it could hold water "as well as our wooden platters." He scorned the fact that they sat on the ground to eat and used their own bodies "for napkins, which are so much more beautiful by how much they are the more greasy." Gorst was fascinated with the grease the Crees spread on their bodies. He believed that they were "borne as white as the English but with grease & paint they spoil their Skins & make themselves look very deformed." That comment put Gorst squarely in a European aesthetic tradition that dated back to the early sixteenth century when Amerigo Vespucci noted that Tupinambas in Brazil destroyed their appearance with paint and piercings.

The Crees' encampment did not last long. When the weather turned colder they dispersed to pursue deer, birds, and the occasional hare. This seasonal migration was not surprising. In eastern North America, native peoples who lived far enough south to rely on farming often remained in the same area during the entire year. But farther north, where indigenous communities needed to rely on what they could capture during the winter hunt, they typically broke up into small, family-based groups. The fact that the Crees visited the English periodically and brought the newcomers meat suggests that relations between them remained positive and that the Americans either did not travel far away or made periodic journeys to their autumn camps.

But it was not only the locals who caught Gorst's attention. He also described how the English managed to cope with the winter. They built a series of houses, and they dug cellars for their beer, pork, beef, and butter. They erected rooms that they managed to keep dry enough to store flour, bread, oatmeal, and peas. The houses "are built of Timber," he noted, "cut into Spars set quite close to one another & caulked with Moss instead of Okam to keep out the wind and the weather." They used marsh grasses for their thatched roofs. They had brought enough bricks with them to make a chimney, but there was no need to haul wood to their settlement, "that Country affording enough to keep always Summer within, while nothing but Ice & snow are without doors." The men also built an oven and used it to cook their venison.

By mid-October, with winter now fast approaching, the English sent a team into the forest to gather wood to last several months. When a small party tried to row out to the *Wyvenhoe* on October 13, they had to push through a wind so bitter that ice formed on their oars even while they were rowing. Within ten days, the desire to make even such a short venture had considerably diminished. A snowstorm starting on October 22 left 4 feet of snow on the ground.

The *Wyvenhoe* had struck rocks after parting from the *Rupert* and straggled to the settlement only on October 12. By the time the men from the *Wyvenhoe* arrived, two of their crew members had died, and Captain Newland would succumb two days later. His crew had a chance to purchase his belongings ten days afterward, but that would have been small solace to men who arrived too late to build sturdy houses for winter and who instead set up what Gorst referred to as a "wigwam," covering it with old sails.

As the men on the expeditions led by Hudson and James had discovered earlier, the winters near James Bay presented a series of challenges. By November 20, Gorst wrote, the Rupert River had frozen over even in the stretch where it was a mile and a half wide. The English were frozen in, but the conditions did not deter the Crees, who continued to hunt deer. They brought venison to the English to trade for the peas they adored—though they despised the sailors' salted beef and pork. In mid-December, the English managed to kill several foxes, and on Christmas they celebrated and thought of home, drinking strong beer and brandy and feasting on venison and partridge, both obtained locally, along with what they had stored in their ships. One man later became ill with scurvy, which

Gorst believed was the only serious disease the English risked, but he soon recovered.

Winter began to ease its icy grip by late March. By then one of the Englishmen had surveyed the nearby forests and re-ported that he had found tall spruce and pine trees with cir-cumferences of up to 5 feet that would make perfect masts. Anyone who read that report would have known that American forests were much more capable of providing naval stores, espe-cially masts, than English woods at the same time, a fact that had proved crucial to the development of the New England economy. By the end of March, the ground had thawed. The English immediately sowed mustard seed and peas, which, Gorst reported, "came up well enough for the time we stayed there & no doubt but all sorts of roots would have grown very well if We had been furnished with seed." The English hogs and chickens, which had survived the winter, flourished with the new season.

April brought even better news. The geese that had mi-grated southward now returned in large flocks and remained in the region until the beginning of June, when they took flight again, destined for their hatcheries even farther north. By mid-May, Gorst complained that the weather had become hot, which also roused the local mosquitoes. Even then, vestiges of winter remained. It was not until May 22 that the river finally shed its last ice floes. Soon after, the English realized it was time to head home.

Setting off from Charles Fort at the end of June, the En-glish sailed toward Point Comfort. There they went ashore to chop wood for the homeward voyage. They presumably gath-ered food, too, though Gorst neglected to mention it, noting only that he and the other English "prepared for our return homewards."

As men gathered supplies, Gorst and a few others boarded a shallop and set out to explore the local area. They paddled out to a nearby island. There, Gorst wrote, "we found an old wigwam not built by Indians, but suppose it rather to be the place where poor Hudson ended his days." Gorst wrote no more about what he saw on the island. On another nearby island they found signs of another English winter camp. They found bones, possibly the remains of men who had died on James's expedition, though perhaps they had stumbled on remains from Hudson's party.

Gorst provided no other details about what he saw on the edges of James Bay. But another member of the expedition would write a note on the back of the last page of Gorst's journal. There, a man named Paul Mercer added a very brief history of what happened to the *Wyvenhoe* after it had parted from the *Rupert*. In addition to the sketch of its troubled journey toward Port Nelson, he provided details about the environment, saying that the English saw excellent supplies of timber and fine marshes. There they found a former Cree settlement, with the "remains of some of the Natives Wigwams & Sweating houses & some pieces of dressed Beaver skins." They guessed that the locals had only recently left, though the English did not understand why. "There is no want of food" there, Mercer noted, adding that they discovered large numbers of deer, rabbits, and fowl along with strawberries, currants, huckleberries, gooseberries, and cranberries.

Stakes driven in the ground, a house built by nonnative peoples, an environment capable of supporting newcomers if they were willing to engage in trade with the locals, an abundance of seasonal birds and fish, summer grasses that could ward off scurvy, forests providing ample supplies for a dwelling, animals whose skins could be used to provide shelter—each may provide a clue about Hudson's ultimate fate.

The report by Gorst and the brief note by Mercer reveal that this territory, even during the winter, was capable of sustaining an English community, as the men on both the Hudson and the James expeditions knew. Neither Gorst nor Mercer spoke of tense relations with the Crees. Each noted the presence of wild foods and animals that could provide sufficient nourishment to supplement any foods that the Americans were willing to trade.

Gorst had written that the island, easily reachable by a shallop, was apparently the final home for Hudson and his companions. If this is so, the tides Hudson had studied at least since 1607 had driven him to the end of his days. But though his life apparently ended in James Bay, his efforts proved crucial for the English state, especially its desire to lay claim to Canada. In May 1687, representatives of King James II informed a group of French commissioners that it was England that owned the "Northern parts of America." They based their claim on the discoveries of Sebastian Cabot in 1497 and, more centrally, of Hudson (and those who followed him). In 1610, as they reminded the French, Hudson had sailed through the strait and into the bay that bore his name, and "took possession thereof, giving names to several places therein by which they have been since call'd and known in the Maps of those parts as well Foreign as English." The French disputed the assertion, arguing that Samuel Champlain had in fact laid claim to all of Canada. But Hudson's careful record of naming places for those he wanted to honor, notably the royal family and his financial supporters, paid enormous dividends. In death, his explorations would provide his country not with the vaunted passage to the east, but something of even more enduring value and significance—lands, bays, and rivers whose fortunes and history would forever link one hemisphere to the other.

❧

So what happened to Henry Hudson and the others on the shallop? Hudson knew enough not to try to sail back to England in a small open boat. Such a journey would have been doomed from the start. Of course, the late summer swarm of mosquitoes and stinging green flies might have driven even sane men to seek extravagant escapes from the torment.

In all likelihood, after failing to catch up to the fast-escaping *Discovery*, the men paddled their shallow craft to a nearby island, quite possibly the one that Thomas Gorst explored six decades later. In June, this island would have shed its winter ice and sprouted cockle and other fast-growing summer plants that could have provided at least some nutrition for hungry humans. Philip Staffe would have built a winter shelter from driftwood and trees, and any able-bodied men would have gathered firewood for the approaching winter. They had ample opportunity to hunt ptarmigan, geese, thick-billed murres, and other migratory birds, which had arrived by the thousands to breed in the brief Arctic summer. The stranded men might also have rigged up seines to drop from the shallop into shallow water, enabling them to gather a plentiful harvest of fish if schools were nearby. This was hardly a certainty, though, given the crew's earlier mixed record hauling in a catch.

Hudson—strong-willed and, as he showed in 1609, at times bellicose—would have realized that he and his men had only two chances for survival and eventual rescue. First, they had to keep a keen eye out for another English vessel looking either for them or for the Northwest Passage. If they survived long enough to signal a passing ship, they would be saved. Hudson could return to London, challenge the crew that had cast him out, win retribution and justice, and maybe even continue his explorations, in spite of the humiliation of losing control of his own ship. Or perhaps, he may have mused, another ship seeking the Northwest Passage would take him and his men along to East Asia. Either way, Hudson knew that a rescue could only take place if they kept guard near the shore.

Hudson's second option was to seek out locals and beg for shelter, food, and protection. Hudson had looked for Crees earlier in his journey, but without luck. Maybe in the perpetual daylight of another summer he could do better. The men had the carpenter's tools with them, which would have tempted Inuit or Crees. Hudson would have known that he would benefit from the Crees' advice about the land and their knowledge of how to take advantage of its resources.

Over the course of the summer, the men could have learned from the locals and built a storehouse for birds, especially those taken in the autumn after the heat had ebbed and the mosquitoes and blood-sucking flies had vanished. They could have fished into the autumn, strengthening themselves with fresh supplies of protein in preparation for the approaching winter. When the first thin layers of ice began to form on the rocks along the shore, they might have been just as prepared as they had been the previous winter, when only one of the men had perished.

But the coming winter would be cruel. Hudson and his men were more exposed and isolated than they had been the previous year. Without English rescuers or help from the Crees they were lost. Hudson and his men probably died on that island during the winter of 1611–1612. Perhaps their desperation drove them to attempt a voyage homeward on the shallop. If so, the fierce storms in the region could have capsized even skilled seamen, erasing any sign of them.

They probably died one after another, succumbing to a brutal chill that never ceased to freeze their bodies. Or scurvy could have killed them if they had failed to lay in enough cockle grass to ward it off. If they fell victim to the disease, their gums would have bled, their teeth might eventually have fallen out, and any bones broken earlier could have fractured again; the men would have become dehydrated from diarrhea, sunk into depression, and eventually expired. Some might have suffered frostbite, leading to gangrene and death. If they chose to burn sea coal, which could have washed up on the shore and was a common source of heat in this era when wood was not available, they might have died of carbon monoxide poisoning, a fate that possibly befell an earlier shipload of English men sailing in search of the Northeast Passage in 1553. Animal attacks, especially by polar bears or wolves, could also have taken them.

At first, the ill or injured could have been tended by those who remained healthy. But eventually, the men still able to nurse others also would have grown so weak that they could do no more than haul the corpses of their companions into the snow. If they lacked the strength to bury the dead, they could have put off the task until the next summer's thaw. One can imagine the bodies dragged out of the hut, their clothes increasingly shredded by wind. Eventually, scavenging bears, wolves, and foxes would have gnawed off the frozen flesh, ultimately obliterating any sign of the men's existence. By the time other English sailors happened by twenty or even sixty years later, nothing was left of Hudson's party but the most meager markings of remarkable lives—sharpened stakes, a ruined shelter.

The mystery of what happened to Hudson and his men became the stuff of legend. One tale claimed that Hudson survived and several years later carved his initials in a rock, which a road crew unearthed in Deep River, Ontario, in 1960. Another told how the Crees adopted Hudson's son. In the small settlement of Wemindji at the mouth of the Maquatua River in northern Quebec, the keepers of oral history reported that a place called Waamistikushiish in the Paint Hills area of James Bay meant "young Englishman"—possibly after John Hudson or his father—and referred to someone who had been buried there long ago. But a recent expedition to find a purported grave proved fruitless. One legend purports that John Hudson trudged southward, where he found Samuel Champlain, who was in the process of establishing New France, but there is no evidence to support it. An examination of a famous 1823 English expedition to the eastern shores of Greenland suggested that a body found there could have been that of one of the men on the shallop— if this man made the rather unlikely trip east hundreds of miles, or his remains drifted there with polar tides.

After Hudson's disappearance, the Canadian Arctic and Hudson Bay continued to lure the English and other Europeans. Two generations after the mutiny on the *Discovery,* the

Hudson's Bay Company established a storehouse along the shores of James Bay. The company men recognized that the area was an ideal staging ground for a trade that would eventually transport hundreds of thousands of furs to eager European customers. Unlike Hudson himself, those traders managed to build ties with northern peoples who brought furs in exchange for European goods such as metal tools, blankets, and alcohol. The success of the Hudson's Bay Company also proved that it was possible for the English to survive in territory much colder than anything they had ever experienced at home. Hudson's Bay Company traders went to Canada with the purpose of establishing permanent residences capable of withstanding the skin- and eye-freezing cold of a James Bay winter. Archaeologists have found traces of the company's early buildings from the 1670s, but nothing that can be attributed to the presence of Hudson and the other men on the shallop.

By the time the Hudson's Bay Company began to control the edges of this vast inland sea, the English had resigned themselves to the fact that they might never find the Northwest Passage. That recognition represented a dramatic shift in English thought about Arctic geography. Even in the early 1620s, after Baffin and others had failed to find the fabled route, English scholars had not yet abandoned hope. The mathematician Henry Briggs, for example, argued in 1622 that rivers somewhere north of Virginia ran into the South Sea and possibly connected with the enormous bay that Hudson had found. Samuel Purchas, the man most responsible for keeping the narratives of Hudson's journeys in circulation, included a map of the Americas in his 1625 edition with the note that one way to the South Sea might be via Hudson Strait and Baffin Bay. The passage did not, he noted, run via Hudson Bay. But none of the texts in his collection offered any proof that the passage could actually be accomplished.

But soon the consensus shifted. In an undated manuscript, Admiral William Monson, who died in 1643, wrote that Hudson's last journey was the most important of any that the English had undertaken to that point. Not content only to read about Hudson's expedition, he interviewed none other than Robert Bylot, the master of the *Discovery* upon its return. Monson reported that Bylot confirmed the findings of other authorities. The Northwest Passage might exist, and it could be a shorter route to East Asia. But the passage would be of little use to English traders "because of the hazard of cold, of ice, and of unknown seas which experience must teach us." Monson wondered if it might be possible to reach the Pacific via a more northerly route, or even directly across the North Pole, a journey that, by his calculations, put the distance from England to East Asia at a mere 1,500 leagues. Even if such a mission failed, those on board could then steer toward the English colony in Newfoundland, where they could purchase fish to trade in the Mediterranean, thus earning back the cost of their effort. But Monson concluded that he could not endorse any further efforts to follow Hudson's route of 1610–1611.

Monson was not the only one in England who found no point in following Hudson's route. By the early 1630s, the Cambridge-based geographer William Watts had concluded that the Spanish had fooled the English with their claims of a Northwest Passage. Watts sarcastically suggested that the Philosopher's Stone, the magical substance long sought by alchemists to turn base metals into gold, could probably be found in the Northwest Passage, too. Watts's speculation could charitably be seen as an effort to instruct Cambridge students about the limits of what Aristotle and the ancients knew about the parts of the world that they never saw. After all, as he pointed out, Charlton Island, where James had wintered, was at almost the exact same latitude as Cambridge itself, yet it was a place "so unsufferably cold, that it is not habitable." But there was no escaping the cynicism and mockery in his dismissal of the possibility of the passage.

The mariner Monson and the scholar Watts understood that Arctic navigations posed challenges that sailors of temperate climes never encountered. The cold was inescapable. As one nineteenth-century physician who visited the Arctic wrote, the climate there "is almost always wintry," and during the frozen months "no one dare venture out, without running great risk of their lives." Over time, those who traveled northward recognized that the climate required humans to find new ways to survive. "When a man journeys into a far country," the American novelist Jack London wrote in 1899, "he must be prepared to forget many of the things he has learned, and to acquire such customs as are inherent with existence in the new land."

Hudson's prior experiences had taught him that Arctic ventures could be difficult, but there is no evidence that he adapted to the challenges of the American environment and the novel stresses suffered by his crew. He thought he knew the risks posed by long-distance travel. Hakluyt had warned of the dangers of the "devouring sea," and pamphleteers had cautioned that Barbary pirates sometimes sold Christian sailors into slavery. He no doubt prepared his ship and his crew to face such dangers, equipping the men with the weapons, tools, and supplies necessary to survive. Yet Hudson was one among the many travelers in this age of discovery who never made it home.

The Europeans who established a secure foothold in the Americas in the sixteenth and early seventeenth centuries tended to have certain advantages over the peoples they met. They had guns and lethal microbes to which native peoples had no immunity. Across much of the Western Hemisphere, the earliest meetings between Europeans and Americans led to devastating epidemics, especially of smallpox, and frequent warfare. Newcomers to the temperate zones in the Americas often survived by pushing indigenous peoples out of their way.

The logic for survival in the Arctic was different. Europeans here needed healthy locals to help them survive. If the newcomers were to extract resources from these northern climes, or (as Hudson had hoped) find a passage to the more temperate waters of the Pacific, they needed to establish lasting ties to the Crees and the Inuit who had learned how to succeed in a land that posed so many challenges.

In the end, as the Arctic autumn gave way to another vicious winter, Henry Hudson could not will his way toward safety. He was a master in northern waters, but not a skilled negotiator on land. It is unlikely that he ever absorbed the lesson that Jack London learned almost 300 years later. Hudson did not change his ways. He could get to the Arctic, but he could not live there, he could not find a way to the Pacific, and he was unwilling to abandon his goal so he could return home. Unlike the Crees of James Bay or the Inuit of Hudson Bay, Hudson could not adapt to the far north. His resolute character had once attracted merchant investors and no doubt also pleased a monarch eager to find new routes to great wealth for the realm. But the corollary of devotion is stubbornness, a trait that doomed Hudson on board the *Discovery* in June 1611. Without assistance from locals, Hudson's chances for survival disappeared when the *Discovery* sailed away.

According to the High Court of Admiralty, the uprising on board the *Discovery* led to the murder of Henry Hudson. No one who survived the journey was ever convicted of the crime. Those seven men and one boy proved more adaptable than the master of the *Discovery*, who in the end almost certainly succumbed in a frozen land that remained beyond English control.

A generation after Hudson's disappearance, a French scholar compared the English captain to the ancient Greek figure of Icarus, who had fashioned wax and feather wings so he could fly. But Icarus flew too close to the sun and plummeted to the sea as the heat melted the wax. No one knew for sure what had happened to Hudson, the Frenchman wrote, but, like Icarus, he succumbed to his ego and went into unknown territory. Hudson left behind few clues about his fate. He never found the Northwest Passage. Today his name marks a strait, a bay, and the river he explored. These are the principal memorials to a man whose ambition ended in the nightmare of betrayal and a lonely death in a windswept Arctic bay.

# Note on Sources

"There is no sea with which our age is so imperfectly acquainted as the Frozen Ocean." That sentiment could have come from any number of those who over the years tried to figure out what happened to Henry Hudson and the others on the shallop set adrift in James Bay in June 1611. But in fact it came from an early nineteenth-century English translation of Gawrila Sarytschew's account of a journey toward Hudson's 1608 destination—the frigid seas north of Siberia. Two hundred years after the mutineers abandoned Hudson in James Bay, northern waters continued to fascinate European observers. But even then, investigating these remote places remained a challenging, if not impossible task.

Sarytschew's problem—how to find a way across this icy region that seemingly defied European understanding and ability—resembles a historian's effort to find out what happened to Hudson. Was he murdered, as the High Court of Admiralty ultimately suspected when it charged four of the survivors in London in 1618? There is in the end no way to know. Samuel Purchas's edition of Abacuk Pricket's self-serving journal of the voyage remains the most comprehensive account of what occurred. But even this text is far from ideal, since it is possible, even if unlikely, that Purchas made alterations in it before printing it in 1625. There is no surviving manuscript copy of any of the documents from James Bay—not Hudson's abbreviated journal, not Wydowse's note, and not Pricket's narrative. But the printed text—when combined with the surviving depositions given to the masters of Trinity House in 1611 and the later depositions from the murder trial at the High Court of Admiralty, and read in the light of other narratives produced by Hudson or other travelers to North America in the early decades of the seventeenth century—does convey the most likely scenario of what happened during the mutiny. We can never forget that Pricket remained under suspicion for the mutiny and murder at least until he and the others were exonerated in 1618. But we also need to bear in mind that Purchas, having learned from Hakluyt that the best way to promote the nation's interest was to reprint travel accounts as he found them, in all likelihood wanted to provide all of the available evidence. He found Pricket a reliable authority.

Hudson himself left only tantalizing clues about what occurred on the *Discovery* in its last months. The surviving fragment of his last journal, at least as it was published by Purchas, ends on August 3, 1610—over ten months before the mutiny. It is likely that a longer version had come to England and been seen by the explorers Robert Fotherby and Thomas Edge; Purchas included brief details suggesting that these men had seen more than the abstract of the journal. That abstract, limited as it is, is closer to a master's log than a full account of a journey. In this sense it resembles the other materials from Hudson, who was a better master of northern waters than he was of quill, ink, and paper. Hudson, like many other mariners, was a man trained to navigate ships across ice-strewn waters and, if possible, to record what he saw and thus add to the stock of European knowledge about the north and to merchants' hopes for a passage to the East Indies. Few of those who went to sea in this era would have seen themselves as members of a literary—or even, in some cases, a literate— society. As Luke Foxe, another ship master who sailed into Hudson Bay, wrote in the mid-1630s, "they breed no Scholars" in "the North-wests cold Clime." Hudson spent more time recording latitude than he did regarding what was happening on his own ships. His inability to tell a riveting tale hardly set him apart from his peers. As one nineteenth-century historian put it in a summary of the primary record for Hudson's third journey, Juet's account "is very long, and very uninteresting, at least in so far as it relates to northern discovery."

The historical question—What happened to Hudson?—is easy to ask and difficult to answer. If, as scholars have long recognized, Pricket's narrative is suspect "from his connection with the mutineers, and his being permitted to remain with them in the ship," as the nautical historian John Barrow put it two centuries later, how much can anyone expect to learn from it? Contemporaries had their doubts, too, including Luke Foxe: "Well, Pricket," he wrote in 1635, "I am in great doubt of thy fidelity to Master Hudson." Even Purchas, who was most responsible for preserving information about the expedition, realized that some readers might not believe Pricket's account, since he had "returned with that Company, which had so cruelly exposed Hudson."

But there are clues in Pricket's journal suggesting that his observations were often quite accurate. Every chronicler would have emphasized the ubiquity of the ice and the dangers that it posed to wooden-hulled ships. All would have reported the fogs that are so common across the Arctic, as Hudson himself had noted on his previous journeys. Yet there are specifics in Pricket's account that reveal him to be astute. He wrote, for example, that ice formed in James Bay by November, which corresponds to modern weather patterns and is similar to Gorst's assessment of the region in 1670. Pricket described abundant flocks of birds in places such as Digges Cape, where hundreds of thousands of fowl, such as thick-billed murres, arrive each year to breed.

Pricket also wrote about the ways that the English and the Cree man, in one pivotal moment, and the Inuit, in another, communicated with each other through signs. Though it is possible that he or Purchas added those details based on the reports of earlier travelers (such as those associated with the Frobisher voyages) who emphasized the importance of such signals, it is more likely that he had observed the ways that Europeans and Americans interacted before they developed a common stock of words and phrases. Acquiring such phrases was crucial at the time; one of Hakluyt's last efforts was to translate a phrasebook allowing Anglophone travelers to speak Malay when they got to the Spice Islands. But there had been no known travel between Europe and this part of the American interior earlier, and so there had been no opportunity to develop the linguistic tool kit that could have helped Hudson and his men speak to the natives they met. Preliminary grammars had begun to appear in English-language books, such as a 1580 translation of accounts from Jacques Cartier's journeys of the 1530s. But it was not until the 1630s that more substantial grammars, such as the one included in William Wood's *New England's Prospect* (London, 1634), began to give English travelers to the northern parts of North America any sense of how to speak to the indigenous peoples they met.

Even more important, there is little in the testimonies gathered after the return of the *Discovery* that contradicts Pricket's account. It is of course possible that the men had ample time to collude and get their stories straight, especially before the murder trial at the High Court of Admiralty. But the inquiry at Trinity House took place soon after the ship's return, and the surviving records do not suggest that the masters believed the men were lying. Samuel Purchas, who had a habit of rewriting travelers' accounts in the first three editions of his collection (published between 1613 and 1617), seems to have made minimal interventions in Pricket's journal, which he published in 1625.

Still, Pricket's report only goes as far as many other travelers' accounts. As such, it can tell only part of the story of Hudson's last expedition. The rest of the story derives from other documents from the time, notably the records of the inquiries at Trinity House and the High Court of Admiralty, reports from other explorers who sailed into Hudson and James bays, and the abundant writings of chroniclers who recognized that the potential opening of direct ties to the Spice Islands would change everyday life in England. To understand not only where Hudson went but what motivated him requires an understanding of his contemporaries. Among them were those who identified the marvelous virtues of domestic and exotic plants—including spices from the East Indies—such as John Gerard and William Langham. Hudson knew mapmakers, too, including Petrus

Plancius, who kept abreast of geographical knowledge in Amsterdam, which was at the time the most important city in Western Europe for cartographic information. Hudson knew Captain John Smith and learned from him that Native Americans claimed there was a water route north of Virginia that led through the interior of North America to the west, which Smith and Hudson believed had to have meant the South Sea. Hudson quite likely was also acquainted with Richard Hakluyt, which would have given the explorer exposure to the man in England most knowledgeable about the Western Hemisphere and the experiences of other travelers. Perhaps it was Hakluyt, who had long argued for the importance of establishing mathematics as a tool for navigation, who suggested that Hudson hire the mathematician Thomas Wydowse. Through Hakluyt, Hudson would have learned about those who had sailed through the North Atlantic and returned, such as Martin Frobisher and John Davis, and those who had perished, such as Sir Humphrey Gilbert. Perhaps most significantly, Hudson had close contact with Sir Thomas Smythe, Dudley Digges, and John Wolstenholme. These men raised the funds needed to outfit the *Discovery* for its journey and also advocated for the importance of the venture at the royal court.

English records from the late sixteenth and early seventeenth centuries often provide details about some of the most prominent people in the nation, but those documents typically tell us less about others. Hudson, after all, had two groups central to his life: his family, and the men who took positions on the ships that he commanded. The documentary record is almost silent about his family, and there are precious few records about the men who went along with him on his major expeditions. Pricket and Bylot joined voyages back to Hudson Bay in the years after 1611, and so can be located in documents of the period. But none of the others left much of a mark, other than Robert Juet with his journal of Hudson's voyage of 1609. Nor are there any surviving written records of the individuals Hudson met in Canada, notably the Cree man, beyond what Pricket recorded. Cree oral history supports Pricket's story, except that the Crees believe that two of their ancestors met the English, not one. Could Pricket have gotten that detail incorrect? Was it possible that two Crees saw *Discovery* but that only one man approached its crew? There is no way to know for sure.

But the absence of certainty does not in itself reduce what we can reconstruct about the experience of the men on the *Discovery* and eventually those on the shallop. Ample sources exist to explain Hudson's motivations and describe the stock of knowledge he carried. Pricket might have embellished his tale, but he did not invent the blood on the decks of the *Discovery*, nor did he write the note hidden in the mathematician's desk. The records from Trinity House and the High Court of Admiralty are less than thorough, but they reveal real interrogations that took place in the metropolis at the heart of a growing maritime power. Hudson's travels made him famous. So did his death, which elicited more commentary than the lives of almost all of his contemporaries.

❧

The notes that follow contain a number of references to scientific studies, which provide confirming evidence for the documentary record. There are also many references to the writings of Hudson's contemporaries, including the most important authorities on English expeditions to the north—William Baffin, Thomas James, and Luke Foxe. Biographical information for Hudson's more famous contemporaries, including his patrons and other prominent explorers, can be found in *The Oxford Dictionary of National Biography,* the *Dictionary of Canadian Biography,* and the *Dictionary of American Biography.* Basic information about ships and shipping can be found in Peter Kemp, ed., *The Oxford Companion to Ships and the Sea* (Oxford: Oxford University Press, 1976), and in Ian Friel, *The Good Ship: Ships, Shipbuilding, and Technology in England, 1200–1520* (Baltimore: Johns Hopkins University Press, 1995). An enumeration of the size of many English ships in this period can be found in R. G. Marsden, "English Ships in the Reign of James I," *Transactions of the Royal Historical Society,* New Series 19 (1905), 309–342. The best starting point for contemporary understanding of navigation is E. G. R. Taylor, *The Haven-Finding Art: A History of Navigation from Odysseus to Captain Cook* (London: Hollis and Carter, 1956).

As Hudson realized, the Arctic posed innumerable challenges to anyone who hoped to sail into it or find a passage through it. Fortunately, it has also attracted the attention of gifted writers, whose books and articles provide details about natural conditions there. Though global warming has changed the Arctic Ocean and decreased the amount of ice in the region, modern writers and photographers have nonetheless depicted the region's fierce climate and natural beauty. This contemporary literature helps to explain the historical documents, which are also abundant, both for the English experience and for continental Europeans, notably the Dutch. The most important sixteenth- and seventeenth-century English sources can be found in Richard Hakluyt, *Principall Voiages, Navigations, and Discoveries of the English Nation* (London, 1589), and his expanded *Principal Voyages, Navigations, Traffiques, and Discoveries of the English Nation,* 3 vols. (London, 1598–1600), which reprinted the crucial narratives relating to Sir Martin Frobisher, among others; and especially in Samuel Purchas, *Purchas his Pilgrimes,* 4 vols. (London, 1625), especially volume 3—which includes all of the surviving narratives for Hudson's four journeys in addition to reports about or by Hugh Willoughby, Richard Chancellor, Willem Barentsz, Robert Fotherby, and William Baffin. The earlier editions of Purchas's collections of travel, published in 1613, 1614, and 1617, are not reliable accounts of Arctic journeys because Purchas rewrote those texts; the 1625 edition, by contrast, follows Hakluyt's model of reprinting texts, presumably accurately—though the absence of manuscripts for most of these accounts makes it often impossible to know what liberties early modern editors took with their materials. Published travel narratives also have to be understood as a genre in which authors and editors normally conformed to certain expectations and in which texts quite often changed from one edition to another, as was the case with Purchas's works. For the larger context, see Peter C. Mancall, ed., *Travel Narratives from the Age of Discovery* (New York: Oxford University Press, 2006).

Arctic exploration fascinated nineteenth-century Europeans, some of whom went into northern climates on expeditions, and many of whom had access to printed materials, including reprints of sixteenth- and seventeenth-century accounts as well as contemporary reports. The Hakluyt Society, founded in 1846 to promote knowledge about earlier English expeditions abroad, played a crucial role in keeping early narratives in circulation. Those interested in Arctic explorations should consult Thomas Rundall, ed., *Narratives of Voyages towards the North-West, in Search of a Passage to Cathay and India, 1496 to 1631,* Hakluyt Society 1st Series 5 (London, 1849); Georg Michael Asher, ed., *Henry Hudson the Navigator,* Hakluyt Society 1st Series 27 (London, 1860); Charles T. Beke, ed., *The Three Voyages of William Barents to the Arctic Regions, 1594, 1595, and 1596, by Gerrit de Veer,* Hakluyt Society 1st Series 13 (London, 1853); Clements Markham, ed., *The Voyages of Sir James Lancaster, Kt., to the East Indies,* Hakluyt Society 1st Series 56 (London, 1877); C. C. A. Gosch, ed., *Danish Arctic Expeditions, 1605 to 1620,* 2 vols., Hakluyt Society 1st Series 96–97 (London, 1897); and Miller Christy, ed., *The Voyages of Captain Luke Foxe of Hull, and Captain Thomas James, of Bristol,* 2 vols., Hakluyt Society 1st Series 88–89 (London, 1894). Readers who want to understand how earlier Europeans understood their encounters in the North Atlantic should consult Robert Kellogg, ed., *The Sagas of the Icelanders* (New York: Viking, 2001), and Magnus Magnusson and Hermann Palsson, eds., *The Vinland Sagas: The Norse Discovery of America* (New York: Penguin, 1965).

For the best sources on the weather of James Bay and Hudson Bay, and how people understood it in Hudson's age, see *The Strange and Dangerous Voyage of Captain Thomas James* (London, 1633); Robert Boyle, *New Experiments and Observations touching Cold, or an Experimental History of*

*Cold* (London, 1665); and E. E. Rich, ed., *James Isham's Observations on Hudsons Bay, 1743,* Hudson's Bay Company Series 12 (Toronto: Champlain Society, 1949).

The two interrogations or trials—in front of the masters of Trinity House and the High Court of Admiralty—took place within institutions that had their own historians. These works provide the context for understanding the actions (or inactions) of these authorities relating to the survivors of the *Discovery*. For Trinity House, see Trinity House Transactions, vol. 1 (1609–1625), Guildhall Library, Ms. 30045/1. These records can also be found in an abstracted form as "The Manuscripts of the Corporation of the Trinity House, Deptford-Le-Strond, at Tower Hill, London," in *Eighth Report of the Royal Commission on Historical Manuscripts. Report and Appendix (Part I)* (London, 1881), and in more complete form in Miller Christy, ed., *The Voyages of Captain Luke Foxe of Hull, and Captain Thomas James of Bristol* (London, 1894) 2:626–634. The surviving records from the High Court of Admiralty testimony and trial can be found in the National Archives of Britain (formerly the Public Record Office) as HCA 1/48, f. 118–121, f. 127, f. 130, and f. 135$^v$–136$^r$ (depositions) and HCA 1/6, f. 88, 90, 133 and HCA 1/7 f. 2 (trial records). These records are printed in Llewelyn Powys, *Henry Hudson* (London: John Lane, 1927), 190–198. For other works on these institutions, see G. G. Harris, ed., *Trinity House of Deptford Transactions, 1609–35,* London Record Society 19 (1983); and Alwyn A. Ruddock, "The Trinity House at Deptford in the Sixteenth Century," *English Historical Review* 65 (1950), 458–476. For the High Court of Admiralty, see Evelyn Berckman, *Victims of Piracy: The Admiralty Court, 1575–1678* (London: H. Hamilton, 1979), and Charles S. Cumming, "The English High Court of Admiralty," *Tulane Maritime Law Journal* 17 (1992–1993), 209–255.

The literature on Hudson himself is voluminous, if somewhat repetitive. Still, reading through these works one can sense how discussion of him has changed from 1860, when Asher put together his collection for the Hakluyt Society, to the present. The most prominent works, listed in chronological order, are: John M. Read, *A Historical inquiry concerning Henry Hudson, his friends, relatives, and early life* (Albany, 1866); B. F. de Costa, *Sailing Directions of Henry Hudson* (Albany, 1869); Thomas Janvier, *Henry Hudson: A Brief Statement of His Aims and Achievements* (New York, 1909); Henry C. Murphy, *Henry Hudson in Holland* (The Hague, 1909); Lleweln Powys, *Henry Hudson* (London: John Lane, 1927); Milton Hamilton, *Henry Hudson and the Dutch in New York* (Albany: University of the State of New York, 1959); Julian Wolfenstein, "Mutiny on the *Discovery*," *de Halve Maen* 40, no. 2 (1965), 9–10; Linden Lundstrom, *The Bay*

*Where Hudson Did Winter* (Minneapolis: James Bell Ford Library, 1980); Philip Edwards, ed., *Last Voyages: Cavendish, Hudson, Ralegh: The Original Narratives* (Oxford: Oxford University Press, 1988); Lawrence Millman, "Looking for Henry Hudson," *Smithsonian* 30, no. 7 (1999), 100–108; and Carl Schuster, "Into the Great Bay: Henry Hudson's Mysterious Final Voyage," *The Beaver* 79, no. 4 (1999), 8–15. Recent works by Donald Johnson (*Charting the Sea of Darkness: The Four Voyages of Henry Hudson* [Camden, Maine: International Marine, 1992]), Douglas Hunter (*God's Mercies: Rivalry, Betrayal, and the Dream of Discovery* [Toronto: Doubleday Canada, 2007]), and Corey Sandler (*Henry Hudson: Dreams and Obsession* [New York: Citadel, 2007]) testify to the enduring attraction of Hudson as a subject for popular writers. Russell Shorto's *The Island at the Center of the World: The Epic Story of Dutch Manhattan and the Forgotten Colony That Shaped America* (New York: Doubleday, 2004) is an ideal introduction to the years following Hudson's journey of 1609.

For an understanding of the world that Hudson entered in the mid-Atlantic in 1609, see the superb work by Anne-Marie Cantwell and Dianna diZerega Wall, *Unearthing Gotham: The Archaeology of New York City* (New Haven, Conn.: Yale University Press, 2001), as well as E. B. O'Callaghan, *History of New Netherland; or New York under the Dutch*, vol. 1 (New York, 1855), and J. Franklin Jameson, ed., *Narratives of New Netherland, 1609–1664* (New York, 1909). A number of recent works have probed the relations between Hudson and the Americans he met; among these the most important are (in chronological order): Paul Otto, "The Origins of New Netherland: Interpreting Native American Responses to Henry Hudson's Visit," *Itinerario* 13 (1994), 22–39; Paul Otto, "Common Practices and Mutual Misunderstandings: Henry Hudson, Native Americans, and the Birth of New Netherland," *de Halve Maen* 72, no. 4 (1999), 75–83; and Evan Haefeli, "On First Contact and Apotheosis: Manitou and Men in North America," *Ethnohistory* 54 (2007), 407–443.

Hudson's efforts need to be understood in the context of the European desire to obtain spices and the English engagement with the wider world. It was the demand for cinnamon, peppers, cloves, and other spices that provided the motivation for seeking new routes from Western Europe to the Southwest Pacific. Among the many studies of the trade, see, especially, John Keay, *The Spice Route: A History* (Berkeley: University of California Press, 2006), and Paul Freedman, *Out of the East: Spices and the Medieval Imagination* (New Haven, Conn.: Yale University Press, 2008). The best work to date on the European drive for a northern water route to the Pacific are Glyn Williams, *The Great South Sea: English Voyages and Encounters, 1570–1750* (New Haven, Conn.: Yale University Press, 1997) and *Voyages of Delusion: The Quest for the Northwest Passage* (New Haven, Conn.: Yale University Press, 2003), though Lawrence Burpee's *The Search for the Western Sea: The Story of the Exploration of North-Western America*, 2 vols. (Toronto: Macmillan, 1935) remains a valuable review of the long-term effort to find the elusive passage. For crucial studies needed to understand the larger context of Hudson's expedition, see (in chronological order) Percival Griffiths, *A Licence to Trade: A History of the English Chartered Companies* (London: Ernest Benn, 1974); Daniel Francis and Toby Morantz, *Partners in Furs: A History of the Fur Trade in Eastern James Bay, 1600–1870* (Kingston and Montreal: McGill-Queen's University Press, 1983); Helen Wallis, "England's Search for the Northern Passages in the Sixteenth and Early Seventeenth Centuries," *Arctic* 37 (1984), 453–472; J. Braat, "Dutch Activities in the North and the Arctic during the Sixteenth and Seventeenth Centuries," *Arctic* 37 (1984), 473–480; Kenneth R. Andrews, *Trade, Plunder and Settlement: Maritime Enterprise and the Genesis of the British Empire, 1480–1630* (Cambridge: Cambridge University Press, 1984); Eleanora C. Gordon, "The Fate of Sir Hugh Willoughby and His Companions: A New Conjecture," *Geographical Journal* 152 (1986), 243–247; W. A. Kenyon, *The History of James Bay, 1610–1686: A Study in Historical Archaeology*, Royal Ontario Museum Archaeology Monograph 10 (Toronto, 1986); Robert C. Ritchie, *Captain Kidd and the War Against the Pirates* (Cambridge: Harvard University Press, 1986); Harry Kelsey, *Sir Francis Drake: The Queen's Pirate* (New Haven, Conn.: Yale University Press, 1998); James McDermott, *Martin Frobisher: Elizabethan Privateer* (New Haven, Conn.: Yale University Press, 2001); Michael Bravo and Sverker Sörlin, eds., *Narrating the Arctic: A Cultural History of Nordic Scientific Practices* (Canton, Mass.: Science History Publications/USA, 2002); and I. S. MacLaren, "'Zealous Sayles' and 'Zealous Sales': Bookings on the Northwest Passage," *Princeton University Library Chronicle* 64 (2003), 253–287. When the English moved out into the wider world they had to confront novel situations, including the risk of death in new climates, at sea, or at the hands of pirates. The literature on the formative period of English expansion is voluminous and includes many recent works, such as (in chronological order): Nicholas Canny, ed., *The Origins of Empire: British Overseas Enterprise to the Close of the Seventeenth Century*, vol. 1 of *Oxford History of the British Empire* (Oxford: Oxford University Press, 1998); Joyce E. Chaplin, *Subject Matter: Technology, the Body, and Science on the Anglo-American Frontier, 1500–1676* (Cambridge: Harvard University Press, 2001); Linda Colley, *Captives: Britain, Empire, and the World, 1600–1850* (New York: Pantheon, 2002); Peter E. Pope, *Fish into Wine: The Newfoundland Plantation in the Seventeenth Century* (Chapel

Hill: University of North Carolina Press for the Omohundro Institute of Early American History and Culture, 2004); Peter C. Mancall, *Hakluyt's Promise: An Elizabethan's Obsession for an English America* (New Haven, Conn.: Yale University Press, 2007); Mancall, ed., *The Atlantic World and Virginia, 1550–1624* (Chapel Hill: University of North Carolina Press for the Omohundro Institute of Early American History and Culture, 2007); and Alison Games, *The Web of Empire: English Cosmopolitans in an Age of Expansion, 1560–1660* (New York: Oxford University Press, 2008).

Many of the biographical treatments of Hudson do little more than retell the story in the documents edited by Asher, many of which came from the 1625 edition of Purchas. Wherever possible I have used original editions of early modern texts, mostly housed in the superb collections of the Huntington Library in San Marino, California, and extant manuscript records of the masters of Trinity House (in the Guildhall Library), the High Court of Admiralty (in the British National Archives, formerly the Public Record Office), the extract of Thomas Gorst's journal (for which the Family History Center of the Church of Latter-Day Saints has a microfilm of the original in the Guildhall Library), and Hatfield House (for Thomas Holland's 1609 letter to the Earl of Salibury). For the indigenous experience, see John S. Long, "Narratives of Early Encounters between Europeans and the Cree of Western James Bay," *Ontario History* 80 (1988), 227–245, and John Bennett and Susan Rowley, eds., *Uqalurait: An Oral History of Nunavit* (Montreal: McGill-Queen's University Press, 2004). The narratives relating to Hudson's journeys only rarely identify specific indigenous peoples and more commonly employ the contemporary European practice of eliding differences between distinct groups by referring to America's natives as "savages." The identifications I use in this book rely on the superb work of other scholars (especially for the peoples who encountered Hudson in 1609) and the locations of traditional territories used in William Sturtevant, gen. ed., *Handbook of North American Indians*, 20 vols. planned (Washington, D.C.: Smithsonian Institution Press, 1978–), esp. vol. 6 (*Subarctic*, edited by June Helm) and vol. 15 (*Northeast*, edited by Bruce G. Trigger).

Historical sources provide evidence to reconstruct Hudson's experience but take on greater meaning if read in the context of the abundant and often brilliant writing about the Arctic. The works most vital for understanding the northern experience include Luke Foxe, *North-West Fox, or, Fox from the North-West Passage* (London, 1635); John Ross, *A Voyage of Discovery* (London, 1819); William Scoresby, Jr., *An Account of the Arctic Regions, with a History and Description of the Northern Whale-Fishery* (London, 1820); Frederick William Beechey, *Narrative of a Voyage to the Pacific and Beering's Strait: To co-operate with the Polar expeditions* (London, 1831); John Barrow, *Voyages of Discovery and Research within the Arctic Regions, from the year 1818 to the present time* (London, 1846); Fridtjof Nansen, *Farthest North* (New York, 1903); Knud Rasmussen, *Across Arctic America* (New York: G. P. Putnam's Sons, 1927); Barry Lopez, *Arctic Dreams: Imagination and Desire in a Northern Landscape* (New York: Scribner, 1986); and Elizabeth Kolbert, ed., *The Ends of the Earth: An Anthology of the Finest Writing on the Arctic* (New York: Bloomsbury, 2007), which is the ideal introduction for anyone interested in how views of the far north have both changed and remained consistent over time. There is a series of spectacular photographs by Robert Glenn Ketchum in *Northwest Passage* (New York: Aperture, 1996). Kolbert's *Field Notes from a Catastrophe: Man, Nature, and Climate Change* (New York: Bloomsbury, 2006) provides a brilliant and sobering account of the ecological changes that have transformed the Artic since Hudson's tragic journey.

Spelling and punctuation were inconsistent in the late sixteenth and early seventeenth centuries. I have silently modernized both in many of the quotations. In addition, spellings of personal names varied considerably from one document to another. For the men on the *Discovery* I have used the spellings provided either by Purchas, in the printed account of Pricket's narrative, or by the masters of Trinity House, who provided a complete list of those involved in the venture (see Trinity House Transactions, vol. 1 (1609–1625), Guildhall Library, Ms. 30045/1, f. 11ᵛ. Place-names are also inconsistent in the documents. Whenever possible I have used the names that appeared on contemporary maps, and provided modern names for identifiable places using the *Times Atlas of the World,* 7th ed., and Derek Hayes, *Historical Atlas of Canada* (Seattle: University of Washington Press, 2002).

There are no portraits of Henry Hudson in this book because none survive from his lifetime. All existing images purporting to depict Hudson are posthumous.

# Notes

CHAPTER I

2    *plow through and circumvent:* For an account of that later expedition, see C. R. Markham, "The Arctic Exploration of 1878," *Proceedings of the Royal Geographical Society and Monthly Record of Geography* 1 (1879), 16–38.

3    *hoped to return to America:* Thomas Holland to the Earl of Salisbury, October 30, 1609, Marquess of Salisbury papers, Hatfield House (CP 128/24).

3    *despondency, fury, and madness:* Jack London, "In a Far Country," *Overland Monthly* 33 (June 1899). During Hudson's second journey the men realized that the season had begun to turn when they needed to use candles to light the ship on July 27, after seven weeks without them. See Samuel Purchas, *Purchas his Pilgrimes,* 4 vols. (London, 1625), 3:580.

4    *Baffin Island and modern Labrador:* For more on the Norse in the North Atlantic, see Kirsten Seaver, *The Frozen Echo: Greenland and the Exploration of North America, ca. A.D. 1000–1500* (Stanford: Stanford University Press, 1996), and William W. Fitzhugh and Elisabeth I. Ward, eds., *Vikings: The North Atlantic Saga* (Washington, D.C.: Smithsonian Institution Press, 2000). For Frobisher, see James McDermott, *Martin Frobisher: Elizabethan Privateer* (New Haven, Conn.: Yale University Press, 2001), and Peter C. Mancall, *Hakluyt's Promise: An Elizabethan's Obsession for an English America* (New Haven, Conn.: Yale University Press, 2007), 47–64, 102–104, 121–127. For Davis, see Richard Hakluyt, *The Principall Voiages, Navigations, and Discoveries of the English Nation* (London, 1589), 776–792.

4    *bark named Discovery:* The size of the *Discovery* as 55 tons is reported in John Barrow, *A Chronological History of Voyages into the Arctic Regions, undertaken chiefly for the purpose of discoverying a North-East, North-West, or Polar Passage between the Atlantic and Pacific* (London, 1818), 187, and *The Arctic Regions: A Narrative of Discovery and Adventure* (London, 1852), 66.

4    *existence and location:* Manuscripts relating to Hudson's voyages came into Hakluyt's hands, quite likely because Hudson realized that Hakluyt was the major promoter of English explorations

abroad and the captain wanted Hakluyt to be aware of his achievements. There are no letters between the two men, but the relationship can be inferred from Samuel Purchas's notes indicating where he obtained the materials he published in 1625; those he got from Hakluyt he marked with an "H" in his book. See Purchas, *Purchas his Pilgrimes*, 3: sig. *3ᵛ, which notes that Hakluyt had all the surviving accounts for all of Hudson's journeys except the one written by Abacuk Pricket. For Hudson's relationship with John Smith, see Emanuel Van Meteren, "On Hudson's Voyage," in J. Franklin Jameson, ed., *Narratives of New Netherland* (New York: Scribner's, 1909), 6. The geographer Petrus Plancius was especially helpful for Hudson; see Purchas, *Purchas his Pilgrimes*, 3:518 (for the loan of a crucial text) and Pierre Jaennin to King Henry IV, January 21, 1609, in Georg Michael Asher, ed., *Henry Hudson the Navigator*, Hakluyt Society 1st Series 27 (London, 1860), 244–254.

6    *illustrious and commercially minded:* Unless otherwise noted, biographical details can be found in the *Oxford Dictionary of National Biography (ODNB)* (Oxford: Oxford University Press, 2004). On Smythe, also sometimes written as Smith, see also J. F. Wadmore, "Sir Thomas Smythe, Knt.," *Archaeologia Cantiana: Being the Transactions of the Kent Archaeological Society* 20 (1893), 82–103. On the connection between the Muscovy Company and the Northwest Passage, see Hakluyt, *Principall Voiages*, 265–292. For an example of Smythe's correspondence reaching a wide audience, see "A Letter of Richard Finch, to the Right Worshipfull Sir Thomas Smith," in Purchas, *Purchas his Pilgrimes*, 3:534–538. The letter, which describes a journey to Pechora for the Muscovy Company in 1611, was among the documents Hakluyt transferred to Purchas. Smythe's management of the Virginia Company came under sharp attack in the 1620s, suggesting that despite his prominence and knowledge of overseas opportunities, he was not immune from criticism. See Nicholas Farrar, *Sir Thomas Smith's Misgovernment of the Virginia Company*, ed. D. R. Ransome (Cambridge: Cambridge University Press for the Roxburghe Club, 1990). Purchas, who played an enormous role in publicizing travels abroad, referred to Smythe as "the stern that with little local stirring guideth so many Ships to many of those Ports." See Samuel Purchas, *Purchas his Pilgrimage* (London, 1614), 744.

6   *evidence that either ventured:* There is considerable mystery about how far either the Portuguese or Frobisher sailed into Hudson Strait, but the historical geographer E. G. R. Taylor cogently argued that surviving maps, especially one drawn by John Dee that made its way to Queen Elizabeth, reveal that either the Portuguese or the English had sailed into the potential passage. Because the Portuguese tried to suppress this information, and because the English did little to make it public—Hakluyt makes an oblique reference to it in an important but unpublished manuscript—there is no way to know how much data Hudson might have had when he guided *Discovery* into these waters. See Taylor, "Hudson's Strait and the Oblique Meridian," *Imago Mundi* 3 (1939), 48–52; Richard Hakluyt, *A Particuler Discourse concerninge the Greate Necessitie and Manifolde Commodyties that are like to growe to this Realme of Englande by the Westerne Discoueries lately attempted, known as Discourse on Western Planting*, ed. David B. Quinn and Alison M. Quinn, Hakluyt Society Extra Series 45 (London: Hakluyt Society, 1993), 27, 64, 111.

8   *and its fabled riches:* "Of Hudsons Discoveries and Death," in Samuel Purchas, *Purchas his Pilgrimage* (London, 1617), 924. Hudson called these "Champaign" lands, signaling their wide open character.

9   *came to regret:* Abacuk Pricket, "A larger Discourse of the same Voyage, and the successe thereof," in Purchas, *Purchas his Pilgrimes* (1625), 3:598.

11   *coasting the shores of James Bay:* See Richard Hakluyt (the elder), "Pamphlet for the Virginia Enterprise," in E. G. R. Taylor, ed., *The Original Writings and Correspondence of the Two Richard Hakluyts*, Hakluyt Society 2nd Series 76–77 (London: Hakluyt Society, 1935), 2:331–335.

11   *rarely rises above 45°F:* For details on the local climate, see Stuart Houston, Tim Ball, and Mary Houston, *Eighteenth-Century Naturalists of Hudson Bay* (Montreal and Kingston: McGill-Queen's University Press, 2003), 115–116.

12   *survive its torments:* On the depth of the snow in the region occasionally preventing even Cree movements, see Houston et al., *Eighteenth-Century Naturalists*, 123. The details about the conditions of the interior of a European enclosure during an over-winter stay come from an account of the Dutch Barentsz voyages; see Edward Pellham, *Gods Power and Providence* (London, 1631), sig. A3$^v$.

12     *no experience trudging through deep snow:* Though there is no record of the supplies for the *Discovery,* another explorer who traveled to the same region provided lamb-skinned coats and socks made of *frieze,* or coarse woolens, for his crew. See Thomas Rundall, ed., *Narratives of Voyages towards the North-West, in Search of a Passage to Cathay and India, 1496 to 1631,* Hakluyt Society 1st Series 5 (London, 1849), 59–60.

13     *attempts to understand other natural phenomena:* For local weather conditions, see *The Strange and Dangerous Voyage of Captain Thomas James* (London, 1633), 54–89; Robert Boyle, *New Experiments and Observations touching Cold, or an Experimental History of Cold* (London, 1665), 522–524, 532, 535–537, and sig. b$^v$ ("Stupendious"); E. E. Rich, ed., *James Isham's Observations on Hudsons Bay, 1743,* Publications of the Champlain Society, Hudson's Bay Company, Series 12 (Toronto: Champlain Society, 1949), 66–72.

15     *". . . nothing is ever really lost":* Elizabeth Kolbert, ed., *The Ends of the Earth* (New York: Bloomsbury, 2007), 3.

16     *went to the gallows:* There was a quickly suppressed insurrection on a ship bound for the Northwest Passage commanded by George Waymouth in 1602, but though notes from the expedition identify this as a "Mutiny," it had little bearing on the journey and only temporarily upset the captain's plans. See Rundall, ed., *Narratives of Voyages,* 66–67. Mutinies became more common later, in all likelihood because of the enormous increase in ships traveling long distances after the sixteenth century. The first relevant act in Britain was the Mutiny Act of 1689 (1 William and Mary, c.5; see *Statutes of the Realm,* 6:55–56), but that was intended to suppress military insurrections on land and did not mention shipboard rebellions; it was related instead to the problems of order in a society without a regular or standing army. For two notable mutinies that preceded the events on *Discovery* and a vivid retelling of the Hudson story built from Pricket's narrative, see Edmund Fuller, ed., *Mutiny!* (New York: Crown, 1953), 3–51; also Irvin Anthony, *Revolt at Sea: A Narration of Many Mutinies* (New York: Putnam, 1937), 14–59. One collection of modern accounts concentrates almost entirely on events after the uprising in James Bay in 1611. See *Fifty Mutinies, Rebellions and Revolutions* (London, n.d.). For the incident with Drake, see Harry Kelsey, *Sir Francis Drake: The Queen's Pirate* (New Haven, Conn.: Yale University Press, 1998), 106–110. Leonard F. Guttridge, *Mutiny: A History of Naval Insurrection* (Annapolis, Md.: Naval Institute Press, 1992), also ignores mutinies before 1700.

17  *newcomers to succeed:* John Murrin, *Beneficiaries of Catastrophe: The English Colonies in America* (Washington, D.C.: American Historical Association, 1997).

## CHAPTER 2

20  *attention of the city:* William Bourne, *A booke called the Treasure for travelers* (London, 1578), sig. *iii^v.

20  *acquisitive impulses:* John Jacob Grasser, "Notes on England, circa 1606," and Justus Zinzerling, "Description of England, circa 1610," both in William Benchley Rye, *England as Seen by Foreigners* (London, 1865), 127, 132–133.

20  "*. . . Kingdom and Nation*": For Hudson's relation to Cope, see Thomas Holland to the Earl of Salisbury, October 30, 1609, Marquess of Salisbury/Hatfield House, CP 128/24; for Cope's cabinet, see Thomas Platter, *Travels in England, 1599*, trans. Clare Williams (London: J. Cape, 1937), 171–173; the quotation is from Edmund Howes, *Annales, Or a General Chronicle of England, begun by John Snow* (London, 1631), 994.

21  *valuable flora:* For the development of Europeans' passion for spices, see Paul Freedman, *Out of the East: Spices and the Medieval Imagination* (New Haven, Conn.: Yale University Press, 2008), esp. 50–75, which describes the use of spices as medicine. On sugar, see Sidney Mintz, *Sweetness and Power: The Place of Sugar in Modern History* (New York: Viking, 1985). On tobacco, see Peter C. Mancall, "Tales Tobacco Told in Sixteenth-Century Europe," *Environmental History* 9 (2004), 648–678.

22  *guiacum from Java:* William Turner, *A New Herball*, 3 vols. (1551–1568), ed. George T. L. Chapman et al., 2 vols. (Cambridge: Cambridge University Press, 1989–1995), 2:746–747 (nutmeg and mace), 2:742–744 (guiacum).

22  *125 recipes featuring cinnamon:* Freedman, *Out of the East*, 24.

23  *infected rat urine:* William Langham, *The Garden of Health* (London, 1597), 141–142 (cinnamon), 149–150 (cloves), 376–377 (mace). For the modern disease, see E. A. S. Reid and R. W. Reid, "Leptospirosis Icterohæmorrhagica, or Weil's Disease," *Canadian Medical Association Journal* 63 (1950), 479–483.

23  *until the patient was healthy again:* Langham, *Garden of Health*, 435–436.

24  *leprous facial sores:* Ibid., 485–489.

25  *illustrations of each:* John Gerard, *The Herball, or Generall Historie of Plants* (London, 1597), 1348–1349 (cinnamon), 1351–1353

(cloves), 1353–1354 (nutmeg), 1357 (bastard pepper), 1358 (cardamom). Europeans had earlier used the phrase "grain of paradise" to refer to malagueta pepper, which they obtained from West Africa in the medieval era; see Freedman, *Out of the East,* 12.

26   *overflowing with delicacies:* Howes, *Annales,* 994; John Chamberlain to Sir Ralph Winwood, January 13, 1610, in *Letters of John Chamberlain,* ed. Norman E. McClure, 2 vols. (Philadelphia: American Philosophical Society, 1939) (hereafter Chamberlain, *Letters*), 1:294–295. For news about ships arriving in London, see Chamberlain to Dudley Carleton, December 30, 1609, in Chamberlain, *Letters,* 292. Howes claimed that the *Trades Encrease* was 1,200 tons, but an enumeration of ships during this period lists it as 1,100 tons; see R. G. Marsden, "English Ships in the Reign of James I," *Transactions of the Royal Historical Society,* New Series 19 (1905), 333.

26   *". . . transplanted into England":* Juan Fernandez de Velasco, "Banquet and Entertainment given by James I to the Constable of Castile at Whitehall Palace" (1604) in Rye, ed., *England as Seen by Foreigners,* 119–120.

27   *English manufactured goods:* Howes, *Annales,* 994; Alison Games, *The Web of Empire: English Cosmopolitans in an Age of Expansion, 1560–1660* (New York: Oxford University Press, 2008), 93–94. On the later journey of the *Peppercorne,* see [Dudley Digges], *The Defence of Trade* (London, 1615), 20. For the East India Company, see also Percival Griffiths, *A Licence to Trade: A History of the English Chartered Companies* (London: E. Benn, 1974), 75–77.

28   *without a special license:* Marsden, "English Ships in the Reign of James I," 309–342; Howes, *Annales,* 894.

28   *clean water to drink:* For conditions in Jamestown, see Carville V. Earle, "Environment, Disease, and Mortality in Early Virginia," in Thad W. Tate and David L. Ammerman, eds., *The Chesapeake in the Seventeenth Century: Essays on Anglo-American Society* (Chapel Hill: University of North Carolina Press for the Institute for Early American History and Culture, 1979), 96–125; Karen Ordahl Kupperman, "Apathy and Death in Early Jamestown," *Journal of American History* 66 (1979), 24–40; Edmund Morgan, *American Slavery, American Freedom: The Ordeal of Colonial Virginia* (New York: W.W. Norton, 1975), 71–91; Mark Nicholls, ed., "George Percy's 'Trewe Relacyon': A Primary Source for the Jamestown Settlement," *Virginia Magazine of History and Biography* 113 (2005), 212–275; Peter C. Mancall, "Savagery at James-

town," *Huntington Library Quarterly* 70 (2007), 661–670. For the Virginia Company reference to cannibalism, see *A True Declaration of the Estate of the Colonie in Virginia* (London, 1610), 38–40.

29    *sustained interest in the business:* See, for example, *A True and Large Discourse of the voyage of the whole fleete set forth the 20 of Aprill 1601 . . . by the Governours and Assistants of the East Indian Merchants in London, to the East Indies* (London, 1603).

29    *alleged routes:* Helen Wallis, "England's Search for the Northern Passages in the Sixteenth and Early Seventeenth Centuries," *Arctic* 37 (1964), 457–467.

29    *Newfoundland in 1583:* "The voyage of M. Hore and divers other gentlemen, to Newfoundland, and Cape Briton, in the yere 1536," in Richard Hakluyt, *Principal Voyages, Navigations, Traffiques, and Discoveries of the English Nation,* 3 vols. (London, 1598–1600), 3:131; Peter C. Mancall, *Hakluyt's Promise: An Elizabethan's Obsession for an English America* (New Haven, Conn.: Yale University Press, 2007), 102–127.

29    *funding explorers could be expensive:* On Hakluyt attending the meeting, see Mancall, *Hakluyt's Promise,* 237–243; Heidi Brayman Hackel and Peter C. Mancall, "Richard Hakluyt the Younger's Notes for the East India Company in 1601: A Transcription of Huntington Library Manuscript EL 2360," *Huntington Library Quarterly* 67 (2004), 423–436. For Weymouth's expenses, see C. C. A. Gosch, ed., *Danish Arctic Expeditions, 1605 to 1620,* Hakluyt Society 1st Series 96–97 (London, 1897), 2: lxxvi.

30    *fabled water route:* For the narratives of the sixteenth-century English journeys to Newfoundland and North America, see Hakluyt, *Principal Voyages,* 3:129–182; for Hakluyt's travel to find the last survivor of Hore's journey, see 3:131. On Weymouth, see "Hessel Gerritz's Various Accounts of Hudson's Two Last Voyages," in Georg Michael Asher, ed., *Henry Hudson the Navigator,* Hakluyt Society 1st Series 27 (London, 1860), 190–191.

30    *inaccuracies of navigational devices:* For the kinds of guides that sailors used, see John Davis, *The Seamans Secrets* (London, 1599); on problems facing those at sea, see Edward Wright, *Errors in Navigation* (London, 1599). George Weymouth, who crossed the Atlantic in 1605, carried five kinds of navigational tools— cross-staff, compass, semisphere, astrolabe, and a "ring instrument"; see James Rosier, *A True Relation of the most prosperous voyage made this present yeere 1605, by Captaine George Waymouth, in the Discovery of the land of Virginia* (London, 1605), sig. E$^v$. For

how such devices worked and their evolution, see J. B. Hewson, *A History of the Practice of Navigation* (Glasgow: Brown, Son and Ferguson, 1951), 43–79.

32 *circumvent the Portuguese and Spanish:* For Thorne's argument about what could be found in the Spice Islands and how to get there, see Richard Hakluyt, *Divers Voyages touching the discoverie of America, and the Ilands adjacent* (London, 1582), sig. B3ʳ (spices), sig. Dᵛ–[D2ʳ⁻ᵛ]. Thorne's map did not extend far enough north to depict this open sea, but Lok's did; both maps were printed separately, as was common at the time, and inserted into the book. The theory of an ice-free sea in the Arctic survived for centuries; see John K. Wright, "The Open Polar Sea," *Geographical Review* 43 (1953), 338–365.

33 *requisite skills and knowledge:* For accounts of Frobisher, see Thomas Churchyard, *A Prayse, and Reporte of Maister Martyne Frobishers Voyage to Meta Incognita* (London, 1578); Dionyse Settle, *A True reporte of the laste voyage into the West and Northwest regions, &c., worthily achieved by Capteine Frobisher* (London, 1577); Thomas Ellis, *A True reporte of the third and last voyage into Mega incognita . . . by Martine Frobisher* (London, 1578); and [George Best], *A True Discourse of the late voyages of discoverie, for the finding of a passage to Cathaya, by the Northwest, under the conduct of Martin Frobisher* (London, 1578). For more on Sir Humphrey Gilbert, see his *A Discourse of a Discoverie for a New Passage to Cataia* (London, 1576); and George Peckham, *A True Reporte of the Late Discoveries and Possession taken in the right of the Crowne of Englande, of the Newfound landes: by . . . Sir Humfrey Gilbert* (London, 1583). For more on Davis, see his *The Worldes Hydrographical Discription* (London, 1595), sig. [C5ᵛ].

33 *ice-free body of water:* William Bourne, *A Regiment for the Sea* (London, 1574), 35ᵛ; Bourne, *A Regiment for the Sea* (London, 1590), f. 77; Thomas Blundeville, *A briefe description of universal mappes and cardes* (London, 1589), sig. C2ᵛ–3ʳ; "Hondius his Map of the Arctike Pole, or Northerne World," in Samuel Purchas, *Purchas his Pilgrimes,* 4 vols. (London, 1625), 3:625; Wallis, "England's Search for the Northern Passages," 454, 470; Wright, "The Open Polar Sea," 338–365. William Scoresby was among those who tried to put the theory of an ice-free passage through the Arctic to rest; see *An Account of the Arctic Regions, with a History and Description of the Northern Whale-Fishery,* 2 vols. (Edinburgh, 1820), 46–49. Plancius's 1594 map, "Orbis Terrarum typis de In-

tegro Multis in Locis Emendatus," circulated widely, including in Jan Huyghen van Linschoten's *Itinerario* (Amsterdam, 1596) and in an English translation, arranged by Hakluyt, entitled *John Huighen van Linschoten: his discours of voyages into ye Easte and West Indies* (London, 1598). Blundeville's lengthy treatise on Plancius's work included details about spices and where they could be found; see *M. Blundeville His Exercises* (London, 1594), 257$^r$–258$^r$, 260$^v$. For Hudson's relationship to Plancius, see "Hessel Gerritz's various accounts of Hudson's two last voyages" and President Jeannin to Henry IV of France, January 21, 1609, both in Asher, ed., *Henry Hudson the Navigator*, 186, 191, 245.

35    *new sources of natural resources:* For the significance of what Europeans found in this region, see, especially, W. Jeffrey Bolster, "Putting the Ocean in Atlantic History: Maritime Communities and Marine Ecology in the Northwest Atlantic, 1500–1800," *American Historical Review* 113 (2008), 19–47, and Nancy Shoemaker, "Whale and Bone," *Common-Place* 8, no. 2 (January 2008). For sixteenth-century views of walrus and the use of their tusks, see Conrad Gesner, *Historiae Animalium Lib. 4* (Frankfurt, 1620); "A briefe note of the Morsse and the use thereof," in Hakluyt, *Principal Voyages*, 3:191.

36    *stratification of this indigenous society:* John Chamberlain to Dudley Carleton, October 15, 1602, in *The Letters of John Chamberlain*, 2 vols., ed. Norman E. McClure (Philadelphia: American Philosophical Society, 1939), 1:164; Thomas Rundall, ed., *Narratives of Voyages towards the North-West in search of a passage to Cathay and India, 1496–1631*, Hakluyt Society 1st Series 5 (London, 1844), 63–63. On Hudson's knowledge of Weymouth, see Hessel Gerritz's 1613 account of Hudson's last voyage in Asher, ed., *Henry Hudson the Navigator*, 190–191. On Maine commodities, see Rosier, *True Relation*, sig. C3$^v$–[C4$^r$].

36    *taught him about the threats:* For Knight's account, see "Journal of the Voyage of John Knight to seek the North-West Passage, 1606," in C. R. Markham, ed., *The Voyages of Sir James Lancaster, Kt., to the East Indies*, Hakluyt Society 56 (London, 1877), 279–294. Purchas published an abridged version of Weymouth's journal in 1625; see Purchas, *Purchas his Pilgrimes*, 3:809–814.

38    *came into the possession of Hakluyt:* Purchas reprinted Hudson's version of the manuscript's history in *Purchas his Pilgrimes*, 3:518; see sig. *3$^{r-v}$ for the mention of Hakluyt's collection of these manuscripts.

38    *profit at their expense:* Wallis, "England's Search for the Northern Passages," 453–456.

39    *slow route around Africa:* Davis, *Worldes Hydrographical Discription,* sig. A2ᵛ and title page.

39    *performances of Shakespeare:* Richmond Barbour, "The East India Company Journal of Anthony Marlowe, 1607–1608," *Huntington Library Quarterly* 71 (2008), 255.

## CHAPTER 3

42    *quicker and less expensive:* John Keay, *The Spice Route: A History* (Berkeley: University of California Press, 2006), 7–17.

43    *genuine maritime empire:* See C. R. Boxer, *The Portuguese Seaborne Empire, 1415–1825* (New York: Knopf, 1969); Sanjay Subrahmanyam, *The Career and Legend of Vasco da Gama* (Cambridge: Cambridge University Press, 1997); Anthony Disney, "Portuguese Expansion, 1400–1800: Encounters, Negotiations, and Interactions," in Francisco Bethencourt and Diogo Ramada Curto, eds., *Portuguese Oceanic Expansion, 1400–1800* (Cambridge: Cambridge University Press, 2007), 255–282.

44    *attractive to potential investors:* A man named Henry Hudson, who might or might not be the Arctic explorer, was mustered for service from Longhaughton and Bowmer on September 30, 1584. If Hudson was about forty in 1607—old enough to gain the command of a ship and the trust of investors, but still young enough to be willing to try his luck on a dangerous mission—he would have been around seventeen in 1584, a time when it was possible he could have fulfilled his family's (and town's) military obligations to the Crown. See Joseph Bain, ed., *Calendar of Letters and Papers relating to the affairs of the Borders of England and Scotland,* 2 vols. (Edinburgh, 1894–1896), 1:160.

44    *stretched from Brazil to Newfoundland:* Richard Hakluyt printed a report of an English expedition to Persia and Media from 1579 to 1581 that included a Thomas Hudson from Limehouse, identified as "maister of the English barke." Thomas Hudson might also have been related to the intrepid Christopher Hudson (also spelled Hoddesdon and Hodsdon), who traveled on expeditions to Muscovy in 1555 and 1570, provided instructions to an English voyage to Brazil in 1580, and was a member of the Muscovy Company committee that advised the explorer Christopher Carleill on his voyage to "the hithermost partes of America"—which

meant Newfoundland—in 1583. For more on Thomas Hudson, see Richard Hakluyt, *Principall Voiages, Navigations, and Discoveries of the English Nation* (London, 1589), 445; for more on Christopher Hudson, see p. 299 (the Muscovy expedition of 1555), pp. 425–426 (the Muscovy expedition of 1570), p. 639 (the voyage to Brazil), and p. 723 (instructions for Carleill).

44  *his father's constant companion:* On his son's emigration to the East Indies, see W. Noel Sainsbury, ed., *Calendar of State Papers Colonial, East Indies, China, and Japan,* 5 vols. (London, 1864), 2:462, and East India Company records for September 1628, in W. Noel Sainsbury, ed., *Calendar of State Papers Colonial, East Indies, China, and Persia, 1625–1629,* 9 vols. (London, 1884), 6:542–554, 8:54–70.

45  *many guilds in London:* [John Stow], *A Survay of London* (London, 1603), 172.

45  *audacious but appealing:* Samuel Purchas, *Purchas his Pilgrimes,* 4 vols. (London, 1625), 3:567.

46  *whims of weather:* Purchas, *Purchas his Pilgrimes,* 3:567; see also James Rosier, *A True Relation of the most prosperous voyage made this present yeere 1605, by Captaine George Waymouth, in the Discovery of the land of Virginia* (London, 1605).

46  *fog had besieged the ship:* Purchas, *Purchas his Pilgrimes,* 3:567.

47  *ship ran closer to the island:* Ibid.

47  *such brutal coastlines:* Ibid., 3:567–568.

48  *difficult and precarious:* Ibid., 3:568.

48  *near modern-day Kap Parry:* Ibid., 3:568.

50  *details about indigenous peoples:* The pursuit of eyewitness testimony was crucial to the argument of the French essayist Michel de Montaigne's essay on cannibalism, first written in the late 1570s and translated into English by the early seventeenth century. Montaigne's essays were translated by John Florio, one of Hakluyt's associates, and published as *The Essayes, or Morall, Politike, and Militarie Discourses* (London, 1603). On the vogue for "true" tales, see Peter C. Mancall, *Hakluyt's Promise: An Elizabethan's Obsession for an English America* (New Haven, Conn.: Yale University Press, 2007), 51–52; for the earlier history of travel narratives, see Mary B. Campbell, *The Witness and the Other World: Exotic European Travel Writing, 400–1600* (Ithaca, N.Y.: Cornell University Press, 1988), and Peter C. Mancall, ed. *Travel Narratives from the Age of Discovery: An Anthology* (New York: Oxford University Press, 2005), 3–9.

50  *English thunderstorm:* Purchas, *Purchas his Pilgrimes,* 3:569.

51     *walruses paddling nearby:* Ibid., 3:569–570. For the possible location of Vogel Hooke, see Georg M. Asher, ed., *Henry Hudson the Navigator,* Hakluyt Society 1st Series 27 (London, 1860), clxxxvi.

51     *increasingly in doubt:* Purchas, *Purchas his Pilgrimes,* 3:570. Purchas added a marginal note indicating that he, too, believed that Hudson was the author from this point forward.

52     *illuminated by the half-light:* Ibid.

52     *rocky, icy coastline:* Ibid., 3:571.

53     *reach this latitude:* No European traveled this far north again until 1827, when Sir William Edward Parry reached 82°45´N. See Samuel F. Haven, ed., "Narrative of a Voyage to Spitzbergen in the Year 1613," *Archaeologia Americana, Transactions and Collections of the American Antiquarian Society* 4 (1860), 270n; F. W. Beechey, *A Voyage of Discovery towards the North Pole* (London, 1843), 204; and William Scoresby, *An Account of the Arctic Regions, with a History and Description of the Northern Whale-Fishery,* 2 vols. (Edinburgh, 1820), 1:41, 82. "The Arctic Voyagers," *New York Times,* October 13, 1855, provides a mid-nineteenth-century review of passages to the North Pole, the Northwest Passage, and the Northeast Passage.

53     *landed at Tilberie Hope:* Purchas, *Purchase his Pilgrimes,* 3:571–574. Purchas's text notes that Hudson identified the "Iles of Farre" at 52°N, but this is an error if he had in mind, as seems likely, the Faeroes.

54     *struggling new English settlement:* John Chamberlain had noted Weymouth's earlier efforts to find the Northwest Passage, as well as ships sailing to or returning from Virginia, but he never mentioned the return of the *Hopewell,* or, for that matter, any of Hudson's expeditions. For his earlier interest in the Northwest Passage, see Chamberlain to Dudley Carlton, May 8, 1602, and October 5, 1602; for his observations of the Virginia enterprise, see Chamberlain to Carleton, July 7, 1608, January 29, 1609, December 18, 1611, August 1, 1613, and May 12, 1614, all in *Letters of John Chamberlain,* ed. Norman E. McClure, 2 vols. (Philadelphia: American Philosophical Society, 1939), 1:144, 166, 259, 283, 324, 470–471, and 529; Edmund Howes, *Annales, Or a General Chronicle of England, begun by John Stow* (London, 1631).

54     *They all had failed:* See the narratives of Sir Hugh Willoughby and of Arthur Pet and Charles Jackman, in Hakluyt, *Principall Voiages,* 265–270, 466–486.

55     *store of knowledge:* For Hudson's knowledge of Barentsz, see Purchas, *Purchas his Pilgrimes,* 3:579. Barentsz was perhaps the most

famous of a series of Dutch explorers who explored the Arctic between 1584 and 1668; see J. Braat, "Dutch Activities in the North and the Arctic during the Sixteenth and Seventeenth Centuries," *Arctic* 37 (1984), 473–480.

55    *tell the tale of what had happened:* For the history of these journeys see Gerrit de Veer, *A True Description of Three Voyages by the North-East towards Cathay and China*, trans. W. Phillip, ed. C. T. Beke, Hakluyt Society 1st Ser. 13 (London, 1853).

56    *learned about the expeditions:* For details about the editions of de Veer's text, see John Alden et al., eds., *European Americana: A Chronological Guide to Works Printed in Europe relating to the Americas, 1492–1776*, 6 vols. (New York: Readex Books, 1980–1996).

57    *past 74°N with relative ease:* Purchas, *Purchas his Pilgrimes*, 3:575.

58    *cost of a future venture:* Ibid., 3:575–578; "A briefe note of the Morsse and the use thereof," in Richard Hakluyt, *Principal Voyages, Navigations, Traffiques, and Discoveries of the English Nation, 3 vols. (London, 1598–1600)*, 3:191.

58    *this magical creature:* Purchas, *Purchase his Pilgrimes*, 3:575. Mermaids, known since antiquity, remained an object of scientific fascination for centuries; see Karl Banse, "Mermaids—Their Biology, Culture, and Demise," *Limnology and Oceanography* 35 (1990), 148–153.

58    *monsters roaming the forests:* See W[alter] Ralegh, *The Discoverie of the Large, Rich, and Bewtiful Empyre of Guiana* (London, 1596), 69–71. The printer Henry Bynneman noted that he lived "in Knight-rider Streat, at the signe of the Mermaid," as he indicated on the title page of Pierre Boaistuau's *Certaine Secrete Wonders of Nature* (London, 1569).

59    *cartographers had posited:* Purchas, *Purchas his Pilgrimes*, 3:578–579.

59    *misread the variation:* Ibid., 3:579.

60    *perpetual summer daylight:* Ibid., 3:580.

60    *reached Gravesend:* Ibid., 3:580–581.

60    *before real problems arose:* Ibid.

62    *overture never resulted:* On Dutch culture of this age, including its commercial orientation, speculative booms, cultural aspirations, and relations with the Spanish see, among other sources, Anne Goldgar, *Tulipmania: Mercy, Honor, and Knowledge in the Dutch Golden Age* (Chicago: University of Chicago Press, 2007); Simon Schama, *The Embarrassment of Riches: An Interpretation of Dutch Culture in the Golden Age* (New York: Knopf, 1988); Jonathan I. Israel, *The Dutch Republic: Its Rise, Greatness, and Fall, 1477–1806*

(Oxford: Oxford University Press, 1995); and Benjamin Schmidt, *Innocence Abroad: The Dutch Imagination and the New World, 1570–1670* (Cambridge: Cambridge University Press, 2001). On the possible French effort to hire Hudson, see Pierre Jeannin to Henry IV, January 21, 1609, in Asher, ed., *Henry Hudson the Navigator*, 244–253.

64    *fewer problems with the weather:* Emanuel van Meteren, "On Hudson's Voyage," in J. Franklin Jameson, ed., *Narratives of New Netherland, 1609–1664* (New York, 1909), 6–7.

64    *water for the long journey:* Purchas, *Purchas his Pilgrimes*, 3:581–582.

64    *Frobisher had been in error:* Ibid., 3:583.

65    *cod from the continental shelf:* See Peter Pope, *Fish into Wine: The Newfoundland Plantation in the Seventeenth Century* (Chapel Hill: University of North Carolina Press for the Omohundro Institute of Early American History and Culture, 2004), 15–44, for a description of the cod trade.

65    *lobster and halibut as well:* Purchas, *Purchas his Pilgrimes*, 3:585–586.

66    *a preemptive raid:* Ibid., 3:585. Harriot's account was the first European depiction of any American population simultaneously published in four languages—English, Latin, German, and French—and the images from it continued to circulate for decades, thereby making it perhaps the best-known account of Americans circulating in Europe at this time. The kinds of exchanges that Hudson had with the Algonquians were already common; see James Axtell, "At the Water's Edge: Trading in the Sixteenth Century," in *After Columbus: Essays in the Ethnohistory of Colonial North America* (New York: Oxford University Press, 1988), 144–181.

66    *"The Land is very sweet":* Ibid., 3:587. On the lure of tobacco, see Peter C. Mancall, "Tales Tobacco Told in Sixteenth-Century Europe," *Environmental History* 9 (2004), 648–678. One nineteenth-century editor identified the fishing area as modern Stage Harbor, south of Chatham, Massachusetts; see Asher, ed., *Henry Hudson the Navigator*, 65n. Juet did not acknowledge that the ship was off Cape Cod, but Hudson reported that location after he returned to England; see Thomas Holland to the Earl of Salisbury, October 30, 1609, in Marquess of Salisbury papers, Hatfield House (CP 128/24).

67    *four men to haul it:* Purchas, *Purchas his Pilgrimes*, 3:589–592.

67    *despite the peaceful exchanges:* Ibid., 3:592. For the initial encounter between Hudson and the Munsees and other indigenous peoples

in the region, see Charles T. Gehring and William A. Starna, "Dutch and Indians in the Hudson Valley: The Early Period," *Hudson Valley Regional Review* 9 (1992), 1–25; Anne-Marie Cantwell and Diana diZerega Wall, *Unearthing Gotham: The Archaeology of New York City* (New Haven, Conn.: Yale University Press, 2001), 119–124; Paul Otto, "Common Practices and Mutual Misunderstandings: Henry Hudson, Native Americans, and the Birth of New Netherland," *de Halve Maen* 72 (1999), 75–83; Paul Otto, "The Origins of New Netherland: Interpreting Native American Responses to Henry Hudson's Visit," *Itinerario* 13 (1994), 22–39; Evan Haefeli, "On First Contact and Apotheosis: Manitou and Men in North America," *Ethnohistory* 54 (2007), 407–443.

68    *a vigilant watch:* Purchas, *Purchas his Pilgrimes,* 3:592. For Coleman's possible participation on Hudson's journey of 1607, see 3:567.

68    *". . . whatever they take a fancy to:* Ibid., 3:592; "Extracts relating to Hudson's third voyage (1609), from John De Laet's Nieuwe Werelt," (1625) in Asher, ed., *Henry Hudson the Navigator,* 160.

69    *beads, knives, and hatchets:* Purchas, *Purchas his Pilgrimes,* 3:593. Europeans often maintained that they traded "trifles" to the indigenous peoples of eastern North America, but the exchange worked only because the newcomers offered goods the locals valued or that had utilitarian benefits. What the natives offered—especially furs—had great value to the English. In other words, though Juet and other observers believed they were getting a good deal because of Indians' economic naïveté, they were instead participants in a system of exchange that benefited each party. See Christopher L. Miller and George R. Hamell, "A New Perspective on Indian-White Contact: Cultural Symbols and Colonial Trade," *Journal of American History* 73 (1986), 311–328.

70    *liquor trade:* On the alcohol trade in eastern North America, see Peter C. Mancall, *Deadly Medicine: Indians and Alcohol in Early America* (Ithaca, N.Y.: Cornell University Press, 1995), esp. 29–61.

70    *treated Hudson with "reverence":* Purchas, *Purchas his Pilgrimes,* 3:593–594.

70    *retrace their route downstream:* Ibid., 3:594.

70    *cut through steel or iron:* Ibid., 3:594–595.

71    *hurried downstream:* Ibid., 3:595. Juet refers to the man who shot the Indian as "our Masters Mate," a possible reference to the Dutch mate on the ship.

71    *headed into the Atlantic:* Ibid.

72  *made northern routes impassable:* Van Meteren, "On Hudson's Voyage," 7–8.

73  *return soon to the American coast:* Holland to the Earl of Salisbury, October 30, 1609.

73  *repaying the debt:* Howes, *Annales,* 894 (festivities, license), 898 (alum), 897 (debt).

74  *end their days at the gallows:* Andrew Saint and Gillian Darley, eds., *Chronicles of London* (London: Weidenfeld and Nicholson, 1994), 86–87. The idea of transporting the unemployed in England to North America had been discussed at least since the publication of Humphrey Gilbert's *A discourse of a discoverie for a new passage to Cataia* (London, 1576).

75  *Hakluyt to provide guidance:* Mancall, *Hakluyt's Promise,* 237–243, 304.

75  *notably the river:* Van Meteren, "On Hudson's Voyage," 8–9.

75  *extend trade and political ties:* B. F. DeCosta, *Sailing Directions of Henry Hudson, Prepared for his use in 1608, from the Old Danish of Ivar Bardsen* (Albany, 1869), 19.

76  *not a potential colonizer:* "Extracts relating to Hudson's Third Voyage," in Asher, ed., *Henry Hudson the Navigator,* 161.


CHAPTER 4

78  *never had the chance:* Dionyse Settle, *A True reporte of the laste voyages into the West and Northwest regions, &c. 1577, worthily achieved by Capteine Frobisher* (London, 1577), sig. [Bviii^v]–Cij^r; James McDermott, *Martin Frobisher: Elizabethan Pirate* (New Haven, Conn.: Yale University Press, 2001), 120–244; Robert McGhee, *The Arctic Voyages of Martin Frobisher: An Elizabethan Adventure* (Seattle: University of Washington Press and the Canadian Museum of Civilization, 2001), 81–88; James Watt and Ann Savours, "The Captured 'Countrey People': Their Depiction and Medical History," in Thomas H. B. Symons, ed., *Meta Incognita: A Discourse of Discovery: Martin Frobisher's Arctic Expeditions, 1576–1578,* 2 vols. (Hull, Quebec: Canadian Museum of Civilization, 1999), 2:553–562. European fascination with the three Inuit extended beyond England; engravings of them appeared on the continent in *La navigation due capitaine Martin Forbisher* (La Rochelle, 1578) and *Beschreibung der shiffart des haubtmans Martine Forbissher* (Nuremberg, 1580). On these and other Inuit travelers, see Richard Hakluyt, *Divers Voyages touching upon America*

and the Ilands adjacent (London, 1582), sig. A3ʳ–[A4ʳ]; Michael Harbsmeier, "Bodies and Voices from Ultima Thule: Inuit Explorations of the Kablunat from Christian IV to Knud Rasmussen," in Michael Bravo and Sverker Sörlin, eds., *Narrating the Arctic: A Cultural History of Nordic Scientific Practices* (Canton, Mass.: Science History Publications/USA, 2002), 37–39; Alden Vaughan, *Transatlantic Encounters: American Indians in Britain, 1500–1776* (Cambridge: Cambridge University Press, 2006), 1–20.

78    *well beyond England's shores:* The map was recopied in 1781 and widely distributed when the account became the object of transatlantic fascination. In November 1790, the French royal geographer Jean-Nicolas Buache de la Neuville told the Académie Royale des Sciences of Paris that Ferrer Maldonado's account was legitimate, though others at the time, notably the extraordinary Spanish explorer Alejandro Malaspina, came to dismiss it as the nonsense that it was. The documents for the Ferrer Maldonado manuscript, including a translation of the original and its late eighteenth-century commentators, can be found in Andrew David, Felipe Fernandez-Armesto, Carlos Novi, and Glyndwr Williams, eds., *The Malaspina Expedition, 1789–1794: The Journal of the Voyage by Alejandro Malaspina*, 3 vols., Hakluyt Society 3rd Series (vols. 8, 11, 13) (London: Hakluyt Society, 2001–2004), 2:427–484.

78    *notably the Spanish and Portuguese:* The primary proponent of the importance of England's maritime past was Hakluyt, who put together his collections of travel accounts in order to prove to others in the realm that the English had a venerable tradition of exploration and should continue to vigorously pursue opportunities. See Peter C. Mancall, *Hakluyt's Promise: An Elizabethan's Obsession for an English America* (New Haven, Conn.: Yale University Press, 2007).

80    *at court, in the streets, and on the docks:* Hugo Grotius, *The Free Sea,* trans. Richard Hakluyt, ed. David Armitage (Indianapolis: Liberty Fund, 2004), esp. 13–49.

80    *some enterprising European:* [Dudley Digges], *Fata Mihi Totum Mea sunt agitanda per orbem* (London, 1611), esp. 4, 23–26. John Chamberlain, who had paid attention to voyages to the northwest since the time of Weymouth, thought Digges's small book was a waste of effort and expense: "[S]ome of his good friends say he had been better have given five hundred pound then published such a pamphlet." See Chamberlain to Dudley Carleton, March

11, 1612, in *Letters of John Chamberlain,* ed. Norman E. McClure, 2 vols. (Philadelphia: American Philosophical Society, 1939), 1:338–339.

80 *"... men of best experience":* [Dudley Digges], "Post-script to the Reader," in his *The Defence of Trade: In a letter to Sir Thomas Smith Knight, governour of the East-India Companie, &c., From one of that societie* (London, 1615), (following p. 48). Smythe, Digges, and the other major investor, John Wostenholme, continued to fund ventures into the North Atlantic even after Hudson's demise; in 1615 and 1616 they were major investors for William Baffin's voyages in search of the Northwest Passage. See Clements Markham, ed., *Voyages of William Baffin, 1612–1622,* Hakluyt Society 1st Series 63 (London, 1881), 103, 138.

81 *Paris in 1584:* Mancall, *Hakluyt's Promise,* 131–132; Mordechai Feingold, *The Mathematicians' Apprenticeship: Science, Universities, and Society in England, 1560–1640* (Cambridge: Cambridge University Press, 1984), esp. 45–85; Katherine Neal, "Mathematics and Empire, Navigation and Exploration: Henry Briggs and the Northwest Passage of 1631," *Isis* 93 (2002), 435–453.

81 *pamphlets describing specific voyages:* Richard Hakluyt, *The Principall Voiages, Navigations, and Discoveries of the English Nation* (London, 1589), 615–635 (on Frobisher), 776–792 (on Davis); James Rosier, *A true relation of the most prosperous voyage ... by Captaine George Waymouth* (London, 1605).

82 *preserve peace with Spain:* For Ralegh, see Kenneth R. Andrews, *Trade, Plunder and Settlement: Maritime Enterprise and the Genesis of the British Empire, 1480–1630* (Cambridge: Cambridge University Press, 1984), 287–299; Sir Walter Ralegh's *Discoverie of Guiana,* ed. Joyce Lorimer, Hakluyt Society 3rd Series 15 (London: Hakluyt Society, 2006); and Walter Ralegh, *The Discovery of Guiana with Related Documents,* ed. Benjamin Schmidt (Boston: Bedford/St. Martin's, 1–44.

82 *when the incident occurred:* Samuel Purchas, *Purchas his Pilgrimes,* 4 vols. (London, 1625), 3:596 (Hudson), 3:597 (Pricket).

83 *ordered the crew to drop anchor:* Ibid., 3:596.

83 *such a frigid region:* Those early outposts planted the seeds for later development. On their creation and early history, see Alfred Crosby, *Ecological Imperialism: The Biological Expansion of Europe, 900–1900* (Cambridge: Cambridge University Press, 1986), 42–56; Helgi Thorláksson, "The Icelandic Commonwealth Period: Building a New Society," in William W. Fitzhugh and Elisabeth

I. Ward, eds., *Vikings: The North Atlantic Saga* (Washington, D.C.: Smithsonian Institution Press, 2000), 175–185.

85    *an unlucky ship:* Purchas, *Purchas his Pilgrimes,* 3:597.

85    *hunted population of birds:* Ibid., 3:596 (Hudson), 3:597 (Pricket), 3:609 (Wydowse).

85    *"little wind Easterly":* Ibid., 3:597.

86    *". . . would scald a Fowl":* Ibid. For the identification of Dyre Fjord, see Georg Michael Asher, ed., *Henry Hudson the Navigator,* Hakluyt Society 1st Series 27 (London, 1860), 99n.

86    *from the cold depths:* Purchas, *Purchas his Pilgrimes,* 3:597.

87    *beasts could be fatal:* Olaus Magnus, *A Description of the Northern Peoples,* ed. P. G. Foote, 3 vols., Hakluyt Society 2nd Series 182, 187, 188 (London: Hakluyt Society, 1996–1998), 3:1081–1109. On the development of the North Atlantic fishing and whaling trades, see *André Thevet's North America: A Sixteenth-Century View,* ed. Roger Schlesinger and Arthur P. Stabler (Kingston and Montreal: McGill-Queen's University Press, 1986), 23–25, 55–58; Peter E. Pope, *Fish into Wine: The Newfoundland Plantation in the Seventeenth Century* (Chapel Hill: University of North Carolina Press for the Omohundro Institute of Early American History and Culture, 2004), 11–44; W. Jeffrey Bolster, "Putting the Ocean in Atlantic History: Maritime Communities and Marine Ecology in the Northwest Atlantic, 1500–1800," *American Historical Review* 113 (2008), 19–47; Nancy Shoemaker, "Oil and Bone," *Common-Place* 8, no. 2 (January 2008).

88    *larger than Discovery:* Edward Topsell, *The Historie of Serpents* (London, 1608), 223–236, quotation at 236.

89    *never exceeded 3,500:* For a description of how the Norse transformed Greenland's environment, see Crosby, *Ecological Imperialism,* 44, 50–51.

90    *ample supply of fish:* Abraham Ortelius, *Theatrum Orbis Terrarum: The Theatre of the Whole World* (London, 1606), 102.

90    *believed would lead them:* Purchas, *Purchas his Pilgrimes,* 3:598.

## Chapter 5

91    *". . . irksome noise of the ice":* Samuel Purchas, *Purchas his Pilgrimage* (London, 1613), 624.

92    *mostly westward course:* Samuel Purchas, *Purchas his Pilgrimes,* 4 vols. (London, 1625), 3:596.

92    *never again sail so close:* Ibid., 3:598.

93     *ample experience in such waters:* Ibid.

93     *Hudson was already persuaded:* Ibid.

94     *"there were some who then spake words . . . ":* Ibid. It is possible that Hudson and the others were not the first Europeans to have sailed this far inland. Archaeologists have found Norse items on the northwestern shores of Hudson Bay. The Norse may have traded these to Inuit, who brought them inland, or the Inuit may have found them after the Norse had abandoned settlements. See Patricia D. Sutherland, "The Norse and Native North Americans," in William W. Fitzhugh and Elisabeth I. Ward, eds., *Vikings: The North Atlantic Saga* (Washington, D.C.: Smithsonian Institution Press, 2000), 238–247.

94     *the only logical way:* Purchas, *Purchas his Pilgrimes* (1625), 3:598.

95     *melted in warmer temperatures:* Ibid. For studies of so-called brine extrusion, see R. A. Lake and E. L. Lewis, "Salt Rejection by Sea Ice during Growth," *Journal of Geophysical Research* 75 (1970), 583–597; and W. S. Reeburgh, "Fluxes Associated with Brine Motion in Growing Sea Ice," *Polar Biology* 3 (1984), 29–33. The process is well explained in Elizabeth Kolbert, *Field Notes from a Catastrophe: Man, Nature, and Climate Change* (New York: Bloomsbury, 2006), 25–26.

96     *cutting off the top of the Americas:* Abraham Ortelius, *Theatrum Orbis Terrarum: The Theatre of the Whole World* (London, 1606), f. 5. Ortelius's map of the world, by comparison, included a depiction of a northwest passage running between North America and the frozen lands to the north, which he labeled "Terra Sept Emtrionalis Incognita," or "unknown empty land" (see f. 1). Earlier mapmakers, it should be noted, included what they imagined to be the northern coasts of North America, and some even included what might be taken as a large indentation in the sea resembling Hudson Bay, though no evidence survives to suggest how they might have come to this knowledge. See Carl Schuster, "Into the Great Bay: Henry Hudson's Mysterious Final Voyage," *The Beaver* 79 (1995), 8–15.

97     *their effort wasted:* Purchas, *Purchas his Pilgrimes* (1625), 3:598.

98     *fascinate Europeans for centuries:* Edward Topsell, *History of Foure-Footed Beastes* (London, 1607), 36.

98     *weapons the men might hurl:* Purchas, *Purchas his Pilgrimes* (1625), 3:598.

99     *tide came in from the north:* Ibid., 3:598–599 (Pricket), 3:596 (Hudson).

100    *mark of the English:* Ibid., 3:599.

101    *take any with their muskets:* Ibid.

102 *despite its bitter taste:* For more about scurvy grass (*Cochlearia offici-nalis*), see Kenneth F. Kiple and Kriemhild C. Ornelas, eds., *The Cambridge World History of Food,* 2 vols. (Cambridge: Cambridge University Press, 2000), 2:1849.

102 *ample supply of food:* Dionyse Settle, *A True reporte of the laste voyage into the West and Northwest regions &c. 1577, worthily achieved by Capteine Frobisher* (London, 1577), sig. C$^{vr}$–[Diii$^r$]; Purchas, *Purchas his Pilgrimes* (1625), 3:599–600.

103 *not soon forget the insult:* Purchas, *Purchas his Pilgrimes* (1625), 3:600.

103 *difficult to land the small craft:* Ibid. On the color and freezing of James Bay, see Environment Canada, "Sea Ice—Where Do We Find It?" http://ice-glaces.ec.gc.ca/.

104 *"though not unscarred":* Purchas, *Purchas his Pilgrimes* (1625), 3:600.

104 *"... Labyrinth without end":* On Hudson's manuscript in Hakluyt's possession, see Purchas, *Purchas his Pilgrimes* (1625), 3: sig. *3$^v$; for "Labyrinth without end," see 3:601.

105 *dead birds hanging:* Ibid., 3:600.

105 *Now that they were trapped:* Ibid., 3:601.

106 *in agreement with the captain:* Ibid.

106 *escape unscathed:* Ibid.

107 *stored in his cabin:* Ibid.

107 *belatedly became evident:* Ibid.

108 *combustible combination:* Ibid.

108 *pleading with Hudson:* Ibid.

108 *built the house:* Ibid.

109 *ready for any encounter:* Ibid.

109 *a coveted position:* Ibid.

109 *discredit the master:* Ibid.

109 *likened the sound to thunder:* Fridjtof Nansen, *Farthest North* (New York: Modern Library, 1999 [1897]), 116.

110 *frozen to a depth: The Strange and Dangerous Voyage of Captaine Thomas James* (London, 1633), 57 (frozen skin), 61 (snow), 63 (frozen ground). James made an accurate assessment of the bay, which is mostly shallower than 20 meters in depth and generally freezes early and stays frozen for about six months. See I. P. Martini, "Morphology and Sediments of the Emergent Ontario Coast of James Bay, Canada," *Geografiska Annater, series A, Physical Geography* 63 (1981), 81–83.

111 *kegs of beer and cider:* James, *Strange and Dangerous Voyage,* 69–73 (winter conditions), 54 (fear of damage to the ship).

112 *still serviceable planks:* Ibid., 56 (shaving), 59–61 (houses), 55–56 (pinnace plans).

112 *former chimney sweeps:* Ibid., 63–64 (ailments), 66–67 (wood).

113 *Three died during the winter:* Ibid., 64–65, 74–76 (deaths).

113 *threatened the human body:* Robert Boyle, *New Experiments and Observations touching Cold, or an Experimental History of Cold* (London, 1665), 523–524, 532–537.

114 *tore their own flesh:* James, *Strange and Dangerous Voyage,* 73 (birds), 75 (peas), 77 (weather), 81 and 87 (mosquitoes).

114 *destination more northerly:* Purchas, *Purchas his Pilgrimes* (1625), 3:601–602.

115 *the drink eased the pain:* Ibid., 3:601–602; see also Samuel Purchas, *Purchas his Pilgrimage* (London, 1626), 818. The tree was in all likelihood a spruce, which has been found even on otherwise barren islands in James Bay. See James M. Macount, "Notes on the Flora of James Bay," *Botanical Gazette* 13 (1888), 117; also Douglas Hunter, *God's Mercies: Rivalry, Betrayal, and the Dream of Discovery* (Toronto: Doubleday Canada, 2007), 114.

115 *communicate ideas:* Purchas, *Purchas his Pilgrimes* (1625), 3:602. Settle had noted that during Frobisher's 1577 expedition the Inuit and English had exchanged "dumb signs and mute congratulations," though such rudimentary communication did not always work effectively. See Settle, *True reporte,* sig. B$^{vv}$–[B$^{vir}$].

116 *He never returned:* Purchas, *Purchas his Pilgrimes* (1625), 3:602.

116 *first day's haul:* Ibid.

116 *leave the others behind:* Ibid.

117 *sail upon his return:* Ibid.


## Chapter 6

120 *realized that he might fail:* Samuel Purchas, *Purchas his Pilgrimes,* 4 vols. (London, 1625), 3:602.

120 "*. . . so many hungry bellies":* Ibid.

120 *last them for about a week:* Ibid., 3:602–603.

121 "*yet the counsel of the Lord shall stand":* Ibid., 3:603.

121 *They had not eaten:* Ibid.

121 "*either to mend or end":* Ibid.

122 *banished from England:* Ibid.

122 "*. . . starved abroad":* Ibid.

123 "*. . . take my fortune in the Shallop":* Ibid. On Pricket's relationship to Digges, see Samuel Purchas, *Purchas his Pilgrimes* (London, 1626), 818.

123 *the unfolding plot:* Purchas, *Purchas his Pilgrimes* (1625), 3:603.

123    *answer for his disobedience:* Ibid.

124    *blood, not food:* Ibid.

124    *immediately seconded him:* Ibid.

125    *tried to halt the mutiny:* Ibid.

125    *"wickedness sleepeth not":* Ibid., 3:603–604.

125    *few men strong enough:* Ibid., 3:604.

126    *". . . whither the Master pleased":* Ibid.

126    *avoid the shallop:* Ibid.

127    *keep watch on Staffe:* Ibid.

127    *onto the shallow craft:* Ibid.

128    *Pricket yelled back:* Ibid.

129    *the repugnance they felt:* Ibid.

129    *voracious predation:* Ibid., 3:604–605.

129    *fend for themselves:* Ibid., 3:605.

129    *to sate their hunger:* Ibid.

130    *"as from an Enemy":* Ibid. The reference to the sail on the shallop comes from the testimony offered by the surgeon, Edward Wilson, to the High Court of Admiralty in 1612. See Thomas A. Janvier, *Henry Hudson: A Brief Statement of His Aims and Achievements* (New York, 1909), 135–139.

131    *apparently squirreled away:* Purchas, *Purchas his Pilgrimes* (1625), 3:605.

132    *"or ever after":* Ibid.

132    *". . . half miles in compass":* Ibid.

133    *for the ship's storehouse:* Ibid.

133    *"Cakes of bread":* Ibid., 3:605.

134    *executed more pirates:* Peter Earle, *The Pirate Wars* (London: Methuen, 2003), 55–58; David D. Hebb, *Piracy and the English Government, 1616–1642* (Aldershot: Scolar Press, 1994), 7–10.

134    *servant had become the master:* Purchas, *Purchas his Pilgrimes* (1625), 3:605.

134    *confessions of the three pirates: Clinton, Purser & Arnold, to their Countreymen wheresoever* (London, [1583]).

135    *interests of his prominent supporters:* Tho[mas] Haywood and William Rowly, *Fortune by Land and Sea. A Tragi-Comedy* (London, 1655 [1605]), 43–44; Claire Jowitt, "Rogue Traders: National Identity, Empire and Piracy, 1580–1640," in Thomas Betteridge, ed., *Borders and Travellers in Early Modern Europe* (Aldershot: Ashgate, 2007), 53–70. See also Claire Jowitt, "Scaffold Performances: The Politics of Pirate Execution," in Jowitt, ed., *Pirates? The Politics of Plunder, 1550–1650* (Houndmills, Basingstoke: Palgrave Macmillan, 2007), 151–168.

135   *ship shouldered free:* Purchas, *Purchas his Pilgrimes* (1625), 3:605. Pricket's text reveals that it was Bylot who was plotting *Discovery's* course.

136   *never had any real experience:* Ibid.

136   *thick-billed murres:* Ibid., 3:606. For the estimate of the murres, see Barry Lopez, *Arctic Dreams: Imagination and Desire in a Northern Landscape* (New York: 1986), 156–157. On Frobisher bringing back a narwhal tusk, see the illustration in George Best, *A True Discourse of the late voyages of discoverie, for the finding of a passage to Cathaya, by the Northwest, under the conduct of Martin Frobisher* (London, 1578).

137   *propel the ship into the rocks:* Purchas, *Purchas his Pilgrimes* (1625), 3:606.

137   *led him inside:* Ibid.

138   *killed up to eight birds:* Ibid.

138   *". . . kind people of the World":* Ibid.

139   *". . . how simple soever . . .":* Ibid.

139   *". . . promised him by signs":* Ibid., 3:606–607.

140   *slashed the man's body:* Ibid., 3:607.

140   *run to their kayaks:* Ibid.

141   *". . . most fearful manner . . .":* Ibid.

141   *organized the mutiny:* Ibid.

141   *"poor number":* Ibid.

142   *ship headed eastward:* Ibid.

142   *thought of as garbage:* Ibid., 3:607–608.

143   *cod-fishing station:* By 1615, there were approximately 250 English ships (with crews totaling 5,000 to 6,000 sailors) routinely plying the waters off Newfoundland. See Peter E. Pope, *Fish into Wine: The Newfoundland Plantation in the Seventeenth Century* (Chapel Hill: University of North Carolina Press for the Omohundro Institute of Early American History and Culture, 2004), 33.

143   *". . . left ashore by them":* Purchas, *Purchas his Pilgrimes* (1625), 3:608.

143   *dreamed about creating a colony:* See George Peckham, *A True Reporte, of the Late Discoveries, and Possession, taken in the right of the Crowne of Englande, of the new-founde landes, by . . . Sir Humfrey Gilbert* (London, 1583).

143   *avoid the jagged shoals:* The dangers of the shoals near Newfoundland would have been well known to Hudson, at least, who would have heard from Hakluyt or others about the loss of one of Gilbert's three ships there in 1583.

144   *"with prosperous winds . . .":* Purchas, *Purchas his Pilgrimes* (1625), 3:608.

144   *"a good dish of meat":* Ibid.

144　*ship managed to dock:* Ibid.

144　*European fishing crews:* Ibid. For details on Bear Haven (Beere-haven or Bearehaven, according to contemporary sources), see [Thomas Stafford], *Pacata Hibernia, Ireland Appeased and Reduced* (London, 1633), 324–325; for the date of the meeting, see Purchas, *Purchas his Pilgrimage* (1626), 819.

145　*their best cable:* Purchas, *Purchas his Pilgrimes* (1625), 3:608.

145　*promised that they would be paid:* Ibid.

145　*investors in the venture:* Ibid.

146　*Only eight men:* The complete list of those who were killed, who were put into the shallop during the mutiny, or who survived to make it back to Europe can be found in Trinity House Transactions, vol. 1 (1609–1625), Guildhall Library, Ms 30045/1, f. 11ᵛ.

## CHAPTER 7

148　*maintain an alms house:* Alwyn A. Ruddock, "The Trinity House at Deptford in the Sixteenth Century," *English Historical Review* 65 (1950), 460–462; G. G. Harris, *The Trinity House of Deptford, 1514–1660* (London: Athlone, 1969), 19–20; G. G. Harris, ed., *Trinity House of Deptford Transactions, 1609–35,* Publications of the London Record Society, vol. 19 (London: London Record Society, 1983), ix.

149　*further rise of Deptford:* Edward Hasted, *The History and Topographical Survey of the County of Kent,* 4 vols. (Canterbury, 1778–1799), 1:2–12, quotation at 8).

150　*aimed to protect commerce:* [John Stow], *A Survay of London* (London, 1598), 10–11. The river, of course, remained crucial to the nation; see Jonathan Schneer, *The Thames* (New Haven, Conn.: Yale University Press, 2005).

150　*primary arbiters:* Harris, ed., *Trinity House of Deptford Transactions,* ix.

151　*returned destitute:* Ibid., 3–5.

151　*". . . Middle Earth sea":* Ibid., 9.

151　*compilations of Hakluyt:* Richard Hakluyt, *The Principall Voiages, Navigations, and Discoveries of the English Nation* (London, 1589), 674–677, 688–699, and Richard Hakluyt, *Principal Voyages, Navigations, Traffiques, and Discoveries of the English Nation,* 3 vols. (London, 1598–1600), 3 (passim).

152　*freedom to fish:* Harris, ed., *Trinity House of Deptford Transactions,* 1–2.

153　*defected from the company:* Ibid., 3–4.

153　*assault by the Inuit:* Trinity House Transactions, vol. 1 (1609–1625), Guildhall Library, Ms 30045/1, f. 11ᵛ.

154   *wasteful as well as unfair:* Ibid., 11$^v$–12$^r$.

154   *prone to violence:* Ibid., f. 12$^r$.

155   "*. . . trending from N. to W.":* Ibid.

155   *drove dangerous floes:* Ibid.

155   "*. . . pestered with ice . . . ":* Ibid., f. 13$^r$.

156   "*. . . as the Whale played . . . ":* Ibid.

156   *northwest of Salisbury's headland:* Ibid.

156   "*. . . between the West and N. West . . . ":* Ibid.

157   *Ravenspurre or Kelsey-upon-Humber:* "The Manuscripts of the Corporation of the Trinity House, Deptford-Le-Strond, at Tower Hill, London," in *Eighth Report of the Royal Commission on Historical Manuscripts. Report and Appendix (Part I)* (London, 1881), 237–238.

158   "*. . . the like mutinies":* "A note found in the Deske of Thomas Wydowse, Student in the Mathematickes, hee being one of them who was put into the Shallop," in Samuel Purchas, *Purchas his Pilgrimes,* 4 vols. (London, 1625), 3:609.

158   *"by Candlemasse":* Ibid.

159   *put behind the insults:* Ibid.

160   *jailed for their crime:* Gerritsz provided four versions of Hudson's story in 1612 and 1613. See Georg Michael Asher, ed., *Henry Hudson the Navigator,* Hakluyt Society 1st Series 27 (London, 1860), 181–194, quotations at 187 ("nothing memorable"), 192 (trade for furs). Gerritsz's writings can also be found in Henry C. Murphy, ed., *Henry Hudson in Holland: An Inquiry into the Origins and Objects of the Voyage which led to the Discovery of the Hudson River* (The Hague, 1909), 142–146; and Fred John Millard, ed., *Detectio Freti Hudsoni, or Hessel Gerritsz's Collection of Tracts by Himself, Massa, and de Quir* (Amsterdam, 1878), 45–46.

160   *most desperate months:* The map can be found in [Hessel Gerritsz], *Descriptio ac delineatio Geographica Detectionis Freti* (Amsterdam, 1612).

160   *John White in 1590:* The images appeared in Thomas Harriot, *A Briefe and True Report of the New Found Land of Virginia* (Frankfurt-am-Main, 1590), and in the same text translated into German, French, and Latin.

160   *De Bry's heirs:* For the workings of the de Bry workshop, see Michiel van Groesen, *The Representations of the Overseas World in the De Bry Collection of Voyages (1590–1634)* (Leiden: Brill, 2008); and Michael Gaudio, *Engraving the Savage: The New World and Techniques of Civilization* (Minneapolis: University of Minnesota Press, 2008).

162   "*. . . expected hour by hour":* Johanne Theodor de Bry, *Indiæ Orientalis Pars X. Qua continetur, Historica Revlatio sive Descriptio Nove ad*

*Aquilonom Transitus, supra terras Americanas in Chinam atq; Iaponem ducturi, quemadmodum is ab Henrico Hudsono Anglo nuper inuentus est* ... (Frankfurt, 1613), sig. B^r–v.

162 *"... murderous companions":* Samuel Purchas, *Purchas his Pilgrimage* (London, 1613), 624.

163 *"last and fatal voyage":* Samuel Purchas, *Purchas his Pilgrimage* (London, 1614), 743.

163 *"... won the passage":* Ibid., 744.

163 *volunteered to remain:* Ibid., 744–745.

164 *"... justice find executioners":* Ibid., 745.

164 *"... where she is most unbridled ...":* Ibid., 745–746.

## CHAPTER 8

166 *sailed off in that direction:* For the charter, see W. Noel Sainsbury, ed., *Calendar of State Papers Colonial, East Indies, China and Japan,* 5 vols., (London, 1864), 1:238–241.

166 *By then it was too late:* Luke Foxe, *North-West Fox, Or, Fox from the North-west passage* (London, 1635), 117–118.

167 *"lost many men":* Ibid., 118–119.

167 *"... after they had exposed ...":* Ibid.

167 *"... as big as Mackerels":* Ibid., 118–119.

168 *water flowing from the Pacific:* Ibid., 120.

168 *escaped the ice:* Ibid., 123–129.

168 *"... Morse [walrus] teeth":* Ibid., 130–131.

169 *extracted from their blubber:* Ibid., 131.

169 *only sixteen days:* Ibid., 136.

169 *Rather than push their luck:* Ibid., 137.

170 *Digges was obsessed:* Sainsbury, ed., *Calendar of State Papers,* 1: 238; Chamberlain to Dudley Carleton, December 18, 1611, in *Letters of John Chamberlain,* ed. Norman E. McClure, 2 vols. (Philadelphia: American Philosophical Society, 1939), 1:321–322.

170 *115 leagues:* John Gatonbe, "A Voyage into the North-West Passage, Undertaken in the Year 1612," in Awnsham Churchill and John Churchill, comps., *A Collection of Voyages and Travels,* 6 vols. (London, 1732), 6:245–247.

171 *"... our mastiff-dogs":* Gatonbe, "Voyage into the North-West Passage," 6:247.

171 *watching them die slowly:* See, for example, the report by the Huguenot Jean de Léry, who watched sailors on a voyage to Brazil laugh at the plight of a shark whose fins they had removed before they threw it back into the sea, in Jean de Léry, *History of a Voyage to*

       *the Land of Brazil,* trans. Janet Whately (Berkeley: University of California Press, 1990 [1578]), 18.

171   *five weeks and two days:* Gatonbe, "Voyage into the North-West Passage," 6:248.

172   *in the form of nails:* Ibid., 6:252 (bears, wolves, deer), 6:251 (foxes), 6:248 (Inuit encounters). On the indigenous desire for iron, see Peter Pope, *Fish into Wine: The Newfoundland Plantation in the Seventeenth Century* (Chapel Hill: University of North Carolina Press for the Omohundro Institute of Early American History and Culture, 2004), 73–74.

172   *"so little did they regard it":* Gatonbe, "Voyage into the North-West Passage," 6:248–250.

173   *find whales in the area:* Ibid., 6:251–252.

173   *killed by Inuit spears:* Ibid., 6:252–253 (death of Hall), 6:250 and 6:254 (Pulley).

174   *avenge Hall's death:* Ibid., 6:253.

174   *". . . good store in the sea . . . ":* Ibid., 6:254–256.

175   *larger than that of an ox:* Samuel Purchas, *Purchas his Pilgrimes,* 4 vols. (London, 1625), 3:831–832.

175   *obvious provocation:* Ibid., 3:832.

176   *the rest of Baffin's journal:* Ibid., 3:833–835.

176   *dogs that resembled wolves:* Ibid., 3:835–836, quotation at 835.

177   *Inuit remained savages:* Ibid., 3:835–836. On the English belief that Inuit only consumed raw fish, see Dionyse Settle, *A True reporte of the laste voyage into the West and Northwest regions, &c. 1577, worthily achieved by Capteine Frobisher* (London, 1577), sig. C$^{vr}$–[Diii$^r$].

177   *journey to the next world:* Purchas, *Purchas his Pilgrimes,* 3:835. The rituals of northern peoples relating to the sun continued to attract the attention of European readers. See Bernard Picart, *Cérémonies et coutumes religieuses de tous les peuples du monde,* 7 vols. (Paris, 1723–1743), 3:2–5.

177   *the idea of confronting them:* Theodor de Bry, *America Tertia Pars* (Frankfurt, 1592); Michel de Montaigne, "Of Cannibals," in *The Essayes or Morall, Politike and Millitarie Discourses,* trans. John Florio (London, 1603), 100–107.

178   *transferred it to Purchas:* Purchas, *Purchas his Pilgrimes,* vol. 3, sig. [*5$^r$], indicates that Hakluyt was the source of this text.

178   *four English ships:* Jonas Poole, "A briefe Declaration of this my Voyage of discovery to Greenland, and towards the West of it," in Purchas, *Purchas his Pilgrimes,* 3:711–713.

178     *Basque whalers:* "A Relation written by Jonas Poole of a Voyage to Greenland, in the year 1612," in Purchas, *Purchas his Pilgrimes,* 3:713–715.

178     *commentary or regret:* William Baffin, "A Journall of the Voyage made to Greenland with six English Ships and a Pinnasse," in Purchas, *Purchas his Pilgrimes,* 3:716–720. There is also a second, anonymous journal of this expedition, probably written by Robert Fotherby, that was not published until the nineteenth century. See "A Short Discourse of a Voyage made in the yeare of our Lord 1613 to the Late-Discovered Countrye of Greenland," *Archæologia Americana: Transactions and Collections of the American Antiquarian Society* 4 (1860), 285–314.

178     *how to hunt whale:* "A Short Discourse of a Voyage made in the yeare of our Lord 1613," 300–303. The images appeared in Purchas, *Purchas his Pilgrimes,* 3:472, and in Edward Pellham, *God's Power and Providence: shewed, in the miraculous preservation and deliverance of eight Englishmen, left by mischance in Green-land anno 1630, nine moneths and twelve dayes* (London, 1631).

179     *". . . New Trades and Discourse":* Ro[bert] Fotherby, "A Voyage of Discovery to Greenland, & c. Anno 1614," in Purchas, *Purchas his Pilgrimes,* 3:720–728.

179     *turned for home:* Robert Fotherbie, "A true report of a Voyage Anno 1615 for Discoverie of Seas, Lands, and Ilands to the Northwards," in Purchas, *Purchas his Pilgrimes,* 3:728–731, quotation at 3:730.

180     *toward its next attempt:* Purchas identified him as Robert Byleth, but the marginal note about his previous journeys indicates that he was the same Bylot who had sailed with Hudson; see William Baffin, "A true Relation of such things as happened in the fourth Voyage for the Discoverie of the North-west passage, performed in the year 1615," in Purchas, *Purchas his Pilgrimes,* 3:836. Foxe identified him more accurately as Robert Bilot: see William Baffin, "The Voyage of Robert Bilot . . . 1615," in *North-West Fox,* 173. A third version of Baffin's journal for this report is reprinted in Clements Markham, ed., *The Voyages of William Baffin, 1612–1622,* Hakuyt Society 1st Series 63 (London, 1881), 103–137.

180     *"Savage Iles":* Baffin, "A true Relation," 836–839. A draft map of Baffin's voyage of 1615, along with other contemporary maps, can be found in Derek Hayes, *Historical Atlas of Canada* (Seattle: University of Washington Press, 2002), 38–41.

180     *"a truer Geography . . .":* Baffin, "A true Relation," 839.

181 *had come to an end:* Ibid., 839 (contributions to geography), 840 (ice), 841 (decision to return).

181 *final proof:* Purchas inserted this italicized note at the end of Baffin's report of his 1615 journey, but did not indicate who wrote it; see Baffin, "A true Report," 842.

181 *named new locales:* "A briefe and true Relation of Journall, contayning such accidents as happened in the fift voyage, for the discoverie of a passage to the North-West ... 1616," in Purchas, *Purchas his Pilgrimes,* 3:844–847. It should be noted that Baffin's name does not appear on the document itself, but the title and placement of the text by Purchas reveals it to be by Baffin.

182 *yet another abortive search:* Ibid., 3:847–848.

182 *perhaps only six weeks:* Baffin to Wolstenholme, in Ibid., 3:843–844.

183 *northern ice shelves:* Ibid., 3:843.

## CHAPTER 9

186 *dealings in the Spice Islands: Dialogues in the English and Malaian Languages: Or, Certaine Common Formes of Speech, First written in Latin, Malaian, and Madagascar tongues, by ... Gotardus Arthusius,* trans. August Spalding (London, 1614). For Hakluyt's role, see Peter C. Mancall, *Hakluyt's Promise: An Elizabethan's Obsession for an English America* (New Haven, Conn.: Yale University Press, 2007), 283.

187 *"... miserably perished":* Thomas A. Janvier, *Henry Hudson: A Brief Statement of His Aims and Achievements* (New York, 1909), 139–140.

187 *threats that pirates posed:* For details on merchants' preferences, see Charles S. Cumming, "The English High Court of Admiralty," *Tulane Maritime Law Journal* 209 (1992–1993), 237.

188 *possible further punishment:* "Ordering Punishment of Piracy against England's Allies," November 17, 1490, in Paul L. Hughes and James F. Larkin, eds., *Tudor Royal Proclamations,* 3 vols. (New Haven, Conn.: Yale University Press, 1964), 1:25–26.

188 *"Robbers of the sea":* This act followed shortly after a similar act (27 Henry VIII c. 4), which can be found in *Statutes of the Realm,* 10 vols. (London, 1810–1828), 3:533–534.

188 *property, not humans:* The text of the law, "An Acte for the punysshement of Pyrotes and Robbers of the Sea" (28 Henry VIII c. 15), can be found in *Statutes of the Realm,* 3:671.

188 *the general pardon:* 18 Elizabeth c. 24, in *Statutes of the Realm,* 4: 653.

190   *the statute declared:* As the act put it, anyone convicted of piracy "shall have and suffer such pains of Death losses of lands goods and cattle, as if they had been attainted and convicted of any treasons felonies robberies or other said offences done upon the lands." For the implications of the act, see Robert C. Ritchie, *Captain Kidd and the War against the Pirates* (Cambridge: Harvard University Press, 1986), 140–141.

190   *". . . uttermost perils":* "Making Unlicensed Shipping Punishable by Death" (30 Henry VIII), February 28, 1539, in Hughes and Larkin, eds., *Tudor Royal Proclamations,* 1:283.

190   *assistance to the deserter:* "Providing Death Penalty for Deserters from Ships" (36 Henry VIII), January 24, 1545, in Hughes and Larkin, eds., *Tudor Royal Proclamations,* 1:346–347.

190   *Irish pirates:* "Ordering Arrest of Irish Pirates" (2 Edward VI), c. January 1449, in Hughes and Larkin, eds., *Tudor Royal Proclamations,* 1:437–438.

190   *succored pirates:* "Providing Death Penalty for Aid to Pirates" (3 Edward VI), February 19, 1549, in Hughes and Larkin, eds., *Tudor Royal Proclamations,* 1:444–445.

191   *banned the sale of ships:* "Prohibiting Sale of Ships to Foreigners" (1 Elizabeth I), August 23, 1559, in Hughes and Larkin, eds., *Tudor Royal Proclamations,* 2:135.

191   *exonerated two others:* "Ordering Peace kept on the Seas, and Pirates Arrested" (6 Elizabeth I), July 31, 1564, in Hughes and Larkin, eds., *Tudor Royal Proclamations,* 2:253–255; for the executions, see Edmund Howes, *Annales, or A Generall Chronicle of England, begun by John Stowe* (London, 1631), 675.

192   *levy a tax:* "Penalizing Offenses against Allied Shipping," February 3, 1591 (33 Elizabeth I), in Hughes and Larkin, eds., *Tudor Royal Proclamations,* 3:71–74. The English struggled with policing privateers for years and only managed to regulate them effectively by the end of the seventeenth century. See Ritchie, *Captain Kidd,* 151–152.

192   *face felony charges:* "Ordering Declaration of Goods Seized upon the Sea" (34 Elizabeth I), December 29, 1591, in Hughes and Larkin, eds., *Tudor Royal Proclamations,* 3:99–100.

192   *expanded the statute:* "Ordering Declaration of Prize Goods under Penalty of Piracy" (34 Elizabeth I), January 8, 1592, in Hughes and Larkin, eds., *Tudor Royal Proclamations,* 3:100–101.

193   *confiscated by the state:* "Ordering Execution of Articles against Piracy" (44 Elizabeth I), March 20, 1602, in Hughes and Larkin, eds., *Tudor Royal Proclamations,* 3:238–241.

194    *taken captive and enslaved:* "The Worthy Enterprise of John Fox, in Delivering 266 Christians Out of the Captivity of the Turks, in Richard Hakluyt, *Principall Voiages, Navigations, and Discoveries of the English Nation* (London, 1589), 150–154; [Anthony Munday?], *The Admirable Deliverance of 266 Christians by John Reynard Englishman from the Captivitie of the Turkes* (London, 1608); Andrew Barker, *A True and Certaine Report of the Beginning, Proceedings, Overthrowes, and now present Estate of Captaine Ward and Danseker, the two late famous Pirates* (London, 1609), sig. A2ʳ⁻ᵛ, 15, 22–23. For the context and scope of redemption narratives, see Daniel Vitkus, ed., *Piracy, Slavery, and Redemption: Barbary Captivity Narratives from Early Modern England* (New York: Columbia University Press, 2001).

194    "... *Christian turn'd Turke*": *Newes from Sea, of two notorious Pyrats* (London, 1609), sig. C3ʳ (punishment for drunken murder); Robert Daborn, *A Christian turn'd Turke: or, The Tragicall Lives and Deaths of the two Famous Pyrates, Ward and Dansiker* (London, 1612).

195    *no mercy for anyone:* Howes, *Annales,* 892–893 (Tunis, executions at Wapping); *The Lives, Apprehensions, Arraignments, and Executions of the 19, late Pyrates* (London, 1609).

195    *testimony of the surgeon:* The testimony can be found in Janvier, *Henry Hudson,* 135–139.

198    *threatened to hang pirates:* Privy Council to Sir Thomas Smith, March 9, 1617, in *Acts of the Privy Council of England, 1616–1617,* 46 vols. (London, 1890–1964), 35:181–182; *Calendar of State Papers ... Venice,* 38 vols. (London, 1864–*1947),* 10:100; David D. Hebb, *Piracy and the English Government, 1616–1642* (Aldershot: Scolar Press, 1994), 9–10. Though these merchants did not mention it, the English, too, were in the habit of taking prisoners off the Barbary coast; see Nabil Matar, "Piracy and Captivity in the Early Modern Mediterranean: The Perspective from Barbary," in Claire Jowitt, ed., *Pirates? The Politics of Plunder, 1550–1650* (Houndmills, Basingstoke: Palgrave Macmillan, 2007), 56–73.

198    *"the best friends he had in the ship":* Pricket's responses to the court's questions are in High Court of Admiralty (HCA) 1/48, f. 118ʳ–120ʳ.

200    *after the two vessels parted:* For Bylot's testimony, see HCA 1/48, f. 120ʳ–121ᵛ.

203    *"slain by the Cannibals":* For Mathews's testimony, see HCA 1/48, f. 127ʳ⁻ᵛ.

204    *pushed off in the shallop:* For Clemens's testimony, see HCA 1/48, f. 130ʳ⁻ᵛ.

205   *recognize the handwriting:* For Wilson's testimony, see HCA 1/48, f. 135$^v$–136$^r$.

206   *vices of the sot weed:* For the debate, see Peter C. Mancall, "Tales Tobacco Told in Sixteenth-Century Europe," *Environmental History* 9 (2004), 648–678.

206   *for shipping to thrive: Acts of the Privy Council of England,* 33 (1613–1614), 228–229 (lighthouses), 142–143 (River Tyne).

207   *facilitate commerce in the realm: Acts of the Privy Council of England,* 34 (1615–1616), 257–258, 611–614.

207   *"... obliged to remain immoveable":* John Ross, *A Voyage of Discovery ... for the Purpose of Exploring Baffin's Bay, and Inquiring into the Probability of a North-West Passage* (London, 1819), [xxxv]–xxxvi.

209   *funds to redeem her son:* G. G. Harris, ed., *Trinity House of Deptford Transactions, 1609–35* (London: London Records Society, 1983), 22–23 (Rudes), 26 (Winterton), 26–27 (new statute), 28 (Cooke family).

210   *The court acquitted them:* The documents relating to the trial and acquittal are reprinted in Llewelyn Powys, *Henry Hudson* (London, 1927), 190–198. The manuscript is incomplete and fragile and lists the not guilty verdicts only for Pricket, Wilson, and Clemens, but Mathews was presumably acquitted as well. The surviving original documents can be found in HCA 1/6, f. 133 (the indictment), f. 88 (Pricket and Wilson), f. 90 (preceding pages), and HCA 1/7, f. 2 (Clemens).

## CHAPTER 10

211   *"last and fatal voyage ... ":* Samuel Purchas, *Purchas his Pilgrimage* (London, 1626), 817.

212   *contemplated sailing homeward:* Susan Rowley, "Frobisher Miksanut: Inuit Accounts of the Frobisher Voyages," in William W. Fitzhugh and Jacqueline S. Olin, *Archaeology of the Frobisher Voyages* (Washington, DC: Smithsonian Institution Press, 1993), 27–40.

213   *"... tradition of their ancestors":* John S. Long, "Narratives of Early Encounters between Europeans and the Cree of Western James Bay," *Ontario History* 80 (1988), 227–231; *Andrew Graham's Observations on Hudson's Bay, 1767–91,* ed. Glyndwr Williams and Richard Glover, Publications of the Hudson's Bay Record Society 27 (London, 1969), 204.

214   *relied on tracking animals:* Daniel Francis and Toby Morantz, *Partners in Furs: A History of the Fur Trade in Eastern James Bay,*

*1600–1870* (Kingston and Montreal: McGill-Queen's University Press, 1983), 3–15.

214  *200 different bird species:* None of the surviving documents from the Hudson voyage identify the natives the English met in the area, but anthropological evidence confirms that they must have been Cree. See Charles A. Bishop and M. Estellie Smith, "Early Historic Populations in Northwestern Ontario: Archaeological and Ethnohistorical Interpretations," *American Antiquity* 40 (1975), 54–63.

214  *its own bounty:* During the eighteenth century, the employees of the Hudson's Bay Company identified more than 140 different species. On the Cree, see Arok Wolvengrey and Jean Okinâsis, "Alphabetic List of Hudson Bay Area Cree Names for Birds, 1770–1830," in Houston et al., *Eighteenth-Century Naturalists,* 210–246; on the HBC sightings, see *Eighteenth-Century Naturalists,* 99–106. One mid-eighteenth-century English explorer left a detailed report about the flora and fauna around Hudson Bay; see *Isham's Observations on Hudsons Bay,* 118–171, *passim.*

215  *berries, seaweed, and shellfish:* Richard J. Preston, "East Main Cree," in June Helm, ed., *Subarctic,* in William C. Sturtevant, gen. ed., *Handbook of North American Indians,* 20 vols. planned (Washington, D.C.: Smithsonian Institution Press, 1978–), 6:197; John Bennet and Susan Rowley, eds., *Uqalurait: An Oral History of Nunavut* (Montreal and Kingston: McGill-Queen's University Press, 2004), 50–85.

215  *dozens of generations:* Stuart Houston, Tim Ball and Mary Houston, *Eighteenth-Century Naturalists of Hudson Bay* (Montreal and Kingston: McGill-Queen's University Press, 2003).

217  *mention of the health:* Samuel Purchas, *Purchas his Pilgrimes, 4 vols.* (London, 1625), 3:603–604.

218  *unleashed deadly contagions:* Some Native peoples along the mid-Atlantic coast quickly blamed European newcomers for spreading disease among them; see Thomas Harriot, *A Briefe and True Report of the New Found Land of Virginia* (London, 1590 [1588]), 29. For the reasons why disease had such a devastating impact among indigenous Americans, see David S. Jones, "Virgin Soils Reconsidered," *William and Mary Quarterly* 3rd Series 60 (2003), 703–742.

218  *traditional material culture:* Francis and Morantz, *Partners in Furs,* 15.

219  *Danish explorer Jens Munk:* For Munk's narrative, see C. C. A. Gosch, *Danish Arctic Expeditions, 1605 to 1620,* Hakluyt Society

1st Series 96–97 (London, 1897), book 2; for the news of his apparent success circulating in London, see John Chamberlain to Dudley Carleton, April 29, 1620, in *Letters of John Chamberlain,* ed. Norman E. McClure, 2 vols. (Philadelphia: American Philosophical Society, 1939), 2:302.

220 *more than a new title:* For a superb study of James's book and its impact, see I. S. MacLaren, "'Zealous Sayles' and 'Zealous Sales': Bookings on the Northwest Passage," *Princeton University Library Chronicle* 64 (2003), 253–287. For contemporary maps from James's expedition, see Derek Hayes, *Historical Atlas of Canada* (Seattle: University of Washington Press, 2002), 43–44.

220 *not to disrupt the mission: North-West Fox, Or, Fox from the North-west passage* (London, 1635), 171–172 (preparations), 173–174 (oath).

220 *filled in the geographical gap:* Ibid., 181 (Frobisher), 183–184 (ice), 268–270 (profits).

221 *"Laboured in vain":* Ibid., 184 (smoke from James), 268 (labored in vain).

221 *reached the same latitude: Strange and Dangerous Voyage of Captain Thomas James* (London, 1633), 112–116; MacLaren, "'Zealous Sayles,'" 256n. James could not have known it, but it is quite likely that his letter could have survived for decades on that post; modern observers have often found signs of earlier expeditions in the Arctic. See Chauncey Loomis, "Murder in the Arctic?" [1971], in Elizabeth Kolbert, ed., *The Ends of the Earth: An Anthology of the Finest Writing on the Arctic* (New York: Bloomsbury, 2007), 14–29.

222 *evidence of Hudson's presence:* James, *Strange and Dangerous Voyage,* 90–91. A nineteenth-century editor of James's text believed that James had found evidence of Staffe's handiwork; see Miller Christy, ed., *The Voyages of Captain Luke Foxe of Hull and Captain Thomas James of Bristol, in Search of a northwest passage, in 1631–1632,* 2 vols., Hakluyt Society 1st Series 88–89 (London, 1894), 2:568–569n.

222 *six canoe loads:* Extract of Mr. Thomas Gorst's Journall in the Voyage to Hudson Bay begun the 31st day of May 1670, Guildhall Library, London; microfilm version at Church of the Latter-Day Saints Family History Center, Salt Lake City (film number 1068847), f. 1 (hereafter Gorst, Extract). A typescript of this extract can be found in Grace Lee Nute, *Caesars of the Wilderness: Médard Chouart, Sieur des Groseilliers and Pierre Esprit Radisson, 1618–1710* (New York: D. Appleton-Century, 1943), 286–292.

223 *eager to trade:* Gorst, Extract, f. 2.

223    *"... any better society":* Ibid., f. 2.

224    *paint and piercings:* Ibid., f. 3. For an earlier view that the indigenous peoples of the Americas marred their appearance, see Amerigo Vespucci, *Mondus Novus,* trans. G. Northrup (Princeton, N.J.: Princeton University Press, 1916 [1504]). Indigenous peoples in North America routinely adopted English kettles and other goods and recognized the utility of cooking vessels that were both lighter and more durable than what they had used earlier; see Calvin Martin, "The Four Lives of a Micmac Copper Pot," *Ethnohistory* 22 (1975), 111–133; and James Axtell, "The First Commercial Revolution," in *Beyond 1492: Encounters in Colonial North America* (New York: Oxford University Press, 1992), 125–151.

224    *their autumn camps:* Gorst, Extract, f. 3. On seasonal migrations of northern peoples, see William Cronon, *Changes in the Land: Indians, Colonists, and the Ecology of New England* (New York: Hill and Wang, 1983), 39–41.

225    *cook their venison:* Gorst, Extract, f. 3–4.

225    *covering it with old sails:* Ibid., f. 4–5.

226    *disease the English risked:* Ibid., f. 5–6.

226    *flourished with the new season:* Ibid., f. 6. For the central importance of naval stores to the establishment of New England, see Michael Williams, *Americans and Their Forests: A Historical Geography* (Cambridge: Cambridge University Press, 1989), 82–94. Gorst's journal suggests that men on this expedition had traveled farther from James Bay than Hudson's men, who never reported finding such tall trees.

226    *time to head home:* Gorst, Extract, f. 6–7.

227    *stumbled on remains:* Ibid., f. 7.

227    *gooseberries, and cranberries:* Ibid., f. 8.

228    *one hemisphere to the other:* Colonial Office (CO) 1/62, no. 49, and CO 135/2, 18–28, for the French reply. The English repudiated the French response; see CO 135/2, 34–48 (July?, 1687), and CO 1/49, no. 92 (November, 1682). See also Hudson's Bay Company to the Lords Commissioners, March 4, 1699, CO 134/3, no. 8.

229    *some nutrition for hungry humans:* One modern observer counted approximately 300 species of flowering plants in James Bay; see James M. Macoun, "Notes on the Flora of James Bay," *Botanical Gazette* 13 (1888), 115–118.

230    *advice about the land:* The area around James Bay was notoriously bad for travel, which would have made any attempt to hike to safety unlikely. Two archaeologists concluded that it was even unlikely that Hudson (or later, James) provided much in the way of

trade goods to the Americans, other than what was mentioned by Pricket. See Chris Vickers and Ralph D. Bird, "A Copper Trade Object from the Headwaters Lake Aspect in Manitoba," *American Antiquity* 15 (1949), 158–159. Cree knowledge of the land began in the childhood ritual of *ithaawsunaauhc*, or walking the land, which helped to teach individuals how to live in the region; see Gail Whiteman and William H. Cooper, "Ecological Embeddedness," *Academy of Management Journal* 43 (2000), 1265–1282, esp. 1277–1278.

230 *Animal attacks:* For the ways that they might have died, see Eleanora C. Gordon, "The Fate of Sir Hugh Willoughby and His Companions: A New Conjecture," *Geographical Journal* 152 (1986), 243–247, and Vilhjalmur Stefansson, *Unsolved Mysteries of the Arctic* (London: G. G. Harrap, 1939).

231 *unearthed in Deep River:* Unfortunately for those who saw historic value in the rock, vandals smashed it into four pieces soon after two enterprising residents mounted it publicly; fortunately, the inscription, "H.H./1612/CAPTIVE," survived; see John R. Colombo, *Mysteries of Ontario* (Toronto: Hounslow, 1999), 67–68.

231 *drifted there with polar tides:* Lawrence Millman, "Looking for Henry Hudson," *Smithsonian* 30 (1999), 100–108. On John Hudson and Champlain, see Douglas Hunter, *God's Mercies: Rivalry, Betrayal, and the Dream of Discovery* ([Toronto]: Doubleday Canada, 2007), 346. On the body found in eastern Greenland, see *Telegraph* (UK), January 4, 1998. For a repository of possible theories, see Ian Chadwick's "The Life and Voyages of Henry Hudson, English Captain and Explorer," www.ianchadwick.com.

232 *company's early buildings:* See W. A. Kenyon, *The History of James Bay, 1610–1686: A Study in Historical Archaeology,* Royal Ontario Museum Archaeology Monograph 10 (Toronto, 1986).

232 *none of the texts:* [Henry Briggs], "A Treatise of the Northwest Passage to the South Sea," in [Edward Waterhouse], *A Declaration of the State of the Colony and Affaires in Virginia* (London, 1622), 45–47. Purchas included this map with a copy of Briggs's already published treatise; see Purchas, *Purchas his Pilgrimes* (1625), 3:852–853.

233 *endorse any further efforts:* William Monson, *Naval Tracts,* 5 vols. (London, 1902–1914), Book 4, 373 (Bylot), 378 (ice), 387–390 (further explorations).

233 *cynicism and mockery:* Watts, in James, *Strange and Dangerous Voyage,* sig. [R4ʳ]–S2ʳ, quotation at sig. S2ʳ.

234 *". . . risk of their lives":* Thomas M'Keevor, *A Voyage to Hudson's Bay, during the Summer of 1812* (London, 1819), 64.

234    *". . . inherent with existence . . .":* Jack London, "In a Far Country," *Overland Monthly* 33 (June 1899).

234    *supplies necessary to survive:* On English shipping to the Mediterranean and beyond, and the taking of English captives and publicity of their experiences, see Linda Colley, *Captives: Britain, Empire, and the World, 1600–1850* (New York: Pantheon, 2003), 23–134; and Alison Games, *The Web of Empire: English Cosmopolitans in an Age of Expansion, 1560–1660* (New York: Oxford University Press, 2008), 47–79. On Hakluyt and the dangers of the ocean, see Peter C. Mancall, *Hakluyt's Promise: An Elizabethan's Obsession for an English America* (New Haven, Conn.: Yale University Press, 2007), 102–127.

234    *Newcomers to the temperate zone:* On the shifting military techniques in early America, see Joyce E. Chaplin, *Subject Matter: Technology, the Body, and Science on the Anglo-American Frontier, 1500–1676* (Cambridge: Harvard University Press, 2001), 79–115. On the spread of diseases, see Jared Diamond, *Guns, Germs, and Steel: The Fates of Human Societies* (New York: W. W. Norton, 1997); Alfred Crosby, *Ecological Imperialism: The Biological Expansion of Europe, 900–1900* (Cambridge: Cambridge University Press, 1996), 199–208; and Jones, "Virgin Soils Revisited," 703–742.

235    *figure of Icarus:* [Isaac de la Peyrère], *Relation du Groenland* (Paris, 1647), 229–230.

## NOTE ON SOURCES

237    *challenging, if not impossible:* Gawrila Sarytschew, *Account of a Voyage of Discovery to the North-East of Siberia, The Frozen Ocean, and the North-East Sea* (London, 1806), [iii].

238    *"the North-wests cold Clime":* Luke Foxe, *North-West Fox, Or, Fox from the North-west passage* [London, 1635], [sig. A3$^r$].

238    *". . . as it relates to northern discovery":* John Barrow, *A Chronological History of Voyages into the Arctic Regions; undertaken chiefly for the purpose of discovering a North-East, North-West, or Polar Passage between the Atlantic and the Pacific* (London, 1818), 186.

238    *". . . fidelity to Master Hudson":* Ibid., 188; Foxe, *North-West Fox,* 117.

238    *". . . cruelly exposed Hudson":* Samuel Purchas, *Purchas his Pilgrimes,* 4 vols. (London, 1625), 3:608–609.

# Acknowledgments

Henry Hudson understood that he had to rely on his crew. The problems he experienced on his last expedition testified to the importance of maintaining the support of comrades as well as to the consequences of losing it. Scholars, obviously, have it much easier—in Southern California we rarely need to fear icebergs—but we, too, are reliant on fellow travelers.

I thank the Huntington Library in San Marino, California, the Yale Center for British Art, and the National Maritime Museum in Greenwich for permission to reprint the pictures that appear in this book. I could not have told Hudson's story without the resources of the Huntington, which possesses one of the great collections of materials relating to the early modern Atlantic world. Just as important, this book developed among the Huntington's community of scholars, and among them I especially thank Roy Ritchie, Tiffany Werth, Sarah Rivett, Luis Corteguera, and Claire Kennedy. Further, I thank those who provided research assistance, particularly Christopher Wittick, Bill Martin, Andrew Jones, Danny Richter, Vicki Perry, Aaron Greenlee, and Tim Wales. For guidance on legal issues surrounding the mutiny on the *Discovery* I am grateful for advice I received from Cynthia Herrup, Dan Klerman, Tica Stanton, and Maryanne Kowaleski. As always, I have relied on a small group of friends and scholars who have provided crucial advice, especially Anne Goldgar, Sherry Velasco, Steve Pincus, Eric Hinderaker, Ian MacLaren, Mary Fuller, Donal Manahan, Daniela Bleichmar, Heidi Brayman Hackel, Carole Shammas, Bill Deverell, Doug Greenberg, Lou Masur, and my incomparable agent Deirdre Mullane. At Basic I want to thank Kay Mariea and Brandon Proia for shepherding this book through production, Kat Bennett for drawing the map depicting Hudson's routes, and my copy editor Kathy Streckfus, and offer my greatest thanks to David Groff and Lara Heimert, who helped give shape to an unwieldy manuscript.

As always, my greatest debt is to Lisa Bitel, who brings warmth and light to the cold and dark and who would never set me adrift on a shallop.

# Index